Thank you to all contributors an
guide; you are a large factor towards helping young
people achieve their goals.

- Department of Energy (DOE)

- Ohio State University Extension Food, Agricultural and Biological Engineering

- Environmental Research Foundation

- John McCarthy Professor of Computer Science at Stanford University

-
  EM U.S. Department of Energy Office Of Environmental Management

- USGS Information Services

- **EPA** United States Environmental Protection Agency — Climate Protection Partnerships Division — Methane and Sequestration Branch

- www.eren.doe.gov/wind

-

- Carie L. Lopatka, Edgewater High School

- Mary Burnett, Edgewater High School

- Dr. Robert W. Smith, Valencia Community College

- Dr. Judith Legault, Lake Highland Preparatory School

Table of Contents

Introduction: Letter to A.P. Environmental Science Students..................2

Chapter 1: About the Exam..................3

    Test taking tips..................3
    Vocabulary Tune Up..................5

Chapter 2: Outline of Topics & Key Concepts..................29

    Climatic Patterns and Species Distribution..................29
    Ecological and Terrestrial Biomes..................29
    Aquatic Ecosystems..................30
    Marine Ecosystems..................30
    Hydrologic Cycle..................31
    Atmospheric Dynamics..................31
    Regions of the Atmosphere..................32
    El Nino / La Nina..................33
    Population Ecology..................33
    Demography..................33
    Birth and Death Rates..................33
    Exponential Growth..................34
    Carrying Capacity..................35

Community Ecology..................35

    Species Interactions and Adaptations..................35
    Ecological Succession..................36
    Aquatic Succession..................37
    Habitat Destruction..................38
    Habitat Fragmentation..................39
    Exotic Species..................40
    Overgrazing/Overharvesting..................40

Evolutionary Concepts..................40

    Natural Selection..................40
    Species Extinction..................40

Ecosystem Ecology..........41

- Energy Flow in Ecosystems..........41
- First / Second Law of Thermodynamics..........41
- Trophic Levels..........42
- Food Chains / Food Webs..........43
- Carbon Cycle..........44
- Nitrogen Cycle..........45
- Phosphorus Cycle..........46
- Land Use Concepts..........48
- Agriculture..........49

Earth Science Principles..........50

- Geological Time Scale..........50
- Plate Tectonics..........52
- Rock Cycle..........53
- Volcanism..........54

Geotechnical Science..........54

- Soil Types..........54
- Erosion..........55

Energy Resources..........56

- Power Generation..........57
- Wood..........57
- Coal..........58
- Oil..........59
- Natural Gas..........60
- Geothermal..........60
- Hydroelectric..........61
- Nuclear Fission..........62
- Nuclear Fusion..........65
- Solar..........65
- Wind..........66
- Tidal..........67
- Biofuels..........68
- Hydrogen..........69

Pollution..........70

    Pesticides..70
    Point and NonPoint Sources..72
    Thermal Pollution..72
    Green House Gases...73
    Ozone...73
    Global Warming..73
    Levels and Loss of Biodiversity.......................................75

  Management of Pollutants..76

    Wastewater Treatment..76
    Municipal Solid Waste...78

  Reduction and Reuse..81

    Toxicology...82

  Environmental Laws, Public Policy and Trade Offs.......................82

    Environmental Choices..82
    Environmental Laws..84
    Environmental Decisions..87

Chapter 3: Laboratory Skills Review..89

    #1 Ecosystem Ecology..89
    #2 Earth Science: Plate Tectonics, Volcanism; Earthquakes
   90
    #3 Earth Science: Soil Structure and the Rock Cycle.........91
    #4 Earth Science: Geotechnical......................................91
    #5 Population Ecology: Env. Factors and Organism Dist....91
    #6 Population Ecology —Calculating Population Data........92
    #7 Population Ecology —Sampling Techniques...................93
    #8 Population Ecology —Human Demographics..................93
    #9 Energy —Calculating Consumption.............................93
    #10 Pollution - Atmospheric...97
    #11 Toxicology...99
    #12 Aquatic Ecology...100
    #13 Enviro Engineering: Potable and Wastewater Treat....101
    #14 Enviro Engineering: Solid Wastes............................104
    #15 Greenhouse Effect...106
    #16 Acid Deposition..106

        #17 Radiation and Growth Factor..108
        #18 Designing a Professional Environmental Impact Study.........109

Chapter 4:   A.P. Environmental Science Practice Test #1..110

        Practice Test #1 Free Response Questions...128

Chapter 5:   A.P. Environmental Science Practice Test #2..132

        Practice Test #2 Free Response Questions...145

Chapter 6:   A.P. Environmental Science Practice Test #3..148

        Practice Test #3 Free Response Questions...164

Appendices:
        Appendix A - Practice Test #1 Answer Sheet Key 167
        Appendix B - Practice Test #1 Subject Index Comparison................168
        Appendix C - Practice Test #1 Answer Key & Rubrics........................169
        Appendix D - Practice Test #1 Free Response Question Answers...179
        Appendix E - Practice Test #2 Answer Sheet Key 184
        Appendix F - Practice Test #2 Subject Index Comparison................185
        Appendix G - Practice Test #2 Answer Key & Rubrics.......................186
        Appendix H - Practice Test #2 Free Response Question Answers.193
        Appendix I - Practice Test #3 Answer Sheet Key 195
        Appendix J - Practice Test #3 Subject Index Comparison................196
        Appendix K - Practice Test #3 Answer Key & Rubrics........................197
        Appendix L - Practice Test #3 Free Response Question Answers205
        Appendix M - Measurement Units..207
        Appendix N - Energy Measurement Units...208
        Appendix O - Important and Helpful Web Sites...................................209
        Appendix P - Practice Test Answer Sheet..211

A.P. Environmental Science Study Guide - Chapter One  Awesome Guides, Inc.

Letter to A.P. Environmental Science Students

Dear Student,

 Completing the A.P. Environmental Science Exam with a 3, 4, or 5 (considered a passing grade) has probably been in the back of your mind since you started the class in August or September. Sometimes it brings trepidation to your life, and rightfully so, it's a tough exam. In other words, you may be in fear of the day the exam arrives. When the time does arrive to prove how much knowledge you have accumulated during the school year, the tension gets even greater. It simply means you have the same feelings and fears that other students across the world, yes world, are experiencing. That's to say, you are normal! Let's face it without a little trepidation you would never have the motivation to prepare for the exam. So how do you get over your anticipation, and apprehension? To start, follow these three rules, 1) review weeks in advance, 2) don't skip any concepts in this guide 3) prepare, prepare and prepare.

By reading this guide, you have taken the first step towards your exam preparation. In the A.P. Environmental Study Guide, you will find the key goals and concepts set by the A.P. College Board. Take the time to read this review guide and strive to learn its contents. Do however keep in mind that this guide, although complete, does not replace the months you have spent in the classroom studying for exams, completing labs and participating in field experiences. If you were going to take the easy way, then you would have never taken this class in the first place. The best supplements to this guide are your A.P. Environmental Science Teacher, and the classroom material that she/he has provided. Be sure to take advantage of these experts' knowledge and experience.

Your A.P. Environmental Science Study Guide is arranged to make the most efficient use of your time. After reading about the exam and the testing tips, you should review your vocabulary. You will have a better understanding of the concepts that follow by knowing the "lingo". From there you can proceed in one of several directions. Either take one of the three sample tests, and time yourself, or go right to the key concepts review. If you go to the practice test first, then you will get an idea of the areas that you are weak in. This may help focus your study efforts. You could also go to the lab review section. Try to study with someone else, and say or write the concepts and vocabulary. Using your motor skills will help you remember the course objectives much better than simply reading them. Like a gymnast who practices a routine over and over until it's imbedded in their memory, so should you go over the material until you know it by heart. This guide was written for you; use it to your advantage and best of luck on the exam and in your future.

                Best Regards,

                Michael I. Lopatka

Awesome Guides, Inc.   A.P. Environmental Science Study Guide – Chapter One

Chapter 1
About the Exam

The Advanced Placement (A.P.) Environmental Science Exam is a three-hour examination consisting of two 90-minute sections; multiple choice and free response. The multiple-choice section has 100 questions and accounts for 60% of your grade. It requires *recall* and *understanding* of material learned in the course. The free response (essay) section has 4 questions and accounts for 40% of your grade. Free response questions require you to *apply principals*, *demonstrate analytical skills*, write clearly, concisely, interpret information from readying an environmental article and recall information from several different sources. You will not be able to bring a calculator to the exam for use in either section; however you should bring several sharpened #2 pencils with good erasers for the multiple choice questions, and one or more black pens to answer the free response questions. The 2003 exam will be given on **Wednesday May 14, 2003**, during the afternoon session. Preparation is the key, because this test may be more difficult than the tests you took in the classroom. Even though the exam may be more difficult than you are used to, by studying most or all of the concepts it is possible to achieve an acceptable grade.

Test Taking Tips

- Be sure that you understand all of the testing instructions that the test proctor has given to you. Ask the proctor to explain anything you do not understand.

- Besides the pencils and pens mentioned above also bring a watch, so that you can keep track of the time.

- Should you finish early, make sure that you have answered ALL of the questions. Make sure that the answer you marked is on the correct line for that multiple-choice question.

    √ **Never panic, you probably won't know everything on the exam. Try to be calm and think. Chances are that you have read or heard something about most of the subjects.**

- Answer questions that you know first, and then go back to complete the rest. By answering questions you know first, you may find that the questions you skipped may be on related topics which, allows you to recall information that will help you answer the skipped questions. Don't forget to go back and answer the ones you skipped. Don't leave any answers blank; these are always marked incorrect.

- Read all of the multiple choice questions carefully, and try to eliminate one or more of the choices in each question. This gives you a better chance of choosing a correct answer. In most cases, random guessing WILL NOT improve your test score. In fact, ¼ of the incorrect answers are subtracted from the correct answers.

    √ **The remainder of the tips apply to the free response questions.**

    - Read the ENTIRE question carefully.
    - Answer **all** of the parts of the question unless you are given a choice of what parts to answer, then answer only your choice

Awesome Guides, Inc. A.P. Environmental Science Study Guide – Chapter One

Make sure that you accomplish what the question requires, such as, explain, graph, calculate, compare, contrast, design, describe, outline, define, provide evidence, etc. Answer the question as it is stated, and don't spend too much time providing answers that are not asked for.

- Define and explain any vocabulary terms that you use.

- If asked to provide a diagram, be sure to label and explain its components. Do not spend a lot time providing diagrams as part of your essay, unless you are asked to do so.

√ **Make your answer concise and complete, don't wander off the point.**

- Include everything you can remember about the subject, as long as it applies to the question. Don't worry if you can't remember the term or process, but instead write what you do know. You **ARE NOT** penalized for wrong answers.

- If asked to design an experiment, include the following components:

    o Hypothesis —Remember this is based on some knowledge, it is an educated guess
    o Be sure to include independent (the treatments applied) and dependent variables (what is being measured)
    o Explain the procedures, and make sure that it is possible to complete the experiment
    o Describe any types of equipment or organisms used
    o Explain how the data will be collected, and analyzed
    o Explain the possible outcomes of the experiment

- If the question has multiple parts, such as a, b, c etc. be sure to label these in your answer.

- Although spelling is important, don't worry if you can't spell everything, do the best you can to allow the reader to understand what you are saying.

- Don't scribble or mark out too much and make sure that you write neatly, clearly, and logically.

Attempt every question, never give-up or quit!

Awesome Guides, Inc.   A.P. Environmental Science Study Guide - Chapter One

Vocabulary Tune-Up

All of the terms that you may have encountered during your AP Environmental Science class won't necessarily be found here. To examine all of the possible terms would fill an entire book in itself. However, **most** of the terms that will provide you with a good understanding of the AP Environmental Science concepts <u>are</u> included. Certain terms such as erosion, hypothesis, or fertilizer, are purposely left out because these definitions are assumed to be known by the vast majority of AP Environmental Science students.

Abiotic   Pertaining to the non-living factors in an ecosystem. Examples include air, water, soil, humidity, pH, wind temperature speed, dissolved oxygen, salinity etc.

Acid deposition   Refers to any kind of release of acid precipitation, over a particular area.

Acid precipitation   Condensed or frozen water vapor that includes acid rain, acid fog, and acid snow. Usually, any pH below 5.5 could be considered acid precipitation. Acid precipitation is anthropogenic (human made) and usually comes form the release of excessive or pollutants i.e. sulfur dioxide SO_2, nitrogen oxides.

Activated sludge   Refers to a material, typically found in the waste water treatment process, made up of a mass of living bacterial organisms feeding on waste material that has settled. Activated sludge is recycled to the aeration tank of secondary wastewater treatment.

Adaptation   An ecological or evolutionary adjustment to environmental changes, that may produce physical or structural changes in an organism, allowing it to cope better with the new conditions. For example; fur color that allows an animal to blend in with ecosystem.

Adiabatic cooling   Cooling that occurs when warm air, such as in the tropics, rises and bumps into lower atmospheric pressure. Adiabatic warming is opposite, where cool air descends into higher pressure. Descending air removes moisture from air, such as over deserts.

Aeration   Occurs in both soil and in the water. In soil it refers to the exchange of oxygen and carbon dioxide. This is necessary for roots to carry on cellular respiration. In water, it is the bubbling of air or oxygen through water to increase the dissolved oxygen.

Aerobic respiration   Pertains to organisms that require oxygen during the break down of organic molecules, the end result is carbon dioxide and water.

Aerosols   Any small (microscopic) liquid or solid particle coming from land or water surfaces that are carried into the atmosphere.

Awesome Guides, Inc. A.P. Environmental Science Study Guide - Chapter One

Aesthetics Refers to the natural beauty of something. This could refer to a forest, ocean, mountain, or even a quite place away from noise.

Agenda 21 A program designed to promote sustainable development. It is the result of the Earth Summit in Rio de Janeiro, Brazil, 1992, and is supported by the United Nations General Assembly.

Age structure Represents the proportions of people of different age groups. For example, it tracks certain groups such as, children, teenagers, young adults, middle-aged, and the elderly. Each similar age group is called a cohort.

Age structure diagrams Graphic representative of the age distribution of a human population. If the base of the graph is narrow then the population is experiencing negative growth because this represents a large elderly population and small young population. Similarly, if the base of the graph is wide then the population is growing, the wider the base, the more rapid the growth. Uniform shape represents a zero population growth.

Alga, or algae Photosynthetic microphytic (small) plants that live and reproduce entirely in aquatic environments Planktonic forms, may be single or colonial. Examples include spirogyra, volvox, or desmids. Some marine algae are very large (100 plus feet) and attached, such as kelp.

Algal bloom A rapid development of plantonic algae, causing water clarity to decrease. Algal blooms usually result from additions of nutrients to aquatic ecosystems

Alkaline, alkalinity Refers to a chemical that has a pH above 7.0. Alkalines absorb hydrogen ions and/or release hydroxyl ions.

Alternative energy Refers to energy sources that do not require fossil fuels or nuclear power. Examples include solar, wind, tidal, and hydrogen.

Ambient standards Air quality standards (set by the EPA) stating that the outside average air should always maintain a certain level of purity. These standards regulate levels of pollution that should not be exceeded to maintain environmental and human health.

Ammonification A process in the nitrogen cycle where soil bacteria convert organic waste to ammonia.

Anaerobic Without oxygen or oxygen-free.

Anthropogenic Refers to human activities such as, pollution or habitat destruction that have impacted our planet.

Appropriate technology Technology that increases the efficiency and productivity of hand labor without displacing workers. Workers improve their security without changing the social or economic system.

Aquaculture A process of aquatic farming, and usually refers to an artificial system.

Awesome Guides, Inc. A.P. Environmental Science Study Guide - Chapter One

Aquifer An underground layer of porous rock, sand, or other material where water moves between layers of nonporous rock or clay. Aquifers are used as a major water supply by sinking wells hundreds of feet below the ground.

Asbestos fibers Crystals of asbestos, that form minute strands. This natural mineral is known to cause cancer.

Assimilation A process in living systems where nutrients are converted into organic molecules, such as proteins.

Autotroph An organism that can produce its own food from raw materials, using light, phtosynthesizers or inorganic chemicals, chemosynthesizers. Examples include, green plants, algae, and some forms of bacteria.

Background radiation Radioactive radiation that comes from natural sources, not caused by human activity. Exposure to background radiation includes sunlight and radon.

Balanced herbivory A diversified plant community held in balance by various herbivores specific to each plant species.

Bedload A load of coarse sediment, mostly coarse silt and sand, that moves along a riverbed (bottom) due to the flowing of water, in contrast to being carried in suspension.

Benefit-cost analysis Analysis and/or comparison of the value of benefits received from a certain project or action in contrast to the costs.

Benthic plant The term benthic refers to the bottom. Therefore, the term includes plants that grow under water rooted or attached to the bottom of a lake, stream or the ocean.

Bioaccumulation Refers to the accumulation of increasing higher and higher concentrations of potentially toxic chemicals in organisms through a food chain. Substances that are ingested, nonbiodegradable, and stored in living tissue are passed along the food chain. This is also known biomagnification.

Biochemical oxygen demand (BOD) The amount of oxygen that is used or demanded as waste material is digested or oxidized in organisms. Higher BOD values remove greater amounts dissolved oxygen (DO) from aquatic ecosystems. Raw sewage has an extremely high BOD values and thus can lower DO very rapidly. BOD is measured in mg/l.

Bioconversion The use of a biomass as fuel, which includes the burning of wood, paper, and plant wastes produce energy. Biomass can also be converted into fuels such as alcohol and methane.

Biodegradable Refers to a substance that can be broken down to natural substances such as carbon dioxide and water by biological organisms. Decomposers typically breakdown these organic substances.

Awesome Guides, Inc. A.P. Environmental Science Study Guide - Chapter One

Biodiversity   Refers to the variety of life. Biodiversity occurs at the genetic, species, and ecosystem levels.

Biogas   Is a fuel that contains about two-thirds methane, one-third carbon dioxide, and small amounts of compounds from anaerobic (without air) digestion. Biogas had a very strong order.

Biological control   The control unwanted pest population by using living organisms. These include, introduction of predatory, parasitic, or disease-causing organisms.

Biological nutrient removal   A process used in sewage treatment that removes nitrogen and phosphorus from the effluent or final process before release to the environment.

Biomagnification   Bioaccumulation of a pollutant occurring through several levels of a food chain.

Biomass   Mass of biological material, usually the total mass of a particular group or category; for example, biomass (or weight) of producers in a certain ecosystem.

Biome   A group of ecosystems with similar vegetation and climatic conditions. Some examples include deciduous forests, arctic tundra, deserts, and tropical rain forests.

Bioremediation   Uses microorganisms to decontaminate soil or groundwater. This can be done by introducing organisms and/or oxygen into contaminated ecosystems.

Biosolids   The organic material removed from sewage effluents. Also known as sludge.

Biosphere   The entire ecosystem of Earth. It is the sum total of all the biomes and smaller ecosystems, which are all interconnected and interdependent through global processes such as water and atmospheric cycles.

Biota   Refers to the living or once living things in an ecosystem.

Biotic   Living or once living things.

Biotechnology   Pertains to genetic engineering (changing DNA sequences) of organisms. This has a practical application in that scientists are able to create new organisms that have more vigor, are more resistant to disease, have a better flavor, produce larger yields, and a host of other possibilities that make the product more valuable.

Biotic potential   Refers to the reproductive potential of a species. It's the maximum rate at which organisms may increase its population without any limiting factors affecting them.

Birth rates   The number live births per thousand individuals.

Birth control   Any means, natural or artificial, that may be used to reduce the number of live births.

Awesome Guides, Inc. A.P. Environmental Science Study Guide - Chapter One

BOD See biological oxygen demand.

Bottle law Also known as the bottle bill, this law that gives cash back for the return of containers, usually bottles. Not all states have a bottle law, and the amount of cash received varies form state to state.

Breeder reactor A nuclear reaction, in a specialized reactor, that converts nonfissionable uranium-238 into fissionable plutonium-239, which in turn can be used as fuel. In other words, it can make it own fuel while still producing power.

Broad-spectrum pesticide Chemical pesticides that kill many different kinds of pests, both the target pests and the nontarget pests (beneficial) ones.

Brownfields Abandoned, industrial sites that are contaminated to the point that new development is curtailed.

BTU An acronym for British Thermal Unit, that is the amount of energy required to raise the temperature of 1 pound of water 1 degree Fahrenheit.

Capillary action Water that moves upward, against gravity, in soil by clinging together with its hydrogen bonds and powered by evaporation.

Carbon dioxide (CO_2) A gas found in small quantities in the atmosphere, and released by organisms, internal combustion, and volcanoes. It is a principle green house gas.

Carnivore An organism that feeds on other animals. Examples include lions, wolves, sharks etc.

Carrying capacity The maximum population of a given species that an ecosystem can support. Populations often fluctuate above and below the carrying capacity, due to migration, resource availability, and competition etc.

Castings Humus-rich pellets made as a result of earthworm activity.

Catalyst A substance that speeds up a chemical reaction without being involved, or changed by the reaction. Examples include enzymes in organisms, and substances used in catalytic converters.

Canalization/canalized The straightening and deepening of stream or river channels to speed up water flow and reduce flooding.

Chlorinated hydrocarbons Also called organochlorides, these are synthetic organic molecules in which one or more hydrogen atoms have been replaced by chlorine atoms. These compounds are extremely hazardous because they are usually nonbiodegradable and tend to biomagnify. Some are also carcinogenic, cause cancer.

Awesome Guides, Inc.  A.P. Environmental Science Study Guide – Chapter One

Chlorination A disinfection process by which chlorine is added to drinking water or sewage effluent to kill bacteria.

Chlorofluorocarbons (CFC's) Synthetic organic molecules that contain one or more of both chlorine and fluorine atoms, and are implicated in ozone destruction.

Clear cutting Cutting of all trees in an area, leaving NOTHING standing. This may lead to severe erosion.

Climate Pertains to all historical data, temperature and rainfall, gathered over a long period of time.

Climax ecosystem The last stage in ecological succession. Climax ecosystems are stable and unchanging, unless acted upon by fire, storms, disease, or human activity.

Cogeneration When both useful heat and electricity are produced through the process of making electricity.

Combined-cycle natural gas unit A process of generating electricity using a natural gas turbine and a steam turbine. Excess heat produced while running the gas turbine is used to run the steam turbine.

Commensalism A relationship between two organisms in which one benefits and the other does not, but is not harmed.

Common pool resources Also referred to, as "commons", are natural resources owned by many people, such as a state park or federal rangeland. This also refers to resources no one owns like the ocean or the atmosphere.

Competitive exclusion principle Occurs when two species compete for the same resource. One will prevail and the other is excluded from the vicinity.

Compost The recycling or organic household waste products, like leaves, food etc. into useable plant fertilizer.

Cone of depression The lowering of the water table in the vicinity of a well.

Conservation The management of a resource to make certain that it provides the greatest benefit to humans in the future.

Consumers Any organism in an ecosystem that does not make its own food. This includes all organisms other than autotrophs or chemotrophs.

Consumptive use Producing just enough resources to provide for the present needs. This is opposite to overproducing.

Awesome Guides, Inc. A.P. Environmental Science Study Guide – Chapter One

Contour farming   Cultivation of land along the contours, that is, across a hill, rather than up and down slopes, to prevent or slow erosion.

Control rods   Neutron-absorbing material that is inserted or removed to control the rate of nuclear fission, located in the core of a nuclear reactor.

Cooling tower   A very large tower, usually parabolic shaped, designed to get rid of thermal wastes from a power plant, or other industrial process, into the atmosphere.

Cost-benefit analysis   Comparing of the value benefits of an action or project in to the costs.

Cost-benefit ratio/benefit-cost ratio   The value of the benefits to be gained from a project divided by the costs of the project. If the ratio is greater than 1, the project is economically justified; if the ratio is less than 1, the project is not economically justified.

Crepuscular   active at dusk and dawn.

Crop rotation   Changing the variety of crops grown every year or two. Many times this is done to enrich the soil by planting legumes that enrich the nitrogen in the soil.

Crude birth rate   Number of births per 1000 individuals per year.

Crude death rate   Number of deaths per 1000 individuals per year.

Cultural eutrophication   Accelerating a lakes natural aging process, eutrophication, by adding human related substances, such as fertilizer.

DDT (dichlorodiphenyltrichloroethane)   A chlorinated hydrocarbon, pesticide, now banned in the US, but still used in other countries. It is very persistent, or long lasting, in the environment.

Death rate   Number of deaths per 1000 individuals, per year.

Decomposers   Organisms that break down or feed on organic material. Most are fungi or bacteria, which recycle organic material.

Deep-well injection   A process that puts chemical wastes into deep human made wells, into at dry strata layer. The practice is somewhat controversial.

Deforestation   The process of removing all the vegetation in an area.

Demography   The study of population trends such as growth, movement, and development.

Denitrification   A process in the nitrogen cycle, where soil bacteria or cyanobacteria (blue-green algae) convert different forms of nitrogen into atmospheric nitrogen, N_2.

Awesome Guides, Inc. A.P. Environmental Science Study Guide - Chapter One

Density-dependent factor Takes into account the density in an ecosystems population, and is related to abiotic and biotic events, such as, parasitism. That is to say, as a population increases, it is more prone to parasitism.

Density-independent factor Does not take into account the density of an ecosystems population. For example, a fire or other catastrophic event will kill proportionately the same number of organisms regardless of the population density.

Deregulation Is typically uses to describe the power industry, where consumers are able to choose what power or utility company they want their electricity to come from. This is similar to being able to choose which cellular phone service you want to use.

Desalinization A processes that takes saltwater and converts it to fresh water, by distillation or reverse osmosis.

Desertification The creation of "desert-like" conditions due to overgrazing, over cultivation, and excessive irrigation. The process where fertile land is converted to desert-like conditions.

Detritus Dead organic matter, such as plant and animal wastes, leaves, etc. in an ecosystem.

Developed countries Industrialized countries such as the United States, Canada, Western European nations, Japan, Australia, and New Zealand where the gross domestic product exceeds $7000 per capita.

Developing countries Countries such as Latin America, Africa, and most of Asia, in which the gross domestic product is less than $7000 per capita.

Dissolved oxygen (DO) Oxygen (O_2) that is dissolved in water. This is probably the most important single parameter in aquatic ecosystem since all aerobic organisms depend on it for their cellular respiration.

Distillation The process of purifying water or other liquids through boiling and recondensing the vapor, leaving the solid material in the boiler.

Doubling time The time takes a population to double in size, assuming the rate of growth is steady. This can be calculated by, the rule of 70, that is, dividing the growth rate by 70.

Ecological succession The process where by an ecosystem changes gradually over time from one stage to another, until a climax ecosystem is reached.

Ecosystem An area that includes all of the plants, animals, and other organisms interacting with each other and with their environment.

Ecotone A transitional zone between two ecosystems.

Awesome Guides, Inc. A.P. Environmental Science Study Guide - Chapter One

El Nino A major climatic phenomenon characterized by the movement of unusually warm surface water into the eastern equatorial Pacific Ocean. It results in extensive disruption of weather around the world.

Endangered Species Act The federal legislation that mandates protection of species and their habitats that are in danger of extinction.

Endangered Species A species where the population is declining, and may be endanger of extinction without positive human intervention. Reasons for organisms reaching this level are, habitat destruction, and pollution. Organisms that are most affected include those that are specialists (have very specific habitat needs), live on islands and who require a large home range (area required to feed, reproduce etc.).

Environment Includes all of the biotic and abiotic factors that can affect an organism.

Environmental resistance The totality of factors such as adverse weather conditions, shortage of food or water, predators, and diseases that will keep populations from growing to their biotic potential.

Environmental science The branch of science that studies environmental issues.

Epicenter The origination point of an earthquake.

Epiphytes Also known as air plants, because they receive some of their nutrients for the air. These, usually tropical plants, grow on trees but are not parasitic. Examples include, spanish moss, pineapple, and bromeliads.

Equilibrium theory The theory that ecosystems have natural checks and balances.

Estuary A bay open to the ocean at one end and receiving fresh water from a river at the other end, hence, mixing of fresh and salt water occurs (brackish).

Euphotic zone An area in aquatic ecosystems where there is enough light penetration to support photosynthesis.

Eutrophic A stage in the ecological succession of a lake, where nutrient-rich water provides abundant growth of algae and/or other aquatic plants. Sometimes called a middle-aged lake.

Eutrophication The natural aging process of a lake, that is greatly accelerated by human actions, called cultural eutrophication, and caused by additions of nutrients mainly nitrogen and phosphorus.

Evapotranspiration The combination of evaporation and transpiration.

Evolution Refers to change over time. The theory of evolution states that all species now on Earth descended gradually from ancestral species through a process known as natural selection.

Exotic species A nonnative species introduced to an area. Exotic species may experience exponential growth due to a lack of natural predators, and take over valuable native species.

Awesome Guides, Inc. A.P. Environmental Science Study Guide - Chapter One

Exponential increase The very rapid growth of a species, only possible if considerable resources are present and limiting factors are held to a minimum. It produces a J-shaped curve.

Extinction The death of all individuals of a particular species. This results in a loss of genes and biodiversity.

Fecal coliform test A test for the presence of the bacteria Escherichia coli, typically found in the gut of humans and other mammals. The test is usually used to determine the contamination of a body of water. The presence of fecal coliform is an indication that harmful bacteria are present.

Fire climax ecosystems Ecosystems that are dependent on the fire for their reproduction and regeneration.

First Law of Thermodynamics Also known as the Law of Conservation of Energy, it states that energy is never created, but only converted from one form to another, such as, light to heat.

Fission The splitting of an atom into two atoms of lighter elements. This is the basis of nuclear energy production.

Fission products Refers to the atoms, usually radioactive, and subatomic particles, resulting from the splitting of atoms in a nuclear reactor.

Food chain A simplified view of the transfer of energy and material from one organism to another. Food chains are never very long due the tremendous energy lost at each step.

Food web Takes into account all the food chains in an ecosystem.

Fossil fuels Energy sources that come from millions of years of heat and pressure acting upon prehistoric photosynthetic organic matter. Examples include crude oil, coal, and natural gas.

Fragmentation Occurs when habitats are divided into a patch work of intact forest land and deforested lands.

Fuel assembly Refers to rods containing nuclear fuel, usually uranium. The chain reaction in the fuel assembly is controlled by these rods.

Fuel wood The wood used in many developing countries for cooking and heating.

Gasohol A blend of 90% gasoline and 10% alcohol, used to help extend gasoline supplies.

Geothermal The naturally hot interior of Earth.

Global warming Used to describe the warming of the Earth's atmosphere.

Gray water Wastewater from sinks and showers, bath tubs, washing machines etc. that does not contain human excrement. This water is sometimes reused, without purification, for irrigation.

Greenhouse effect Describes the mechanism of global warming, due to heat trapped near the earth's surface because of green house gases, such as, carbon dioxide which forms a blanket around the planet.

Greenhouse gases Gases such as carbon dioxide, water vapor, methane, nitrous oxide, chlorofluorocarbons and other halocarbons that absorb infrared energy.

Green revolution Pertains to the development and introduction of new varieties of high yield wheat, rice and other crops.

Grit chamber Pertains to the preliminary treatment phase in wastewater-treatment plants, where the velocity of flow is slowed down to a point where large materials can settle out.

Gross primary production The total energy that primary producers, autotrophs produce organic matter.

Groundwater remediation The repurification of contaminated groundwater.

Habitat The specific environment in which an organism lives. This is sometimes called an organism's address.

Hadley cell An atmospheric system of vertical and horizontal moving air circulation predominantly in the tropics, producing the major weather patterns on the earth.

Half-life The time it takes for half of a radioactive substance to decay.

Halogenerated hydrocarbon A synthetic organic compound that has one or more atoms of the halogen family, such as chlorine, fluorine, and bromine.

Hard water Pertains to water that contains relatively high amounts of calcium carbonate.

Hazardous materials (HAZMAT) Any material that is either ignitable, corrosive reactive, or toxic.

Heavy metal A metal with a high atomic weight, such as lead, mercury, cadmium, and zinc. These are considered to be very serious water and soil pollutants.

Herbicide A chemical that kills or inhibits growth of plants.

Herbivore An organism feeds on plant material, also known as a primary consumer.

Heterotroph An organism that cannot manufacture its own food, and therefore depends on other organisms for its nutrition.

Host-specific Referring to organisms such as insects, or fungal diseases that can affect only one particular host.

Humidity The amount of water vapor in the air.

Humus A dark brown or black, soft, spongy residue of organic matter, found at the surface of soils. Humus forms due to the decay of leaves or other organic materials.

Hydrocarbon A natural or synthetic organic substance that is made up mostly of carbon and hydrogen. Examples include carbohydrates, fats, crude oil, and coal. Release of hydrocarbons through the burning of fossil fuels is a major cause of air pollution.

Hydroponics The cultivation of plants without soil, and where a water solution replaces the minerals found in soil.

Hypoxia In aquatic ecosystems, a condition where dissolved oxygen is greatly lowered, where life can no longer be supported.

Incineration A process of burning municipal solid wastes, MSW, to reduce the amount of waste going into a sanitary landfill. The heat produced in the process can be used as an energy source, but may produce toxic wastes to the air, if not controlled.

Indicator organism Any organism that can determine or indicate a certain environmental condition, such as, trout living and breeding in a mountain stream, indicates a good supply of dissolved oxygen. Also see indicator species.

Industrial Revolution A time in history, the 19th century, where factories used fossil fuels and produced large amounts of products.

Indicator species A species, that if present in an ecosystem, confirms a particular abiotic or biotic condition, such a soil pH or the presence of a pollutant. Also see indicator organism.

Infant mortality An indicator of the number of babies that die before age 1, per 1000 babies born.

Infiltration When water percolates into soil. The more the infiltration, the less the runoff.

Infrastructure A system of roads, bridges, sewer and water systems, power plants, etc. in a community, state, etc.

Inorganic compounds Includes nonliving chemicals in air water, soil etc. Also refers to compounds that do not contain carbon.

Insecticide A chemical that is used to kill insects.

Awesome Guides, Inc.   A.P. Environmental Science Study Guide - Chapter One

Integrated waste management   The use of several options for the handling solid wastes. This includes recycling, waste reduction, composting, landfilling, and others.

Intrinsic value   An idea that things are valuable, without "$$" value, just for their own being.

Keystone species   An organism that is absolutely necessary for the survival or many other species.

Kinetic energy   Refers to energy of motion.

K strategist   A reproduction approach where an organism has few offspring that are born at one time, and then the young are carefully cared for. This is typical of mammals and birds. Also see R strategist.

La Nina   A major climatic phenomenon characterized by intense easterly trade winds in the eastern equatorial Pacific Ocean. It results in extensive disruption of weather around the world, often opposite to El Nino.

Lacey Act   The first national act, passed in 1900, that gave protection to wildlife by forbidding interstate commerce in illegally killed wildlife.

Landfill   A site where wastes (municipal, industrial, or chemical) are disposed of and sealed in large under or above ground cells.

Land subsidence   The phenomenon where land gradually sinks, due to excessive removal of ground water or oil.

Law of Limiting Factors   Also known as Liebig's Law of Minimums. An ecosystem can be limited by the absence or minimum amount of any one vital factor.

LD 50   Stands for lethal dose 50%, where ½ of organisms are killed due to an application of a pollutant.

Leachate   The mixture of water and materials that are leaching (moving) through the ground. Typically pertains to the landfills.

Legumes   A group of land plants that have the ability to fix nitrogen. Examples include, peas, beans, alfalfa and clovers.

Limiting factor   A single factor that an organism must have for survival, regardless of how much of the other resources are present. For example O_2.

Limits of tolerance   The absolutes extreme of any factor, e.g., temperature or pressure that an organism can tolerate, before it will die.

Litter   In an ecosystem it refers to leaves, twigs, and other dead plant material.

Awesome Guides, Inc.  A.P. Environmental Science Study Guide - Chapter One

Loam A soil consisting of a mixture of about 40% sand, 40% silt, and 20% clay. Loam is considered the best soil for agriculture.

Maximum sustainable yield The maximum amount of a renewable resource that can be taken year after year without depleting the resource.

Meltdown When a nuclear reactor loses its cooling water and melts from the excessive heat produced. This is also known as the China Syndrome because it was once jokingly said that a complete meltdown would cause radioactive substances to melt to China.

Methane A natural gas, CH_4 that is produced through the decomposition of organic material.

Microbe Any microscopic organism, such as, bacteria, viruses, and protozoan.

Mitigation Used in restoring or moderating the quality or condition of an ecosystem. This may reduce the intensity of a pollutant, or include replanting a clear cut forest to moderate or alleviate an environmental problem. Mitigation may also include a punishment, or penalty.

Microclimate Abiotic conditions of particular location in an ecosystem, that may include, a shaded area, a pond etc.

Monoculture The growing a single crop with the same genetic makeup over a very large area.

Monsoon Seasonal heavy rainfall.

Morbidity The occurrence of disease in a population.

Mortality The occurrence of death in a population.

Mutagenic Causing mutations, genetic deformities, and cancer.

Mutualism A relationship between two organisms in which both organisms benefit from the relationship.

Muncipal Solid Waste Refers to trash that is thrown away, mostly paper, from communities.

Natural biological control Used in sewage treatment to remove nitrogen and phosphorus.

Natural chemical control Using of one or more natural chemicals such as hormones or pheromones to control a pest.

Natural selection States that, organisms which are best suited for the environmental conditions of an ecosystem, have a better change of survival and passing their genes on to the next generation.

Awesome Guides, Inc. A.P. Environmental Science Study Guide – Chapter One

Net primary production The available energy in the form of organic material that is available for transfer to the next level of the food chain. This is equal to the gross primary productivity of an organism minus the energy used by that organism.

Niche The role an organism has in an ecosystem. Sometimes referred as an organism's job. NO two organisms can occupy exactly the same niche.

NIMBY Acronym for 'not in my back yard.' NIMBY refers to a common attitude regarding undesirable facilities such as incinerators, nuclear facilities, and hazardous waste treatment plants etc.

NIMTOO An acronym for "not in my term of office".

Nitric acid (HNO_3) An acid found in acid rain.

Nitrification A process in the nitrogen cycle where ammonia is converted into nitrate ions (NO_3), the form of nitrogen that plants uptake.

Nitrogen fixation The process of directly converting nitrogen gas (N_2) from the atmosphere into nitrates (NO^-_3) or ammonia (NH_3), that green plants use for their nutrition.

Nocturnal The term for organisms that are active at night.

Nonbiodegradable Refers to substances that can be either consumed or broken down by living things. Examples include plastics, aluminum, nuclear wastes, and many types of chemicals.

Nonconsumptive water use Refers to water that is not consumed, like, bathing water, dish water, etc.

Nonpersistent Any chemical that will quickly break down into harmless compounds.

Nonpoint sources Types of pollution that the source is usually difficult to locate and manage, such farm or urban runoff of fertilizers, pesticides, and oils.

Nonrenewable resources Resources that cannot be replaced because they take long periods of time to generate. Examples include fossils fuels and metal ores.

No-till agriculture An agriculture process where weeds are killed, usually with chemicals, without tilling the land to reduce erosion.

Nuclear power Energy that uses a nuclear reactor, and nuclear fuel, usually uranium, as a source to run a steam turbogenerator.

Nutrient cycle Also known as a biogeochemical cycle, it represents the pathway of nutrients in an ecosystem, through the soil, air, water, and organisms. The major cycles are represented by the carbon cycle, the nitrogen cycle, the phosphorus cycle.

Awesome Guides, Inc. A.P. Environmental Science Study Guide – Chapter One

Oil sand A sedimentary tar-like hydrocarbon, containing bitumen, that can be mined, and used as fuel, when heated, then refined as crude oil.

Oil shale A sedimentary rock containing kerogen that can be mined and refined into oil.

Oligotrophic Refers to a lake that is unproductive and low in nutrients. It is characterized by low biodiversity, and usually refers to a new lake, during the first stage of aquatic succession.

Omnivore An animal that consumes other animals.

OPEC An acronym for the 'Organization of Petroleum Exporting Countries'.

Optimal range Refers to an abiotic condition that will best support a particular kind of organism. This also refers to populations of organisms, thus the term optimum population.

Organic food Is food that is produced without the use of synthetic fertilizers, synthetic pesticides, genetic engineering etc.

Organic phosphate Phosphate bonded to any organic molecule.

Over cultivation Is the farming practice that overuses the land by repeatedly growing crops faster than the soil can be regenerated. This practice may lead to desertification.

Overgrazing Is the grazing of livestock in greater numbers than the land can sustain, leading to destruction of the land.

Ozone A natural atmospheric gas formed by three oxygen molecules O_3, found in the stratosphere, that shields the earth from damaging electromagnetic radiation. Ozone may also be used for disinfecting water.

Ozone hole A large area over the Antarctic, where stratospheric ozone air is severely depleted of its normal levels. The possible cause is CFCs.

PANs (peroxyacetylnitrates) Compounds that are present in photochemical smog. These air pollutants are very harmful to plants and cause eyes, nose and throat irritation to humans.

Parent material The original rock, which after weathering, produces the minerals in soil.

Particulates Air pollutants that are made up of suspended solid and liquid particles.

Passive solar heating system Solar heating that uses convection currents instead of pumps or other mechanical means to transfer heated air or water.

Percolation The process of water soaking into the soil.

Awesome Guides, Inc. A.P. Environmental Science Study Guide - Chapter One

Permafrost   A permanent layer of solid ice just under the soil, which is present even during the summer, and found in the tundra biome.

Persistent   Refers to pesticides or other chemicals that breakdown in the environment very slowly. This is also known as being nonbiodegradable.

Pesticide   A chemical that kills pests. Pesticides are often categorized according to what they will kill. For example, herbicides kill plants, insecticides kill insects, fungicides kill fungi, and rodenticides kill rodents.

Phosphate   A compound that has four oxygen atoms attached, such as PO4's. Phosphate is a major plant nutrient, and limiting factor in water. Too much added phosphate may cause an algae bloom.

Photochemical smog   Air pollution from automobile exhaust that is formed by sunlight causing chemical reactions with nitrogen oxides and hydrocarbons. It forms a brownish haze.

Photovoltaic cells   A piece of equipment that can convert light energy directly into an electrical current.

Plant community   A group of plant species that occupies a given area.

Plate tectonics   A scientific theory stating that the earth's crust is composed of many individual plates that move over and under each other causing geological activity such as, earthquakes, volcanic activity, continental drift.

Point sources   Pollutants that have a specific point of origin. For example, a pipe that directly flows into a river.

Pollutant   A contaminate to air, water, or soil.

Pollution   Contamination of air, water, or soil with undesirable amounts of hazardous materials or even heat.

PCBs (polychlorinated biphenyls)   A group of synthetic chlorinated hydrocarbon chemicals that are nonbiodegradable, contaminate food chains, and are carcinogenic (cause cancer).

Population   Groups within a single species, the individuals of which can and do freely interbreed, and produce fertile offspring.

Population density   The numbers of individuals per unit of area.

Potable water   Water that is suitable for consumption (drinking water).

Awesome Guides, Inc.   A.P. Environmental Science Study Guide - Chapter One

Potential energy   The energy that is stored either in a chemical such as in crude oil, or because of position such water on top of a dam, that has the ability to perform work.

Power grid   The combination of all power plants generated electricity that is bought or sold to utility companies.

PPM   An acromyn for 'parts per million'.

Predator-prey relationship   A feeding relationship between animals, where one feeds on another.

Preliminary treatment   The first stage of sewage treatment where large debris, such as sticks, grit, and rags pass through a screen followed by and grit chamber, where the flow of water is slowed down enough to allow for sedimentation.

Preservation   The idea that land should be left in its natural state, never touched or developed.

Primary consumer   Also known as a herbivore and occupies the second trophic level, and more or less feeds exclusively on green plants or their products.

Primary treatment   The second stage of sewage treatment, where the sewage water flows very slowly allowing particulate organic material to settle out. The settled material is raw sludge.

Producers   Organisms, such as green plants, that use light energy, photosynthesis, to make their own food.

Quadrant sampling   A method of studying an ecosystem, where a representative, or group of representative square sections are selected. This is done when it is impossible to study an entire ecosystem "inch by inch".

Radioactive decay   The natural reduction of radioactivity in unstable (radioactive) isotopes that gives off radiation until it becomes stable.

Radioisotope   An isotope of an element that is unstable and may tend to gain stability by giving off radioactive emissions.

Radon   A natural radioactive gas produced by the decay of rock material. This has been of major concern because it may seep into buildings, and cause cancer to occupants.

Rain shadows   An area of low rainfall due to its position on the leeward (downwind) side of mountain ranges. The height of the mountain range prevents precipitation from falling on the leeward side.

Range of tolerance   The range of abiotic conditions within which an organism or population can survive and reproduce.

Awesome Guides, Inc. A.P. Environmental Science Study Guide - Chapter One

Recycle Recovery of materials that would otherwise be buried in landfills or combusted, and refers to the reusing of the recovered products.

Remediation The return of a contaminated ecosystem to its original uncontaminated state. Sometimes known as bioremediation.

Renewable resources Usually refers to energy resources that can be renewed or regrown.

Resilience An organisms ability to repopulate an area after a catastrophe.

Resistance Refers to organisms that become immune to certain pesticides, antibodies or other treatment, that was suppose to kill them.

Resource partitioning When one or more species compete for a resource, and due to this competition, the species will move or separate to different habitats. This is true for example, when different species of anoles (tropical lizards) can be found in different positions on a tree, some on lower branches, some in the middle and other at the top of trees.

R strategist A reproduction approach where an organism has many offspring born at one time and these offspring are not cared for. This is typical of reptiles and insects. Also see K strategist.

Restoration ecology A branch of ecology that involves the restoring of degraded or altered ecosystems back to their natural state.

Reuse A system of using old items to produce new ones, in contrast to throwing them away, otherwise known as recycling.

Riparian woodlands A wooded area that grows along rivers or lakes.

Replacement fertility level The number of children a couple must have to just replace themselves. In developing countries this number is 2.7, while in developed countries, it is 2.1 children per couple.

Saltwater intrusion Occurs when seawater moves into underwater aquifers or estuaries causing these to become salty. This occurs at or near coastal towns and is the result of drawing groundwater down to the point where it can no longer hold back the saltwater, from the oceans or other salt or brackish (semi salty) sources.

Sand Mineral particles 0.2-2.0 mm in diameter.

Savanna The name used for the grassland biome.

Secondary consumer An organism that feeds on herbivores, and is on the 3rd or higher trophic level in am ecosystem.

Awesome Guides, Inc. A.P. Environmental Science Study Guide - Chapter One

Secondary succession A step-by-step process that ecosystems go through after a catastrophe such as a fire, clear-cutting etc. Also known as old-field succession because abandoned farmlands go through the same process, of changing their plant communities over a period of time.

Secondary treatment Also known as biological treatment, it is the third major step in the sewage treatment process. Using a trickling filter, or activated-sludge process, bacteria break down the organic wastes.

Second generation pesticide A synthetic (human made) pesticide.

Second Law of Thermodynamics States that in every energy conversion (e.g., electricity to light) some energy is converted to heat and some heat always escapes. Therefore, in every energy conversion, a portion of energy is lost, and since energy cannot be created (First Law of Thermodynamics) any system requires the input of energy.

Sediment Refers to sand, silt and clay particles, that have settled or are being carried by rivers and streams.

Seep An area where groundwater comes to the surface of the soil, or cracks in rock, from many different places and/or over a large area.

Seismograph (S&P waves) A graphic representation of S and P waves that travel through the earth due to geological activity such as from earthquakes.

Septic system A method of treating sewage, usually where municipal sewage is not available, where sewage is treated on site in a septic tank and drain field.

Sievert A unit of measurement that measures the amount of penetration radioactive emissions have on biological tissues. 1 sievert = 100 rem.

Slash-and-burn agriculture A method of clearing land, usually done in the tropics, where trees and shrubs are cut and burned for the purposes of agriculture.

Soft water Water with little or no calcium, magnesium, or other ions.

Soil A dynamic system involving biotic and abiotic components such as mineral particles, detritus, and soil organisms.

Soil horizons Distinct layers in soil that contains different properties such as percolation rate and minerals.

Solid waste Any discarded materials that are not flushed down toilets or sinks.

Special interest group An organized group of people who lobby government for a particular issue, or concern.

Awesome Guides, Inc. A.P. Environmental Science Study Guide - Chapter One

Specialization A species that is adapted to take advantage of only one particular resource. These species are practically vulnerable to changes in an ecosystem.

Storm water Water from rainfall.

Stratosphere The second layer of Earth's atmosphere above the troposphere, about 10 and 30 miles up, containing an ozone (O_3) shield.

Strip cropping An agriculture method used to reduce erosion, where crops are grown in strips, fluctuating with hay at right angles to prevailing winds or slopes.

Strip mining A mining technique where all the soil and earth far below the ground surface is removed. Coal and phosphate mining typically uses this technique. Strip mining is very destructive to land.

Subduction Takes place when an oceanic plate slides under a continental plate.

Subsistence farming Is when farmers produce enough food to meet the needs their family. It is common practice in developing countries and usually involves hand labor, in contrast to machines.

Subsoil A soil layer that is just below the topsoil, that has little to no humus or other organic material.

Succession The gradual, or sometimes rapid, change in a species that occupies an ecosystem. The mechanism behind succession is a change in abiotic or biotic factors that facilitates (helps) some species and inhibit others. Succession can be either primary (bare rock) or secondary (old field). Primary succession begins with bare rock and ends with a climax ecosystem. Secondary succession begins with a disturbed area such as an abandoned field, and ends with its climax ecosystem.

Sulfur dioxide (SO_2) An air pollutant that usually comes from the burning of coal for the production of energy.

Surface water Water that is from lakes, rivers, ponds, streams etc.

Sustainability Refers to whether a process can be continued indefinitely without depleting the energy or material resources on which it depends.

Sustainable agriculture The technique of growing crops that maintains the qualities of the land's resources, theoretically, indefinitely.

Sustainable development The concept that maintains the world's ecosystems, while still allowing people to use the land's resources.

Symbiosis The relation between two organisms where there is some kind of interaction, either positive or negative.

Awesome Guides, Inc.  A.P. Environmental Science Study Guide - Chapter One

Synthetic fuels   Also known as synfuels; these are fuels produced from natural gas, coal, oil shale, or tar sands.

Tar sands   Mined material that contains bitumen, and when heated can be refined like crude oil.

Tectonic plates   Pertains to the individual blocks of rock found on the Earth's crust. Movement of these blocks, or plates causes most of the geological activity on the Earth.

Temperature inversion   Also called a thermal inversion, is a weather phenomenon where a warm layer of air is on top of a cooler layer of air. Temperature inversions trap pollutants in the lower atmosphere.

Terracing   A farming technique used where there is a hillside, where the land is graded perpendicular to the slope to prevent or slow down erosion.

Territoriality   An animal behavioral characteristic where animals mark and defend a particular area. Territory size varies greatly from animal to animal.

Thermal pollution   Is pollution caused when hot water, or heat, is added to water or air, usually from power plants. Addition of heat in water usually has detrimental effects, because it lowers dissolved oxygen, DO (DO is inversely proportional to temperature), and may cause algae blooms. An exception is the Crystal River Nuclear Power Plant, in Florida where warm water is released to the Gulf of Mexico, and along with the natural springs, attracts numerous manatees (an endangered species) to the area.

Threatened species   A category given to some organisms when their populations are declining. Threatened species may be numerous in some areas but have low numbers over their entire range.

Threshold level   The maximum exposure to adverse environmental effects, such pollution, with out being killed. Other physical effects may result by reaching the threshold level.

Topsoil   The surface layer of soil, rich in humus and other organic material.

Toxicology   The study of the toxic substances and their impact on human health. Toxicologists (people that study toxicology) investigate the source of toxins and their effects on the environment and human health.

Transect sampling method   A technique of studying an ecosystem where all organisms are cataloged several feet on either side along a straight line. This method gives the researcher a good sampling of the ecosystem, because it is usually impossible, or too time consuming, to study an entire area.

Transpiration   The loss of water from plants, through leaf pores (stomata) in the form of vapor.

Treated sludge   Typically refers to the solid organic wastes of sewage treatment that is nonhazardous.

Trickling filter system   A wastewater treatment method where sewage trickles over porous rocks, allowing microorganisms to breakdown the organic material.

Awesome Guides, Inc. A.P. Environmental Science Study Guide - Chapter One

Trophic level Refers to an ecosystems feeding level, such as autotrophs (green plants) are at the first trophic level, followed by primary consumers on the second level, secondary consumers on the third level, etc.

Troposphere Is the part of Earth's atmosphere that begins at the surface and goes to about ten miles up, where all of the planet's weather takes place.

Turbid Is a determination of a waters transparency, that is, a measure if the visibility.

Turbine A type of 'paddle wheel' that rotates at high speeds, usually in a magnetic field to produce electricity.

Turbogenerator A turbine that drives an electric generator. Driven by steam, gas, or water, it produces electricity.

Ultraviolet radiation Also known as UV radiation, it comes from the sun and has a smaller wavelength than visible light, and causes damage to living tissue.

Upwelling A phenomena that occurs in the oceans where diverging currents and off shore winds cause water from depths to raise to the surface bringing lots of nutrients to the surface. These areas usually attract a great number of fish.

Urban blight The wasting away of the inner city that occurred when many city dwellers moved to the suburbs, lowering the tax base, and causing loss or shortest of services such roads, bridges, building, education etc. General deterioration of structures and facilities such as buildings and roadways, and also the decline in quality of services such as education, that has occurred in inner city areas as growth has been focused on suburbs and exurbs.

Urban sprawl The rapid growth of areas surrounding the inner city, that spreads out housing, shopping, and businesses around outside of the city.

Volatile organic compounds Otherwise known as, VOC, these chemicals vaporize into the air. Examples include, gasoline, paint solvents, many cleaning agents, and are a major factor in the formation of photochemical smog.

Waste-to-energy The use of solid wastes as a fuel to generate electricity.

Water-holding capacity The ability of a soil to hold water so that it will be available to plants.

Water logging Occurs when water completely saturates soil. Some plant roots can tolerate water logging, but many root systems can't, due to lack of oxygen and the growth of fungus, causing root rot and eventual death or weakening of the plant.

Watershed The total sum all the land that will drain directly or indirectly a body of water such as a river or stream.

A.P. Environmental Science Study Guide - Chapter One  Awesome Guides, Inc.

Water table   The upper surface or level of groundwater that changes its level according to season and amount of rain an area receives. Wetlands typically have their water table at or near the surface of the topsoil.

Weathering   The erosion of rock into smaller pieces and eventually soil minerals. This is caused by natural chemical acids found in lichens, physical changes(freezing and cracking), and biological factors (plants growing in rock).

Wetlands   Areas that are wet for at least most of the year, and are a natural control to flooding, and home to numerous organisms.

Wind turbines   Modern 'windmills' used for the purpose of generating electricity.

Zooplankton   The group of small organisms that include, protozoa, and the larvae of crustaceans, worms, mollusks, and cnidarians, that drift with the oceans currents.

While many inner cities are experiencing blight........

........buffalos are returning to our nation's prairies.

Awesome Guides, Inc. A.P. Environmental Science Study Guide - Chapter Two

Chapter 2
Outline of Topics & Key Concepts

Climatic Patterns and Species Distribution

Ecological Terrestrial Biomes

- **Deserts** – **Rainfall:** Less than 10" per year **Climate:** Hot days/cold nights **Soils:** Rich, thin, and permeable **Geographical distribution:** Occurs on every continent except Europe. **Dominant animals:** Arthropods, reptiles, mammals (mainly rodents) and numerous insects. **Dominant plants:** Cactus, thorny bushes, and shrubs. **Supplementary:** Desert plants are known as xerophytes, some plants remain dormant during times of no rainfall, many mammals are nocturnal or crepuscular, seasonal torrential rains cause flash floods in some areas.

- **Grasslands** – **Rainfall:** 10"-60" **Climate:** From hot to cold depending on location. **Soils:** Rich and usually deep. **Geographical distribution:** Central North America (prairie), Central Asia (steppes), Africa (veldt or savanna) South America (Pampas), Australia (Outback), and southern India. **Dominant animals:** Large grazing animals that vary greatly depending on which grassland area they occur. In the U.S. bison, pronghorn antelope, wild horses, cattle, and sheep. Africa has rhinos, warthogs, lions, and hyenas. In Australia kangaroos, carnivores such as: wolves, cougar, foxes, eagles, coyotes, and jackals. **Dominant plants:** Tall grasses in areas where there is more rainfall, and smaller grasses where less rainfall occurs, and small woodlands in some. **Supplementary:** Maintained by grazing animals and fire.

- **Temperate Deciduous Forest** – **Rainfall:** 30"-100" **Climate:** Four seasons, all about equal in length. Warm, humid summers, and cold, below freezing in winter. **Soils:** Well developed, with rich leaf litter. **Geographical distribution:** Western and Central Europe, Eastern Asia, Eastern North America. **Dominant animals:** Numerous varieties of song birds, ducks, raptors, skunks, opossum, mice, white tailed deer, raccoons, foxes, squirrels, black bears, snakes, and amphibians **Dominant plants:** Large variety of broad leaved, deciduous trees, some conifers, ferns, lichens, mosses, liverworts, and herbaceous plants. **Supplementary:** Marketable pines have replaced much of the native hardwood in eastern U.S..

- **Tropical Rain Forest** – **Rainfall:** 90"-180" frequent and heavy, average 92". **Climate:** Nonseasonal, with temperatures around 80 degrees F year round, and humid. **Soils:** Thin and low in nutrients due to leaching after frequent rains. **Geographical distribution:** Northern South America (Amazon), Central America, West/Central Africa (Congo), South East Asia, Burma, Philippines. **Dominant animals:** Extremely high numbers of birds, insects, frogs, fish, monkeys, small mammals, tigers, jaguars, ocelot, and many other endemic and colorful species. **Dominant plants:** No one plant dominates, a vast biodiversity of thick canopy formed form broad leafed trees, vines (lianas), numerous epiphytes (air plants, such as orchids and bromeliads), little to no

A.P. Environmental Science Study Guide - Chapter Two    Awesome Guides, Inc.

under story, except near the many rivers and streams. **Supplementary**: Numerous forms of fungi and bacteria on the forest floor promote rapid decomposition.

- <u>Taiga (Coniferous Forest)</u> ***Rainfall***: 20"-40", with moist winters, and more rain in summer. Some get as much as 90" and more. ***Climate:*** Seasonal with long cold winters, short summer growing season. ***Soils:*** Acid, with leaf litter and humus. ***Geographical distribution:*** Northern North America, Northern Europe and Asia and the upper elevations of tall mountains. ***Dominant animals:*** Large herbivores, moose, elk, mule, hares, deer, and carnivores such as, lynx, foxes, fishers, and martens. ***Dominant plants:*** Conifers, such as, spruce, hemlock, fir, pine, and deciduous trees such as birch, popular, willow, and maple with a poor under story. ***Supplementary:*** The coastal redwood forest of California and Oregon provides a nesting area for ducks and other neotropical birds, as well as a large source of timber.

- <u>Tundra</u>   ***Rainfall:*** Less than 10". ***Climate:*** Long, bitter and cold winters with a 10-week annual growing season. ***Soils:*** Thin with permafrost, which prevents large shrubs or trees from growing. ***Geographical distribution:*** North of the coniferous forest in the northern hemisphere, and on the tops of tall mountains above the timberline. ***Dominant animals:*** Lemmings, musk ox, lynx, caribou, artic hares, artic foxes, and great numbers of insects in the summer. ***Dominant plants***: Small shrubs, lichens, mosses grasses and sedges. ***Supplementary:*** Breeding ground for large numbers of geese, shorebirds, and ducks.

Aquatic Ecosystems

- <u>**Lakes and ponds**</u> – Fresh water bodies of standing water that have rooted littoral (shore) and floating plants. In addition, they have numerous species of algae (older eutrophic lakes) or few species of algae (newer oligotrophic lakes). Northern lakes usually experience spring and fall overturn, where the top and bottom portions will mix with each other.

- <u>**Streams and rivers**</u> – Flowing water with low levels of dissolved solids and high dissolved oxygen, due to the water coming in contact with the air. Algae and insect larvae usually attach themselves to the bottom of rocks and aquatic plants are strongly rooted.

- <u>**Inland wetlands**</u> – Water levels vary from standing water in the wet season to none during the dry season or during droughts. Water table is always near the surface. These include marshes, swamps, and bogs.

Marine Ecosystems

- <u>**Coastal**</u> – Occur near shore where tides and currents are always changing causing a mixing of nutrients. These zones are found from the high tide mark of shorelines out to the continental shelf. Among the organisms found in these regions, are corals (tropical regions), zooplankton, phytoplankton, crustaceans, echinoderms, dolphins, sharks, whales, shellfish, turtle and eel grasses benthos algae, gulls, sea lions, seals, marine turtles, jellyfish, and terns.

- **Estuaries** — Occur where rivers meet the oceans. These will sometimes form bays, inlets, and form behind barrier islands (sandy islands between the coastal ocean and the terrestrial mainland). Animals in these areas must be able to adapt to rapidly and constantly changing salinity. These areas are rich in nutrients and provide excellent spawning and breeding grounds for numerous fish, crustaceans, and wading birds.

- **Open ocean** — These areas occur beyond the continental shelf in deep water up to 11,000 meters. The zones below 200 meters are dark, cold and poor in nutrients. Open oceans cover 70% of the earth's surface, and contain phytoplankton, zooplankton, whales, tuna, sharks, squid, flying fish, and seabirds.

Hydrologic Cycle (Water Cycle)

The hydrological cycle describes the movement of water into and out of the atmosphere. The cycle consists of water rising through two processes, evaporation and transpiration. Water vapor returns to the oceans and the land through condensation and precipitation. When precipitation or condensation occurs it has four possibilities, 1) run-off into lakes, streams or oceans 2) to infiltrate and percolate into the ground adding to the water table 3) reabsorbtion by plants 4) or to simply evaporate.

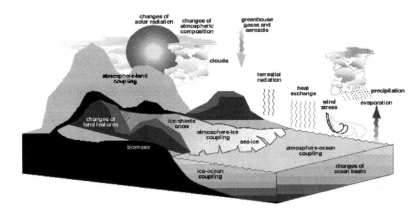

Atmospheric dynamics

The atmosphere is a collection of gases, and composed of four layers. 1) The layer closest to earth is the troposphere. This layer varies from 5 miles up to 10 up miles in the tropics. The troposphere is where our weather occurs, and thus contains most of the water vapor. The temperatures in this layer generally get cooler with increasing altitude except in the case of thermal inversions. 2) The next layer is the stratosphere, which is about 45 miles above the earth's surface. This layer contains ozone, O_3, which is important to all life on earth because it absorbs high-energy radiation from the sun. Ozone concentrations cause the temperatures to increase with altitude 3) The mesosphere occurs next. Ozone becomes less and less concentrated in this layer, and oxygen levels are very low. 4) The next layer is the thermosphere. Like the mesosphere, ozone concentrations become less and less in this layer, and oxygen levels continue to be very low.

The gases in the troposphere include 78% nitrogen (N_2), 21% oxygen (O_2), 0.035% of carbon dioxide (CO_2), water vapor, and trace elements. Increasing levels of carbon dioxide, also known as a greenhouse gas, are thought to contribute to global warming.

A.P. Environmental Science Study Guide – Chapter Two  Awesome Guides, Inc.

Weather represents the day-to-day fluctuations in the atmosphere, such as humidity, temperature, precipitation, and air pressure. Climate tracks these fluctuations over long periods of time, and it represents historical weather data.

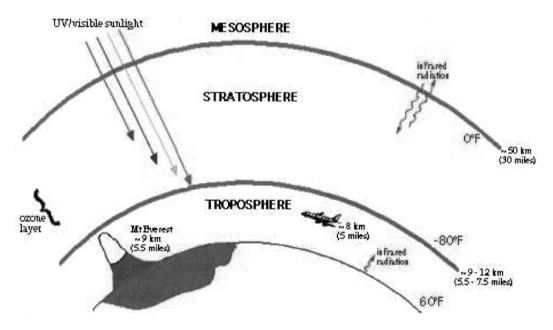

- **Solar heating** - The sun gives us energy in two forms: light and heat.

- **Convection** - The upward motion of a warm fluid or gas spreading through a cooler one.

- **Concepts:**

    o Convection - is the organized motion or movement of large groups of molecules based on their relative densities or temperatures.
    o Weather - is the state of the atmosphere and its conditions such as: dry or wet, cold or hot, stormy or calm, cloudy or clear. In plain terms, we can say that weather happens when wet air travels up through the atmosphere.

- **Principles:**

    o Weather activity happens when wet air goes up into the atmosphere and cooler air comes down from the atmosphere.
    o One cause of rising air in our atmosphere is the process called convection.
    o Warm air rises above cold air by convection.
    o Clouds form when water vapor condenses and molecules cling to each other.
    o While convection is happening and warm, moist air is going upwards, there is also the sinking of denser and cooler molecules from the atmosphere moving downward.

Awesome Guides, Inc. A.P. Environmental Science Study Guide - Chapter Two

- **Facts:**
    - Convection happens because warm air is less dense than the cold air around it. Warm air is lighter and rises in the atmosphere.
    - Evidence of convection is seen with the formation and growth of cumulus clouds.
    - We see evidence of sinking motions of heavier and cooler air falling to the earth when the sky is clear and without clouds.
    - Warm, moist air rises and forms clouds in the atmosphere.
    - There is a constant balancing act going on all the time in our atmosphere as moist, warm air travels upward and cooler, denser air moves down. Air is constantly moving up and down, creating our "weather."

- **El Nino**
    - A weather phenomenon that occurs when there is a major shift in atmospheric pressure over the central equatorial Pacific Ocean.
    - Unusually warm ocean temperatures in the Equatorial Pacific characterize El Nino.
    - This causes the trade winds to relax in the central and western Pacific leading to a reversal of trade winds from a westerly direction to an easterly direction.
    - Among these consequences are: increased rainfall across the southern tier of the U.S. and in Peru, (which has caused destructive flooding), and drought in the West Pacific, and is sometimes associated with devastating brush fires in Australia.

- **La Nina**
    - A weather phenomenon that is characterized when unusually cold ocean temperatures occur in the Equatorial Pacific.
    - It is characterized by warm winters in the Southeastern United States, colder than normal winters from the Great Lakes to the Pacific Northwest, and unsettled winters in the Northeast and Middle Atlantic states.
    - La Niñas occur after some (but not all) El Niño years.

Population Ecology

- **Demography** — Keeps track of human populations. The data collected is used to show age structures (number of people in various age brackets), and is separated by gender (male and female). Population profiles (graphs) are used to determine age structures (proportions of people in each age bracket), and are used to make predictions of future population trends. The age structure histogram on this page shows the percentage of population for both male (left) and female (right) for three nations, Mexico (rapid growth), U.S. (slow growth) and Sweden (zero growth). The shaded areas on each graph show people in their childbearing years.

- **Birth and death rates** — The birth rate refers to the number of live births per thousand in a given year, while the death rate is the number of deaths per thousand in a given year.

A.P. Environmental Science Study Guide - Chapter Two  Awesome Guides, Inc.

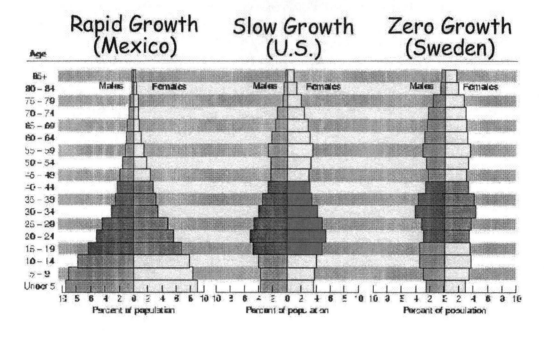

- **Exponential growth** —is extremely rapid growth. The human population is currently experiencing exponential growth. Birth rates FAR outnumber death rates. From the first humans on earth to the early 1800's human population increased very slowly. By 1830 the population reached 1 billion. In the next 100 years, the human population doubled to 2 billion and by 1975 (only 45 years later), the human population had doubled again to 4 billion. In 1999, world population reached 6 billion and is growing at a rate of 80 million per year. When an exotic species is introduced into an area other organisms experience exponential growth. The lack of natural predators and abundance of resources explain this rapid growth.

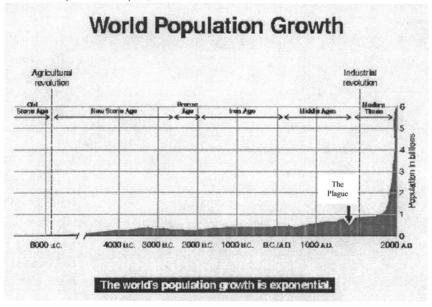

Awesome Guides, Inc. A.P. Environmental Science Study Guide - Chapter Two

- **Factors that affect population growth and resources** – All organisms require resources and have natural enemies. Any deficiency of resources, called a **limiting factor**, can lower the population numbers of a species. The opposite is also true, if resources are abundant, then populations have the potential to increase. Predation, competition, moisture, salinity, pH, light, fire, temperature extremes, and disease can all affect a population's growth rate. These biotic and abiotic factors contribute to **environmental resistance**. Biotic potential acts to increase population size. These factors include: reproduction rate, adaptations to changing conditions, and the ability to migrate or disperse. Once a population reaches its **carrying capacity** (maximum number of a particular organism that an ecosystem can maintain) then populations tend to stabilize.

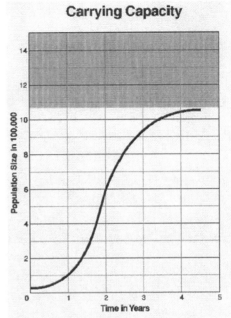

- **Density characteristics** – Population density is the number of organisms in a given area. Density factors that affect populations of organisms are: density-dependent and density-independent. **Density-dependent** factors are those that effect population size as the density increases. For example, as the population of a group of organisms increases in number, then less resources are available, and the population declines. Most environmental factors are density-dependent. **Density-independent** factors are those that are unaffected by the density of a population. For example, if a catastrophic event occurs in an ecosystem, such as a hurricane or fire, then organisms will be killed at the same rate regardless of their population density.

Community Ecology

Species interactions and adaptations –

Among organisms, all interactions with each other can be divided into two major groups: intraspecific and interspecific. Intraspecific interactions of organisms are those that are within the same species. This type of interaction is most intense because both organisms have similar niches (roles or jobs). That is they are looking for the SAME resources and mates. Interspecific interactions occur among different species. A good way to remember the difference between the two types is to think of the U.S. interstate road system. These roads are called **inter**state highways because they travel through **different** states. Interspecific interactions are less intense than intraspecific, because the two organisms have different niches. Other interactions among organisms, called symbiosis, include:

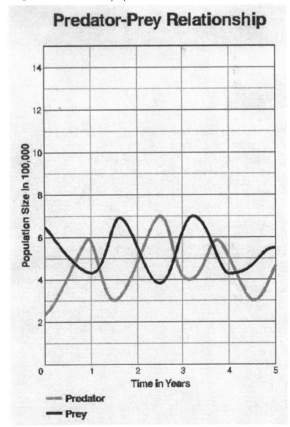

www.awesomeguides.com   35   Copyrighted material – do not duplicate!

- **Mutualism** — An interaction between two species where both species benefit. Some types of mutualism are necessary for the survival of the organism, while other types are beneficial but not essential to life. Examples of mutualism that are necessary for survival include: a) lichens (a fungus and an algae) b) rumen ciliates and cattle, and c) trichonympha found in the gut of termites. Examples of mutualism that are not essential for life include: clown fish and sea anemones, flowers and pollinators. Many types of mutualism have shown evolutionary relationships.

- **Commensalism** — An interaction between two species where one species benefits and the other is unaffected. Examples include: a) oak tree and Spanish moss, b) shark and remora c) animal species that live in the burrows of gopher tortoises.

- **Parasitism** — An interaction between two species where one species benefits and the other is harmed. This is a special form of predation where the predator is much smaller than the prey. Examples include: a) tapeworm and human b) heartworm and dog c) root knot nematode and tomato d) leech and fish e) tic and deer.

- **Predator/prey** — An interaction between two species where one species benefits while the other is harmed and usually killed. Examples include: a) lynx and snowshoe hare b) lion and wildebeest c) wolves and elk.

- **Neutralism** — An interaction between two species where there is no direct relationship. Examples include: a) rose bush and bison b) clam and dragonfly c) gazelle and field mouse.

- **Amensalism** - An interaction between two species where the growth of one species is inhibited while the other species is unaffected. Examples include: a) cyanobacteria (some produce toxins) and the animals that drink from infected waterways.

- **Ecological succession** — This is the step-by-step change that a biotic community goes through over time. The process is gradual and occurs in a predictable series of steps. The three major kinds of succession described by environmental scientists are: primary, secondary, and aquatic. As the plant community changes overtime, so do the animals, soil characteristics, and abiotic factors. Succession continues until the community reaches a final stage called the climax community. A climax community is stable and unchanging unless disturbed by fire, human activity (such as clear cutting), or catastrophic events such as disease, floods, hurricanes, etc.

- **Primary succession** — This type of succession is also known as "bare rock" succession, because it begins with bare rock that starts after volcanic activity, or from receding glaciers. In both cases, no previous plant communities have existed in the ecosystem. The steps are as follows: 1) Mosses and lichens grow on the bare rock (parent material), and invade cracks slowly. With the help of natural weathering, they break down the rock into soil. 2) Small plants begin to grow in the soil, further breaking down the rock into soil. This may take many years. 3) Larger plants begin to grow until a climax community is reached. See secondary succession below for details.

Primary succession of bare rock.

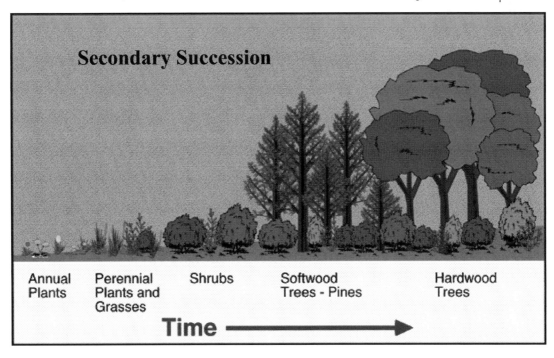

- **Secondary succession** — This type of succession is also known as "old field" succession, because it can be compared to a farmer abandoning his crops after a harvest and letting nature take over. Any ecosystem disturbed by fire, human activity, or a farmer abandoning his field starts secondary succession. The steps are as follows: 1) Land is cleared and then left alone. 2) Annual plants begin to grow during the first year. 3) During years 1-3 both annuals and perennials grow in the area. 4) Between years 3-30 fast growing pines create a pine forest. 5) Somewhere around the 25th year, hardwood trees invade the pine forest. 6) After about 70-100 years a hardwood climax forest is established.

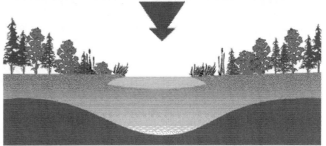

- **Aquatic Succession** — This type of succession involves lakes and ponds. New lakes and ponds are formed by processes such as geological activity and sinkholes. Lakes and ponds, like terrestrial succession, change over time. The steps are as follows: 1) Oligotrophic lakes are also known as new lakes. These lakes are usually clear, deep, low in nutrients and biodiversity, and high in dissolved oxygen. 2) Mesotrophic and eutrophic lakes contain more aquatic plants and as the plants die they decompose and form detritus on the lake/pond bottom. Nutrient levels increase, biodiversity increases, and dissolved oxygen levels drop. 3) Hypereutrophic lakes have excessive levels of detritus, are usually shallow, and have low levels of dissolved oxygen. The types of organisms that can live in these lakes are different than oligotrophic, mesotrophic or eutrophic due to the low oxygen levels. 4) The final stage is when the lake/pond becomes a marsh and then eventually turns into terrestrial habitat or dry land.

Habitat destruction — This is the most common and singly most important aspect of preserving the earth's resources. It makes sense, that by protecting the earths' habitats, valuable resources can also be preserved. The loss and destruction of habitat is the principle cause for decline in **biological diversity.** Habitat destruction and loss outranks - over exploitation, introduction of exotic species, predation, competition, and natural disasters. Inadequate laws as just as much a cause of species extinctions and those threatened with extinction.

- Furthermore, habitat loss and destruction is a direct result of the ever-increasing human population. The greatest destruction of habitats and largest surge of species extinctions have occurred over the past 150 years. In 1850, the global population was approximately 1 billion people and increased to 2 billion by 1930 (80 years); in 1990 (60 years), it was 5.3 billion and reached over 6.0 billion by the year 1999. This alarming growth in human populations has been possible due to the significant progress in medicine. This lowered infant mortality rates, increased life expectancy, and advances in modern agriculture made food plentiful.

- In many countries of the world, substantial portions of natural habitats have already been destroyed; on island countries where human densities are particularly high, most of the original habitat is gone. In 49 out of 61 countries in Africa and Asia, more than 50% of the original habitat has been destroyed.

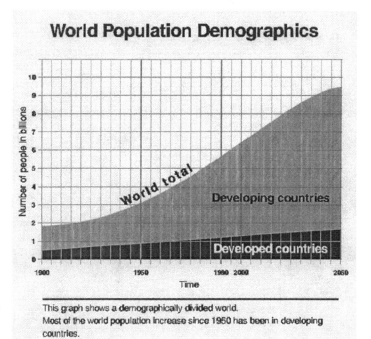

This graph shows a demographically divided world.
Most of the world population increase since 1950 has been in developing countries.

- The fundamental reason for the degradation and loss of habitat is the explosive growth of the human population. Since 1900 the world's population has more than tripled and since 1950 it has more than doubled to 6 billion. Every year 90 million more people (which equals 3 times the population of California) are added to the planet. All of these people need places to live, work, and play, and they ALL contribute to habitat loss and global pollution.

Threatened Habitats

- **Deforestation** of rain forests is of particular concern due to the high **biodiversity** in these habitats. Tropical rain forests make up approximately 7% of the earth's surface area, yet they contain over 50% of the plant and animal species. For example, about 30% of the world's bird species occur in tropical forests of Asia, Africa, and South and Central America (2,600 species). Approximately 180,000 km² of rainforest are lost each year, which represents an area larger than the State of Florida. At the current rate of destruction, rainforests will be virtually eliminated by the year 2040. The conversion of native lands for agriculture, commercial logging, and fuel wood production are the principle causes of deforestation.

- **Wetlands** and aquatic areas are also species-rich habitats that are being destroyed. Wetlands are critically important habitats for a large number of vertebrate species and wetlands make up approximately 5% of the land area in the United States. They also contain approximately 15% of the threatened and endangered species. Wetlands are converted and drained worldwide for development projects or for agriculture. Wetland and aquatic habitats are also altered or transformed by canalization of waterways and dam projects. In the United States, over 50% of the wetlands have disappeared in the last 200 years.

- **Mangrove forests** are unique and important habitats that are being destroyed for wood production, agriculture and aquaculture. Mangroves are special forest habitats that occur in shallow, intertidal coastal areas in the tropics. These habitats are critically important as a breeding area for many aquatic organisms and are important for preventing erosion damage from storms. Between 50 and 60% of the commercial species of fish and shrimp caught in the tropics are dependent on mangrove areas. These areas are also important breeding habitats for many bird species. Mangroves are cleared for the production of rice and aquaculture, and for fuel wood and construction materials. In some Asian countries, over 30% of these habitats have been destroyed or degraded.

- **Temperate grasslands** are biologically important habitats that have been destroyed or degraded primarily through agricultural practices. Because grasslands typically occur on well-developed soils and level terrain, they are prime spots for crop production. Sites that are not converted for crop production are highly desired as grazing land for livestock. Crop production destroys grassland habitats while overgrazing degrades these habitats, allowing the invasion of exotic and early successional stage species. The net result is habitat areas that no longer support the diversity of vertebrates that they once did.

Habitat Fragmentation

Habitat fragmentation is not an apparent category of habitat destruction; however it results in a large decline in biodiversity. Habitat fragmentation is a process by which contiguous habitats are reduced in size leaving ecosystems in two or more pieces. The pieces that do remain are separated from each other. Roads, agriculture, urbanization, and other **anthropogenic** changes on an ecosystem cause habitat fragmentation. Habitat fragmentation has been identified as a principle cause in the decline of many species native to North America.

Fragmented habitats differ from the original contiguous habitats in several important ways. Not only are the original habitats reduced in total area, but the remaining pieces of habitat have a greater amount of **edge** relative to their area. These habitat pieces have smaller central areas that influence the survival and reproduction of species living there. Some tropical rain forest animals for example are considered specialists and require an intact forest for their survival. The pieces might be too small to be used by other wildlife species as well. As the pieces become more and more isolated, animal travel between the pieces is reduced or entirely eliminated and present hazards such as predators, automobiles become more prevalent.

- **Exotic species** — Also known as introduced species, these species are not native to a particular ecosystem. Exotic species have been of concern to ecosystems in many parts of the world. Exotic species thrive in their new ecosystems, due to the lack of natural predators. They can compete aggressively for resources with native species and usually cause a decline in these natives. In addition they can cause widespread habitat destruction because of their exponential growth. Examples are numerous, and unfortunately in the thousands. The following represent some of the more notable exotics: a) fire ants in the Southeastern U.S. b) rabbits in England and Australia c) Kudzu vine to the Eastern U.S. d) Chestnut blight (fungus) in New England e) Meleluca tree in Florida f) Feral cats to the Galapagos Islands g) zebra mussel into the Great Lakes h) Purple loosestrife in the U.S. and Canadian wetlands.

- **Overgrazing and over harvesting (deforestation)** —Overgrazing occurs when too many stock animals are placed in an ecosystem. Grasses are used up faster than they can be replaced causing the land to become barren. Barren land promotes wind and water erosion causing desertification. Similarly, over harvesting (known as deforestation) clear cutting, and slash and burn, cause desertification if the land is not replanted.

Evolutionary Concepts

- **Natural selection** —All organisms experience selective pressures, that is, coping with environmental resistance. Those individuals that are best able to cope with these pressures have a better change of passing their genes on to the next generation. If abiotic conditions change in an ecosystem, because of the vast individual differences within its genes some animals within a species will have a greater survival rate. This process occurs naturally, thus the term natural selection. Certain traits that an individual has may have no advantage, until a change in the ecosystem occurs. For example, if a mosquito population is treated with a certain insecticide, then most may die; leaving a population that is resistant to the insecticide. Since many were eliminated with the initial pesticide application, the remaining population of resistant mosquitoes increases exponentially producing catastrophic effects.

- **Species extinction** —refers to the loss of an organism (species) "for good". Most of the organisms (99%) that have ever lived on this planet are now extinct. Throughout the history of life, extinction has been a natural part of the Earth's fluctuating biodiversity. Environmental changes and interspecific competition produce organisms that are not well suited for survival in a particular niche. The result of such a condition is either evolutionary adaptation or extinction. In the latter case, an evolutionary line is ended, and, as is often the case, new lines emerge to fill the vacated niches. Thus, life forms appear and disappear; biodiversity is maintained through a complex balance of speciation and extinction.

- **Background Extinction Rate vs. Mass Extinction Rate** - The background extinction rate is the relatively constant rate at which organisms have been disappearing from the fossil record over the course of geological time and has been variously estimated at between five and ten marine families per million years. Occasionally, mass extinctions occur, the most notable being the dinosaurs. In this case, many species disappear at once, resulting in a major loss of biodiversity. If extinctions are a natural occurrence on earth, then why are environmental scientists so concerned? Currently, the rate of species extinction is much greater than any other time in the know history of the earth, and organisms are becoming extinct at a rate much greater than the normal background rate. Human populations have been able to drive many common species with high population size to extinction in a very short period of time. Some examples include the: passenger pigeon (1914), dodo bird (1681), Steller's Seacow (1768), Ivory-billed woodpecker (considered extinct as of 1969).

- **Genetic diversity** —within a species of organism is vast. That is, there are many individual differences within a single species. The diversity of genes in individual species' accounts for differences in adaptations and responses to the environment. This intraspecific diversity is the foundation of the ecological and evolutionary processes. Genetic diversity allows species' to adjust to a changing world, and can be naturally anthropogenic.

- **Biodiversity** —is the variety of life. Environmental scientists define biodiversity as the variety of all life forms including the different plants, animals and micro-organisms, their genes, and the ecosystems of which they are part of. Thus, biodiversity occurs at the genetic level, the organism level, the community level and the ecosystem level. The loss of biodiversity means a loss of possible cures for disease, a loss of entire species and all of the organisms that depend on them.

Ecosystem Ecology

Energy Flow in Ecosystems —is one way. That's to say, energy must always be put into an ecosystem. Important energy relationships include:

- The First Law of Thermodynamics states that energy can neither be created nor destroyed but only changed in form. This applies to ecosystems in that energy enters an ecosystem as high quality (useable by organisms) and leaves as low quality (not usable by organisms). Thus energy must always be put into an ecosystem.
The Second Law of Thermodynamics states that when energy is converted into different forms, such as: light into chemical, and high quality energy changed into lower quality energy. Most of the useful, high quality energy in ecosystems leaves a low-grade heat, not usable by organisms.

- The Second Law of Thermodynamics states that when energy is converted into different forms, such as: light into chemical, and high quality energy changed into lower quality energy. Most of the useful, high quality energy in ecosystems leaves a low-grade heat, not usable by organisms.

- Flow of energy and inorganic nutrients through ecosystems, can be generally thought of as:

   1. The ultimate source of energy (for most ecosystems) is the sun
   2. The ultimate fate of energy in ecosystems is that it is lost as heat.
   3. Energy and nutrients are passed from organism to organism through the food chain as one organism eats another. When this energy is passed along the food chain, only a small percent is transferred. This is often referred to as the 10% rule, which states that on the average only 10% of the available energy is transferred from one organism to another. **(see diagram on next page)**
   4. Decomposers remove the last amount of energy from an organism's remains.
   5. Inorganic nutrients are cycled; energy is not.

A.P. Environmental Science Study Guide - Chapter Two  Awesome Guides, Inc.

Energy Flow Pyramid

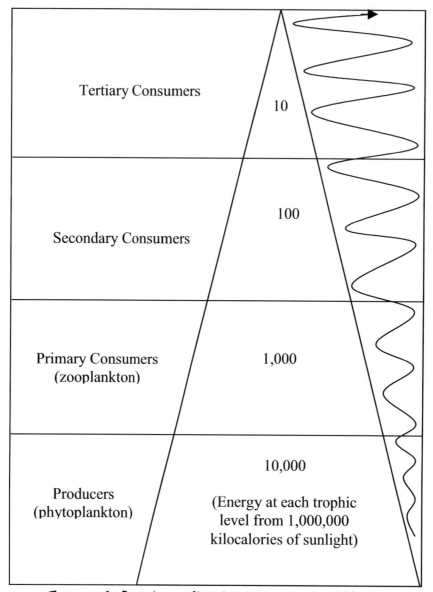

Energy only flows in one direction; it is not cyclic, 10% rule.

Trophic Levels - Refers to an organism's position in the food chain. Autotrophs are at the bottom. Organisms that eat autotrophs are called herbivores or primary consumers. An organism that eats herbivores is a carnivore and a secondary consumer. A carnivore that eats a carnivore which eats a herbivore is a tertiary consumer, and so on. It is important to note that many animals do not specialize in their diets. Omnivores (such as many humans) eat both animals and plants. Except for some specialists, most carnivores don't limit their diet to organisms of only one trophic level. Frogs, for instance, don't discriminate between herbivorous and carnivorous bugs in their diet. If it's the right size, and moving at the right distance, chances are the frog will eat it.

Awesome Guides, Inc. A.P. Environmental Science Study Guide - Chapter Two

The diagrams that follow show the relationships between different trophic levels on the food chain, and their relationship between nutrients and energy. Many times this relationship is shown as a pyramid depicting that in most ecosystems, there are more numbers, biomass and energy available at the lower trophic levels.

Energy Movement Through Ecosystem Trophic Levels

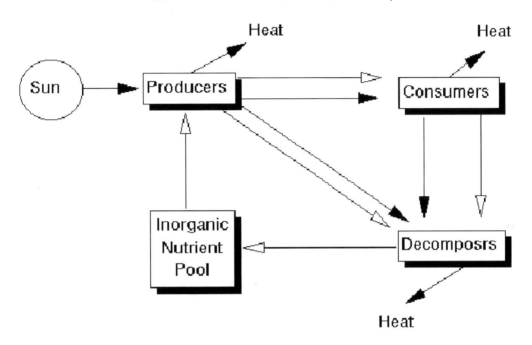

Food Chains and Webs - A food chain follows the path of food through the various trophic levels from the producers (autotrophs) to the consumers. A typical food chain in a field ecosystem might be represented as:

grass ---> grasshopper ---> field mouse ---> garter snake ---> red tailed hawk

In this food chain, the grass is the autotroph and all others represent heterotrophs. Of the heterotrophs, the grasshopper is a primary consumer (herbivore), the field mouse is the secondary consumer (carnivore), the garter snake is a tertiary consumer and the red tailed hawk is a quaternary consumer.

The real world, of course, is more complicated than a simple food chain. While many organisms do specialize (specialist) in their diets, such as anteaters and snail kites, many organisms do not. Hawks don't limit their diets to garter snakes, snakes eat food other than field mice, mice eat grass as well as grasshoppers, and so on. A more realistic depiction of who eats whom is called a food web; an example is shown on the next page.

A **food web** consists of interlocking food chains, and the only way to untangle the chains is to trace *backwards* along a given food chain to its source. The previous food web represents a series of grazing food chains, beginning with the producers. While grazing food chains are important, in

A.P. Environmental Science Study Guide - Chapter Two 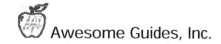 Awesome Guides, Inc.

nature they are outnumbered by detritus-based food chains. In detritus-based food chains, decomposers are at the base of the food chain, and sustain the carnivores, which feed on them. In terms of the weight (or biomass) of animals in many ecosystems, more of their body mass can be traced back to detritus than to living producers.

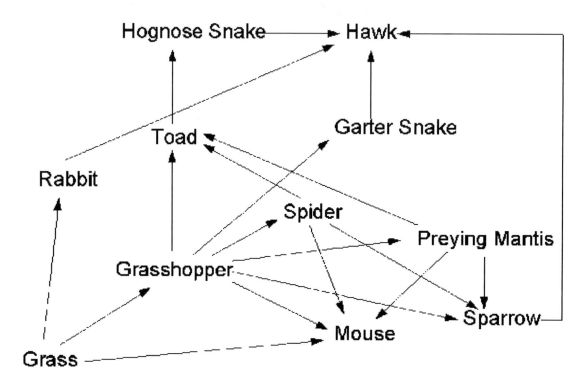

Biogeochemical Cycles —represent how organic material moves through an ecosystem. Remember that energy DOES NOT cycle in an ecosystem, however organic nutrients and minerals do. The three major biogeochemical cycles are the carbon cycle, nitrogen cycle, and the phosphorus cycle.

Carbon Cycle —traces the path of carbon through an ecosystem. Carbon is a major component of organic molecules. It is involved in the reactions of respiration and photosynthesis. Respiration takes carbohydrates and oxygen and combines them to produce carbon dioxide, water, and energy. Photosynthesis takes carbon dioxide and water and produces carbohydrates and oxygen. The outputs of respiration are the inputs of photosynthesis, and the outputs of photosynthesis are the inputs of respiration. The reactions are also complementary in how they deal with energy. Photosynthesis takes energy from the sun and stores it in the carbon-to-carbon bonds of carbohydrates; and respiration releases that energy.

Both plants and animals carry on respiration, but only plants (and other producers) can carry on photosynthesis. The chief reservoirs (sinks) for carbon dioxide are in the oceans Carbon dioxide dissolves readily in water. Once dissolved, it may precipitate (fall out of solution) as a solid known as calcium carbonate (limestone). Corals and algae encourage this reaction and build up limestone reefs in the process. On land and in the water, plants take up carbon dioxide and convert it into carbohydrates through photosynthesis. This carbon in the plants has 3 possible fates: it can be released into the atmosphere by plants through respiration; an animal can eat it, or it can remain with the plant.

Animals obtain all their carbon from the food they eat and this carbon also has three possible fates. Carbon from plants or animals that is released into the atmosphere through respiration will either be taken up by a plant in photosynthesis or dissolved into the oceans. When an animal or a plant dies, two things can happen to the carbon: 1) it can be respired by decomposers (and released to the atmosphere) or 2) it can be buried and ultimately form fossil fuels, after hundreds of thousands of years. These fossil fuels are mined and burned in the future; releasing carbon dioxide into the atmosphere. Otherwise, the carbon in limestone or other sediments can only be released into the atmosphere when they are subducted (brought down) and released only by volcanoes, or when they are pushed to the surface and slowly weathered away. Humans have a great impact on the carbon cycle. When we burn fossil fuels we release excess carbon dioxide into the atmosphere. This means that more carbon dioxide goes into the oceans, and that more is present in the atmosphere. The latter condition contributes to global warming, since the carbon dioxide in the atmosphere allows more energy to reach the Earth than it allows carbon dioxide to escape from the Earth into space. **In short, a lot of processes put carbon dioxide into the atmosphere, and only photosynthesis and the oceans can remove it.**

Carbon Cycle

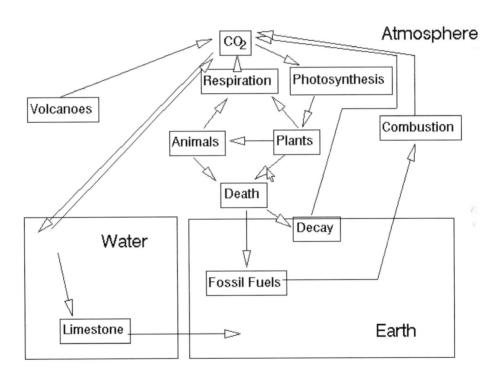

Nitrogen Cycle - The nitrogen cycle involves many important forms of nitrogen, as well as bacterial organisms. Nitrogen is critically important in forming the amino acids, which in turn form proteins. The chief source of nitrogen is the atmosphere, containing about 78%. Nitrogen gas (N_2) in the atmosphere is composed of two nitrogen atoms bound together with a triple covalent bond. This makes N_2 a very non-reactive gas; it takes a tremendous amount of energy to break the bonds of a nitrogen gas molecule.

Nitrogen gas can be taken from the atmosphere (or fixed) in two basic ways: 1) lightning which produces enough energy to break the triple covalent bond, and change it into the form of nitrate (NO_3) and 2) nitrogen fixation through bacteria, which use special enzymes fix nitrogen.
These nitrogen-fixing bacteria come in three forms:

1. Those free-living in the soil, some of which form symbiotic, (mutualistic) associations with the roots of bean plants and other legumes

2. Rhizobial bacteria

3. Photosynthetic cyanobacteria (blue-green algae), which are commonly found in water.

All of these bacteria fix nitrogen, which means they change atmospheric nitrogen into forms that plants can use. Most plants can take up nitrate and convert it into amino acids. Animals acquire all of their amino acids when they eat plants (or other animals). When plants or animals die (or release waste) the nitrogen is returned to the soil. The usual form of nitrogen returned to the soil in animal wastes or in the output of the decomposers, is ammonia. Ammonia is rather toxic, but fortunately there are nitrifying bacteria in the soil and in the water to take up ammonia and convert it to **nitrite** (NO_2). Nitrite is also somewhat toxic, but another type of bacteria, nitrate bacteria, take the nitrite and convert it to **nitrate** (NO_3), which can be taken up by plants to continue the cycle. Additionally, there are denitrifying bacteria, which take the nitrate and combine the nitrogen back into nitrogen gas.

Nitrogen Cycle

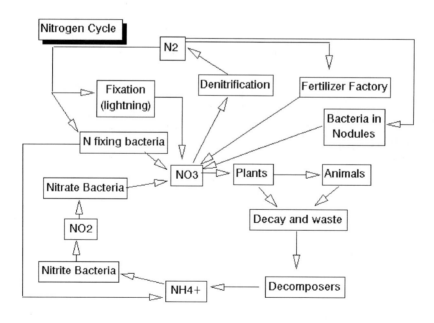

Phosphorous Cycle - The phosphorous cycle is the simplest of the cycles. Phosphorous in ecosystems exist in the form of phosphate (PO_4). Phosphate is found in organisms, dissolved in water, or in rock. When phosphate rock is exposed to water (especially if the water is slightly acidic), the weathered rock releases its phosphate. Autotrophs use phosphorous in several ways, for production of cell membranes, DNA, RNA, and ATP. Heterotrophs (animals) obtain their phosphorous from the plants they eat. Although one type of heterotroph, the fungi, excel at taking up phosphorous and may form mutualistic relationships with plant roots. These fungi are called mycorrhizae; the plant gets phosphate from the fungus and the fungus obtains sugar from the plant. Animals use phosphorous as a component of bones, teeth and shells. When animals or plants die (or when animals defecate), the phosphate may be returned to the soil or water by the decomposers. There, it can be taken up by another plant and used again. This cycle will occur over and over until all the phosphorous is lost at the bottom of the deepest parts of the ocean, where it becomes part of sedimentary rock. Ultimately, this phosphorous it will be released into ecosystems when the rock is brought to the surface and weathered.

In Florida, which was once a sea floor, there are extensive phosphate mines, or more correctly pits, where phosphate is taken for use in fertilizers. Mining of phosphate greatly accelerates the phosphorous cycle and may cause a local overabundance of phosphorous. Local overabundance of phosphate can cause an overgrowth of algae in the water; the algae can use up all the oxygen in the water and kill other aquatic life. This is called eutrophication. The other animals that play a unique role in the phosphorous cycle are marine birds. These birds take phosphorous containing fish out of the ocean and return to land, where they defecate. Their guano contains high levels of phosphorous and in this way marine birds return phosphorous from the ocean to the land. The guano is also mined for use as a fertilizer.

Phosphorous Cycle

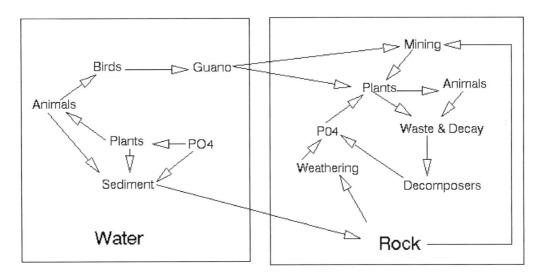

Changes in ecosystems - The biosphere consists of diverse ecosystems that vary widely in complexity and amount of productivity. Ecosystems directly provide forage, timber, fish, food, fiber, as well as other services such as the cycling of water, climate regulation, recreational opportunities, and wildlife habitat. The functioning of ecosystems and sustaining their natural resources is a great concern to environmental scientists. Many ecosystems may be threatened due to several different types of global environmental changes. The stresses or disturbances that have the greatest immediate potential to ecosystems adversely altering their capability to support organisms include:

- Changing land use, land cover, and habitat destruction
- Direct effects of rising greenhouse gases and other pollutants

A.P. Environmental Science Study Guide - Chapter Two  Awesome Guides, Inc.

- Changes in global populations and exponential human growth
- Species invasions to new areas
- Loss of biodiversity

Additionally, subjecting ecosystems to one or more of these stresses simultaneously builds significant negative impact on an ecosystem's function.

Land Use Concepts - The public owns approximately 30 % of U.S. land. In the 11 contiguous states west of the 100th meridian, approximately 50 % is owned by the federal government, including 80 % of Nevada. About 2/3 of the land in Alaska is owned by the federal government. The east and Midwest, have large areas of publicly owned land, particularly Louisiana (20 %), New Hampshire (13 %), Florida (10%), Michigan (10 %) and Virginia (7 %). Although the federal government owns most of these public lands, many states also have large parks and state forests; and most coastal wetlands below mean high water are owned by the state.

The nation's publicly owned lands are put to a variety of uses. About 80 million acres are managed by the Park Service for the "enjoyment of future generations." Over 95 million acres, much of which is in Alaska, is part of the Wilderness Preservation System of "road less" areas that Congress directed should remain "untouched by humans." Another 84 million acres are part of the Fish and Wildlife Service's National Refuge system. About 200 million acres, (9 percent of the nation) is part of the National Forest system, and the Bureau of Land Management holds approximately 260 million acres. Commercial grazing is an important use on 100 million acres of National Forest land and 160 million acres managed by the Bureau of Land Management.

The United States has a land area of about 2.3 billion acres, of which 2.2 billion acres (or 97 %) can be categorized as rural and 66 million acres (or 3 %) is urban. Rural land includes agricultural (range, cropland and pasture, farmsteads, and roads), forest, and other land. Urban land includes residential, commercial, utilities, mixed, transitional, and other urban land.

Major uses of land (U.S.)

Land uses —
1. Rangeland
2. Forest Management
3. Ski Area Management
4. Multiple Use Management

- Urban land - 66 million acres (3 %)
- Cropland - 455 million acres (20 % of the land area)
- Forestland - (total forest land exclusive of forested areas in parks and other special uses), 642 million acres (28%)
- Special uses - (parks, wilderness, wildlife, and related uses), 286 million acres (13 %)
- Miscellaneous other land (deserts, wetlands, and barren land) 235 million acres (10 %)

These proportions vary greatly from region to region due to differences in climate, geography, and population levels. The Northeast, for example, has 12 % of its area in cropland, compared with 60 % in the Corn Belt. However, nearly 60 % of the Northeast is in forest compared with only 2 percent in the Northern Plains. National and regional proportions are also skewed by the land area of Alaska, which has very little cropland and pasture but large areas of forest-use, special-use, and miscellaneous other land.

Major land use changes (U.S.) - by comparing the following information to the major uses of land (previous section) you can see that major land uses have changed little, during the past decade.

- The parks and wildlife component of special uses increased 9 million acres from 1992-1997, but a 4-million-acre decrease in defense and related areas left special uses with an overall increase of 5 million acres (4 %). Urban area increased 6 million acres (11 %). The 1992-1997 rate of urban area increase, 1.4 million acres per year, is above the historic 1950-92 rate of about 1 million acres per year, indicating a slight speedup in urbanization.

- Cropland (455 million acres in 1997) decreased by 1 percent (5 million acres) from the 1992 total. This continues a longer downward trend from 1978, when cropland totaled 470 million acres, a 3% drop. However, the amount of cropland has remained relatively constant from 1945-1997. It ranges only between 444 and 471 million acres with an average of 463 million acres.

- Forest-use lands also decreased by 1 %, from 559 to 552 million acres. Forest-use acres have trended downward since 1954 to 615 million acres (a 10-percent decrease over 43 years). Forest-use land excludes forested areas in special uses, which increased from an estimated 33 million acres in 1954 to 105 million acres in 1997.

Miscellaneous Land Uses - marshes, swamps, bare rock areas, deserts, and transitional areas have increased 10 million acres during the past decade. This residual includes land not included in any other major land use categories. In 1997, a new category named "rural residential" was identified as part of miscellaneous uses. Rural residential land increased, accounting for some of the overall increase in miscellaneous uses.

Forestry, wilderness, and recreational land use — Public owned lands throughout the United States have varied uses. Activities such as hunting, fishing, logging, cattle grazing, camping, boating, etc. etc. are available for businesses or individuals to participate. Public lands have different categories of use that require various fees and have certain restrictions put on them. The National Park Service administers the national parks and the Fish and Wildlife Service administer the National Wildlife Refuges. The following represents the major types of public land and their general uses.

- National Resource and National Forest lands —Multiple use public lands that are used for grazing, logging, mining, recreation, and the protection of watersheds and wildlife.

- National Wildlife Refuge lands —Moderately restricted land that may be used for hunting, recreation, and management of wildlife. The National Wildlife Refuge System administers a national network of lands and waters for the conservation, management, and where appropriate, restoration of the fish, wildlife, and plant resources and their habitats within the United States for the benefit of present and future generations of Americans.

- National Parks and National Wilderness Preservation lands are restricted to limited recreational use.

Agriculture — had its beginnings somewhere around 10,000 years ago. Until about 150 years ago many people in the US lived on small farms. Today's farms are large, sophisticated, and use machinery rather than animal labor to plow and harvest fields. Today's farms also use vast amounts of pesticides, fertilizers, and irrigation in comparison to farms of the past. Agricultural practices, which include both farming and livestock, have greatly affected ecosystems through the degradation of land by:

- Desertification
- Slash and burn techniques
- Salinization of soils due to over irrigation
- Deforestation

Other Agriculture Facts:

- Cropland has remained relatively stable over the past 10 years in the US.
- Four crops— corn for grain, soybeans, wheat, and hay— accounted for 80.1 percent of all crops harvested in 2000.
- An additional 15 principal crops account for another 15.3 percent of harvested area. Vegetables, fruits, nuts, melons, and all other crops account for 4.6 percent of the crop area harvested in 2000.

Effects of urbanization on agriculture in metropolitan areas:

Increased access to labor. Being closer to more people means that farmers are likely to have access to a larger labor pool. This may contribute to farmers' decisions to shift to specialty crops that are labor intensive.

Problems with nonfarm neighbors. Conflicts arise between urban neighbors using secondary roads as commuter routes and farmers traveling to and from distant fields with farm equipment. Other problems for farmers can include increased incidence of vandalism and theft, including damage to crops from urban neighbors driving through fields. Nuisance complaints may also increase as more neighbors voice opposition to the sounds and smells of typical agricultural operations.

Increased 'amenity value' of farmland. As more farmland is converted, the remaining farmland becomes more 'valuable' to the local population due to the amenities that farmland provides in the form of open space, scenic views, and the contribution to rural amenities. These rural amenities associated with farmland are generally not captured in the market value of land. Because farmland has an incentive to delay the conversion of farmland to developed users, owners are not compensated for the rural amenity value of their land.

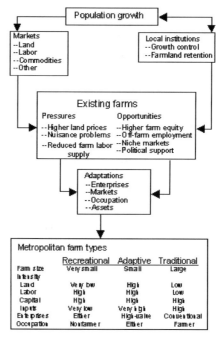

Conceptual model of agricultural adaptation to urbanization

Source: Heimlich and Brooks, 1989

Earth Science Principles

Geological time scale — Represents points in the time history of planet earth. The earth is estimated to be 4.5 billion years old, and its time history is divided into specific areas of significance. The chart, on the following page, shows a breakdown of the major categories of geological history, and includes

Awesome Guides, Inc. A.P. Environmental Science Study Guide - Chapter Two

Eon	Era	Period	Epoch	Age (MY)	Age of	Events
Phanerozoic	Cenozoic	Quaternary	Holocene	0-2	Mammals	Humans
			Pleistocene			Scabland Floods
		Tertiary	Neogene — Pliocene	2-5		
			Neogene — Miocene	5-24		Columbia Basalts
			Paleogene — Oligocene	24-37		
			Paleogene — Eocene	37-58		
			Paleogene — Paleocene	58-66		Extinction of Dinosaurs
	Mesozoic	Cretaceous		66-144	Reptiles	Flowering Plants
		Jurassic		144-208		1st Birds/Mammals
		Triassic		208-245		1st Dinosaurs
	Paleozoic	Permian		245-286	Amphibians	Extinction of Trilobites
		Carboniferous — Pennsylvanian		286-320		1st Reptiles
		Carboniferous — Mississippian		320-360		Large Primitive Trees
		Devonian		360-408	Fishes	1st Amphibians
		Silurian		408-438		1st Land Plants
		Ordovician		438-505	Invertebrates	1st Fish
		Cambrian		505-540		1st Shells, Trilobites
Proterozoic		Precambrian		540-2,500		1st Multicelled organisms
Archean				2,500-3,800		1st One-celled organisms
Hadean				3,800-4,600		Origin of the Earth

Plate tectonics- is a relatively new theory that has revolutionized the way geologists think about the Earth. According to the theory, the surface of the Earth is broken into large plates. The size and position of these plates changes over time. The edges of these plates, where they move against each other, are sites of intense geologic activity, such as earthquakes, volcanoes, and mountain building. Plate tectonics

A.P. Environmental Science Study Guide - Chapter Two  Awesome Guides, Inc.

Plate tectonics - is a relatively new theory that has revolutionized the way geologists think about the Earth. According to the theory, the surface of the Earth is broken into large plates. The size and position of these plates changes over time. The edges of these plates, where they move against each other, are sites of intense geologic activity, such as earthquakes, volcanoes, and mountain building. Plate tectonics is a combination of two earlier ideas, continental drift and sea-floor spreading. Continental drift is the movement of continents over the Earth's surface and their change in position relative to each other. Sea-floor spreading is the creation of new oceanic crust at mid-ocean ridges and movement of the crust away from the mid-ocean ridges.

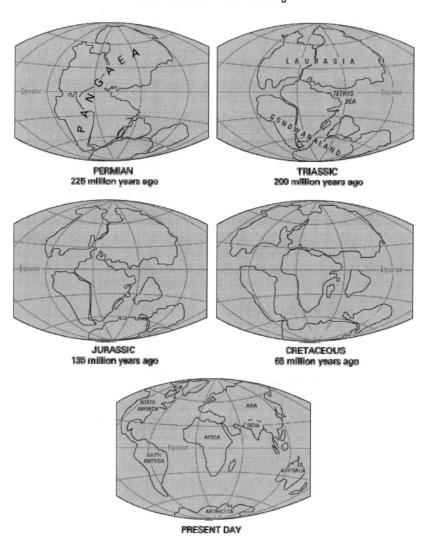

Scientists now have a fairly good understanding of how the plates move and how such movements relate to earthquake activity. Most movement occurs along narrow zones between plates, where the results of plate-tectonic forces are most evident.

There are four types of plate boundaries:

1. Divergent boundaries -- where new crust is generated as the plates pull away from each other.
2. Convergent boundaries -- where crust is destroyed as one plate dives under another.

3. Transform boundaries -- where crust is neither produced nor destroyed as the plates slide horizontally past each other.
4. Plate boundary zones -- broad belts in which boundaries are not well defined and the effects of plate interaction are unclear.

Volcanic Activity Map

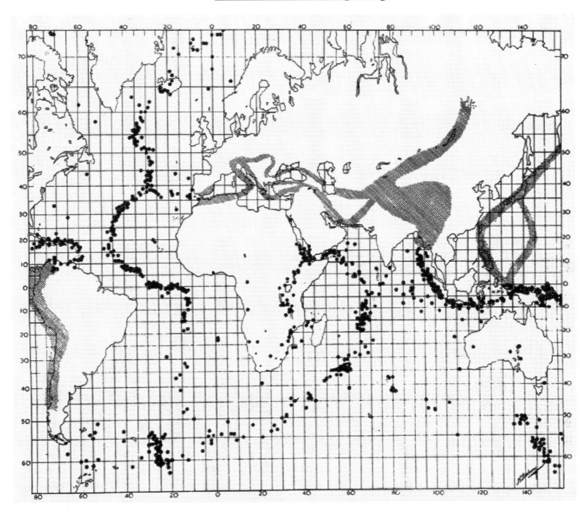

Location of Tectonic Plates showing earthquake or other geological activity.

Rock Cycle -Liquid (molten) rock material solidifies at depth or at the earth's surface. Uplift and exposure of rocks to the Earth's surface destabilizes mineral structures. These minerals break down into smaller grains, which are transported and deposited (either in solution or by lowering the hydraulic energy regime) as sediments. The sediments are lithified (compacted and cemented), and sedimentary rocks are formed. Changes in temperature, pressure, and/or rock or fluid chemistry can allow igneous and sedimentary rocks to change physically or chemically to form metamorphic rocks. At higher temperatures, metamorphic (or any other rock type) rocks may be partially melted, and crystallized. This crystallized melt will create igneous rocks. Uplift and erosion can expose all rock types to the surface, re-initiating the cycle.

A.P. Environmental Science Study Guide - Chapter Two  Awesome Guides, Inc.

In terms of plate tectonics, the rock cycle begins with igneous rock at the sea floors' spreading ridges. Fluid intrusion of these rocks, both during and after formation, results in some low-grade metamorphism. As the rock cools, and more magma is introduced from below, the plate is forced away from the spreading ridge, and acquires a sediment cover. The plate is eventually subducted under a continental plate. In the trenches of the subduction zone, at relatively shallow depths, high pressure —low-high temperature metamorphism of the plate and its sediment cover occur. As the plate travels deeper, high temperature conditions cause partial melting of the crustal slab. Fluid intrusion plays a key role in partial melting.

Volcanism - Volcanism is the process of bringing the earths' minerals from the deep interior, and depositing it on the surface. Volcanic eruptions also release new molecules into the atmosphere. Geysers and hot springs are also part of the volcanic process, involving water and hydrothermal activity.

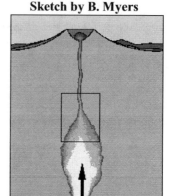

Movement of the earth's minerals by volcanism.

There are several ways in which a volcano forms, just as there are several different kinds of volcanoes. On Earth, the most general cause of volcanism is caused by subduction of the Earth's crust. Volcanoes form when hot material below the earth rises and leaks into the crust. This hot material, called magma, comes from melted, subducted, crustal material, which is light and buoyant after melting. Magma rises and gathers in a reservoir through a weak portion of the overlying rock called the magma chamber. Eventually, but not always, the magma erupts onto the surface. Strong earthquakes accompany rising magma, and the volcanic cone may swell in appearance, just before an eruption. Scientists often monitor the changing shape of a volcano, especially prior to an eruption.

Geotechnical Science

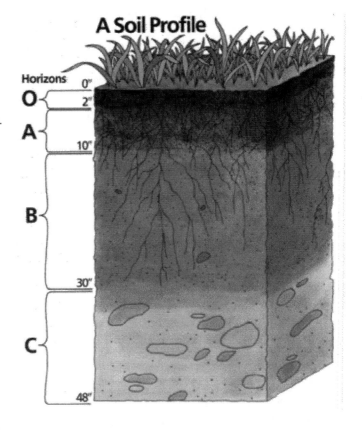

Soils types - Soil types are often described as sandy, clay, loam, or silt. Soil scientists describe soil types by how much sand, silt and clay or loam is present; this is called texture. It is possible to change the texture of a soil by adding different quantities of sand, silt or clay. Changing the soil texture can help provide the right conditions needed for plant growth.

- **Sand** - has the largest particle size than other soil types. When you rub it, it feels rough. This is because it has sharp edges. Sand has good water infiltration, poor water holding capacity, poor nutrient holding capacity, and good aeration.

Copyrighted material – do not duplicate!   www.awesomeguides.com

Awesome Guides, Inc. A.P. Environmental Science Study Guide - Chapter Two

- **Silt** - is a soil particle whose size is between sand and clay. Silt feels smooth and powdery. When wet it feels smooth but not sticky. Silt has medium water infiltration, medium water-holding capacity, medium nutrient holding capacity, and medium aeration.

- **Clay** - has the smallest of particle size of the soil types. Clay is smooth when dry and sticky when wet. Soils high in clay content are called heavy soils. Clay has poor water infiltration, good water holding capacity, good nutrient holding capacity, and poor aeration.

- **Loam** — is considered to be a perfect soil for agriculture. It is roughly composed of 40% sand, 40% silt, and 20% clay. Loam has medium water infiltration, medium water holding capacity, and medium aeration.

Particle size has a lot to do with a soil's drainage and nutrient holding capacity. To better understand how big these three soil particles are, think of them like this: if a particle of sand were the size of a basketball, then silt would be the size of a baseball, and clay would be the size of a golf ball.

Erosion - is the detachment and movement of soil material. The process may be natural or accelerated by human activity. Depending on the local landscape and weather conditions, erosion may be anywhere between very slow to very rapid. Natural erosion has sculptured landforms on upland ecosystems, and built landforms on lowland ecosystem. The rate and distribution of erosion over time can control the age of the land surfaces. When soil is left unprotected (bare) it is highly subject to erosion. Erosion is the loss of topsoil. Natural erosion is an important process that affects soil formation and, like human-induced erosion, may remove all or part of soils formed in the natural landscape. Accelerated erosion is largely the consequence of human activity. The primary causes are tillage, overgrazing, over cultivation, and cutting of timber (deforestation).

The rate of erosion can be increased by activities other than those of humans. Fire that destroys vegetation and triggers erosion has the same effect. The spectacular episodes of erosion, such as the soil blowing on the Great Plains of the Central United States in the 1930's (The Dust Bowl), have not all been due to human habitation. Frequent dust storms were recorded on the Great Plains before the region became a grain-producing area. "Natural" erosion is not easily distinguished from "accelerated" erosion on every soil.

Erosion from water - results from the removal of soil by moving water. A part of the process is the detachment of soil material by the impact of raindrops. The soil material is suspended in runoff water and carried away. Four kinds of accelerated water erosion are commonly recognized: sheet, rill, gully, and tunnel (piping).

- **Sheet erosion** is the more or less uniform removal of soil from an area without the development of conspicuous water channels. The channels are tiny or tortuous, exceedingly numerous, and unstable; they enlarge and straighten as the volume of runoff increases. Sheet erosion is less apparent, particularly in its early stages, than other types of erosion. It can be serious on soils that have a slope gradient of only 1 or 2 percent; however, it is generally more serious as slope gradient increases.

- **Rill erosion** is the removal of soil through the cutting of many small, but conspicuous, channels where runoff concentrates. Rill erosion is intermediate between sheet and gully erosion. The channels are shallow enough that they are easily obliterated by tillage; thus, after an eroded field has been cultivated, determining whether the soil losses resulted from sheet or rill erosion is generally impossible.

- **Gully erosion** occurs when water cuts down into the soil along the line of flow. Gullies form in exposed natural drainage ways, in plow furrows, in animal trails, in vehicle ruts, between rows of crop plants, and below broken human-made terraces. In contrast to rills, they cannot be obliterated by ordinary tillage. Deep gullies cannot be crossed with common types of farm equipment.

- **Tunnel erosion** may occur in soils where the subsurface horizons or layers are more subject to the entrainment of moving free water, than the surface horizon or layer. The free water enters the soil through ponded infiltration sites into surface-connected macropores. Desiccation cracks and rodent burrows are examples of macropores that may initiate the process. The soil material entrained in the moving water travels downward within the soil and may move out of the soil completely if there is an outlet. The result is the formation of tunnels (also referred to as pipes), which enlarge and coalesce. The portion of the tunnel near the inlet may enlarge disproportionately to form a funnel-shaped feature often referred to as a "jug." Hence, the term "piping" and "jugging." The phenomenon is favored by the presence of appreciable exchangeable sodium.

Erosion from wind — occurs in regions of low rainfall, and can be extremely widespread, especially during periods of drought. Unlike water erosion, wind erosion is generally not related to slope gradient. Removing or reducing the vegetation in an ecosystem increases wind erosion.

When winds are strong, coarser particles are rolled or swept along on or near the soil surface, kicking finer particles into the air. These particles are deposited in places sheltered from the wind. When wind erosion is severe, the sand particles drift back and forth, while silt and clay are carried away.

Deposition of sediment carried by water occurs when the velocity of running water is reduced at the mouth of gullies, at the base of slopes, along stream banks, on alluvial plains, in reservoirs, and at the mouth of streams. Rapidly moving water, when slowed, drops stones, then cobbles, pebbles, sand, and finally silt and clay.

Minerals are materials extracted from the Earth are necessary to produce our most fundamental needs: food, clothing, and shelter. Materials are needed to maintain and improve our standard of living. Understanding the whole system of materials flow, from source to ultimate disposition, can help us better manage the use of natural resources and protect the environment.

Loss of topsoil through erosion, coupled with the periods of dry weather causes soils to loose their water-holding capacity and results in desertification.

Energy Resources

History of energy use in the U.S.

- Coal overtook wood in 1885.
- Oil overtook wood by 1915
- Oil overtook coal in 1950.
- Energy from hydropower overtook wood in about 1968.

Awesome Guides, Inc. A.P. Environmental Science Study Guide - Chapter Two

- Nuclear overtook wood in 1972
- Nuclear overtook hydro by 1973.

Power Generation — all electrical power generation is generally produced in the same way regardless of the fuel that is used. There are variations in the processes but the principle is similar. If a coil of wire is passed through a magnetic field, the field induces electricity to flow along the wire. The most commonly used electricity production is that of an electrical generator. The steps include:

1. Water is boiled to create a high-pressure steam
2. The generated steam to used drive a turbine that is coupled to a turbogenerator.

Many different types of fuels can be used to accomplish this task, such as coal, oil, refuse, solar energy, geothermal energy or nuclear energy. Other types of turbogenerators use either natural gas, where high-pressure gas turns the turbine or hydroelectric, where high-pressure water held behind a dam drives a hydroturbogenerator.

Wood

General Concepts: For over a century, from the founding of the country, wood was the primary source of energy in the US. Wood energy (fuel wood and charcoal) is, and will remain, an important source of energy in South and Southeast Asia. In most countries between 20% and 80% of energy demand is met by wood. The use of wood fuels is still increasing though not as fast as the use of fossil fuels.

Although wood fuels are often considered 'non-commercial', they are widely traded, particularly in urban areas, where wood fuels are most relevant, markets for fuel wood and charcoal are thriving. Many people, both in urban and rural areas, earn their main income from the wood fuel business. This can involve growing, harvesting, processing, trading, transporting or retailing. Unfortunately, over harvesting of fuel wood has destroyed tropical ecosystems. However with proper management, fuel wood is a sustainable and versatile fuel.

Most of the wood fuel originates from non-forest land and is managed sustainably. The main uses are: domestic, commercial and industrial sectors. Applications can be traditional, or modern or an intermediate type.

Most charcoal is produced from wood, but other sources may be coconut shells and crop residues. Charcoal is produced in kilns by a process called pyrolysis, i.e. breaking down the chemical structure of wood under high temperature in the absence of air.

Advantages:
1. Managed properly, wood is a sustainable resource
2. It is available world wide and is relatively inexpensive

Disadvantages:
1. Can not provide enough energy to supply large demands
2. Causes deforestation and loss of biodiversity

A.P. Environmental Science Study Guide - Chapter Two  Awesome Guides, Inc.

Nonrenewable Resources (Fossil Fuels)

Coal - is used primarily in the United States to generate electricity. It is burned in power plants and produces more than half of the electricity in the US. If your house were powered by a coal power plant, then you would consume:

- ½ ton to power an electric stove,
- ½ ton to power a refrigerator
- 2 tons for an electric water heater.

Even though you probably never see coal, you use several tons of it every year!

The material that forms fossil fuels varies greatly over time as each layer was buried. As a result of these variations and the length of time, several types of coal are created. Depending upon its composition, each type of coal burns differently and releases different types of emissions

The four types (or "ranks") of coal mined are: anthracite, bituminous, subbituminous, and lignite.

- **Lignite**: The largest portion of the world's coal reserves are made up of lignite, a soft, brownish-black coal that forms the lowest level of the coal family. You can even see the texture of the original wood in some pieces of lignite that is found west of the Mississippi River in the United States.

- **Subbituminous**: Next up the scale is sub bituminous coal, a dull black coal. It gives off a little more energy (heat) than lignite when it burns. It is mined mostly in Montana, Wyoming and a few other western states.

- **Bituminous**: Still more energy is packed into bituminous coal, sometimes called "soft coal." In the United States, it is found primarily east of the Mississippi River in Midwestern states like Ohio and Illinois and in the Appalachian mountain range from Kentucky to Pennsylvania.

- **Anthracite**: Anthracite is the hardest coal and gives off a great amount of heat when it burns. Unfortunately, in the United States, as elsewhere in the world, there is little anthracite coal to be mined. The U.S. reserves of anthracite are located primarily in Pennsylvania.

Coal is the most abundant fossil fuel in the US.

Sulfur is a yellowish substance that exists in tiny amounts in coal. In some coals found in Ohio, Pennsylvania, West Virginia and other eastern states, sulfur makes up from 3 to 10 percent of the weight of coal. For example, in some coals found in Wyoming, Montana and other western states (as well as some mines in the East), the sulfur can be only 1/100ths (or less than 1 percent) of the weight of the coal. Even with low sulfur coals it is important that most of this sulfur be removed before it goes up a power plant's smokestack.

Coal is often cleaned before it arrives at the power plant. This is done is by crushing the coal into small chunks and washing it. Some of the sulfur that exists in tiny specks in coal (called "pyritic sulfur" because it is combined with iron to form iron pyrite, otherwise known as "fool's gold") can be washed out of the coal

Awesome Guides, Inc. A.P. Environmental Science Study Guide – Chapter Two

in this manner. Typically, in one washing process, the coal chunks are fed into a large water-filled tank. The coal floats to the surface while the sulfur impurities sink. There are facilities around the country called "coal preparation plants" that clean coal in this way.

Not all of coal's sulfur can be removed like this. Some of the sulfur in coal is actually chemically connected to the coal's carbon molecules, and not found on the coal's surface. This type of sulfur is called "organic sulfur." Washing won't remove it. Several processes have been tested to mix the coal with chemicals that break the sulfur away from the coal molecules, but most of these processes have proven too expensive. Scientists are still working to reduce the cost of these chemical cleaning processes.

Most modern power plants, and all plants built after 1978, are required to have special devices that clean sulfur from the coal's combustion gases before the being released into the atmosphere, through the smokestack. The technical name for these devices is "flue gas desulfurization units," more commonly known as "scrubbers" – because they "scrub" the sulfur out of the smoke released by coal-burning boilers.

- **Scrubbers** - Most scrubbers rely on a very common substance found in nature called "limestone." Under the right conditions, limestone has the ability to absorb sulfur gases. In most scrubbers, limestone (or another similar material called lime) is mixed with water and sprayed into the coal combustion gases (called "flue gases"). The limestone captures the sulfur and "pulls" it out of the gases. Limestone and sulfur combine with each other to form a wet paste or in newer scrubbers, a dry powder. In either case, the sulfur is trapped and prevented from escaping into the air.

Advantages:
1. Coal is very abundant in the US
2. Provides high grade energy pound for pound

Disadvantages:
1. High sulfur coals can cause air pollution
2. Mining of coal is dangerous to workers and causes environmental damage.

Oil - is a fossil fuel that exists underground as tiny droplets trapped inside the open spaces, called "pores," inside rocks. The "pores" and the oil droplets can be seen only through a microscope. The droplets cling to the rock, like drops of water cling to a windowpane. Also known as petroleum, it is a very versatile fuel. When pumped from the ground, it is called crude oil. The crude oil is refined into gasoline, jet fuel, propane, motor oil, heating oil, and road tar. Petroleum is the most widely used fossil fuel.

Advantages:

1. Currently available
2. Simple combustion process that can directly heat or generate electricity
3. Inexpensive
4. Easily distributed, handled and stored
5. Mainly used in technologies such as plastics, lubrication, etc.

Disadvantages:

1. Dependence on foreign sources
2. Pollution caused by spills and off-shore drilling

3. Air pollution caused by burning
4. Probably a contributor to global warming
5. Questionable availability over a long period of time
6. Major price swings based on politics

Natural gas - is colorless, shapeless, and in its pure form, odorless. Natural gas can be found in a variety of different underground formations, including:

1. shale formations
2. sandstone beds
3. coal seams
4. deep, salt water aquifers (underground ponds of water)

Once used solely in aviation applications, the gas turbine has evolved into a workhorse in industry and has become the premier electric generation system for peak and intermediate loads. Gas turbines are compact, lightweight, easy to operate, and come in sizes ranging from several hundred kilowatts to hundreds of megawatts. A gas turbine produces a high-temperature; high-pressure gas working fluid, through combustion, to induce shaft rotation by impingement of the gas upon a series of specially designed blades.

The shaft rotation drives an electric generator and a compressor for the air used by the gas turbine. Many turbines also use a heat exchanger called a recuperator to impart turbine exhaust heat into the combustor's air/fuel mixture.

Advantages:

1. Burns cleanly compared to other fossil fuels
2. Less nitrous oxides and sulfur oxides
3. Less particulate matter

Disadvantages:

1. CO_2 is released into the air
2. Lower availability than coal or oil
3. Difficult and costly to transport

Geothermal - Geo (Earth) thermal (heat) energy is an enormous, underused heat and power resource that is **clean** (emits little or no greenhouse gases), **reliable** (average system availability of 95%), and **homegrown** (making us less dependent on foreign oil).

Geothermal resources range from shallow ground to hot water and rock several miles below Earth's surface, and even farther down to the extremely high temperatures of molten rock called magma.

Earth's energy can be converted into heat and electricity. The three technology categories are geothermal heat pumps, direct-use applications, and power plants.

Almost everywhere, the upper 10 feet of Earth's surface maintains a nearly constant temperature between 50 and 60 degrees F (10 and 16 degrees C). A geothermal heat pump system consists of pipes buried in the shallow ground near the building, a heat exchanger, and ductwork into the building. In winter, heat from the relatively warmer ground goes through the heat exchanger into the house. In summer, hot air from the house is pulled through the heat exchanger into the relatively cooler ground. Heat removed during the summer can be used as no-cost energy to heat water.

In the U.S., most geothermal reservoirs are located in the western states, Alaska, and Hawaii. Hot water near Earth's surface can be piped directly into facilities and used to heat buildings, grow plants in

Awesome Guides, Inc. A.P. Environmental Science Study Guide - Chapter Two

greenhouses, dehydrate onions and garlic, heat water for fish farming, and pasteurize milk. Some cities pipe the hot water under roads and sidewalks to melt snow. District heating applications use networks of piped hot water to heat buildings in whole communities.

Mile-or-more deep wells can be drilled into underground reservoirs to tap steam and very hot water that can drive turbines and drive electricity generators. Three types of power plants are operating today:

- Dry steam plants, which directly use geothermal steam to turn turbines;
- Flash steam plants, which pull deep, high-pressure hot water into lower-pressure tanks and use the resulting flashed steam to drive turbines; and
- Binary-cycle plants, pass moderately hot geothermal water by a secondary fluid with a much lower boiling point than water. This causes the secondary fluid to flash to steam, which then drives the turbines.

Advantages:

1. Very clean (does not burn fuels)
2. Conserves fossil fuels
3. No air pollution
4. Very reliable (runs 24 hours a day)
5. No transportation involved
6. It's renewable and sustainable

Disadvantages:

1. Can not provide our current energy needs
2. Can only be used in certain geologically active areas
3. Possible hot water leaks into surrounding ecosystem
4. Hazardous minerals may be produced which are difficult to safely dispose of
5. Hydrothermal water and brines are often corrosive

Hydroelectric -
Hydropower converts the energy of flowing water into electricity. The volume of water flow determines the quantity of electricity generated and the amount of "head" (the height from turbines in the power plant to the water surface) created by the dam. The greater the flow and head, the more electricity produced.

A typical hydropower plant includes a dam, reservoir, penstocks (pipes), a powerhouse and an electrical power substation. The dam stores water and creates the head; penstocks carry water from the reservoir to turbines inside the powerhouse; the water rotates the turbines, which drive generators that produce electricity. The electricity is then transmitted to a substation where transformers increase voltage to allow transmission to homes, businesses and factories.

Hydropower plants can significantly impact the surrounding area— reservoirs can cover towns, scenic locations and farmland, as well as affect fish and wildlife habitat. To mitigate impact on migration patterns and wildlife habitats, dams maintain a steady stream flow and can be designed or retrofitted with fish ladders and fish ways to help fish migrate upstream to spawn.

Advantages

1. Fuel is not burned so there is minimal pollution.

A.P. Environmental Science Study Guide - Chapter Two

2. It's a renewable resource. Rainfall renews the water in the reservoir, so the fuel is almost always there
3. Minimal environmental impact.
4. Hydroelectricity produces no gas emissions or waste.
5. It is more reliable than some other forms of renewable energy, such as solar or wind power.
6. Hydroelectric stations are not very expensive to run and have a long life expectancy. Water to run the power plant is provided free by nature.
7. Many dams built for hydroelectricity were built for flood control or irrigation as well, thus communities share the construction costs.
8. Dams are popular for sightseeing, water sports and other recreational activities
9. It's a high quality electric source, producing useful levels of energy.

Disadvantages

1. Smaller power plants depend on availability of fast flowing streams or rivers, and it cannot be used worldwide because of availability of the resource.
2. Plants that depend on running water can impact the mobility of fish and other river organisms. However, this impact is minimized by building fish ladders that allow the typical migration of certain fish species.
3. Large-scale dams cause considerable impact upstream. They may displace animals living in the area, and can take up large areas of land.
4. Water quantity and quality downstream can be reduced, having a negative effect on plant life. This is caused by excessive evaporation behind the dam causing the water to have a higher salt content.

Nuclear Fission -
is probably the least understood and most controversial source of power generation. Nuclear power comes from the fission of uranium, plutonium or thorium or the fusion of hydrogen into helium. The majority of power generation uses all uranium. Fission of an atom of uranium produces 10,000,000,000 times the energy produced by the combustion of an atom of carbon from coal.

- Natural uranium is almost entirely a mixture of two isotopes, U-235 and U-238. U-235 can fission in a reactor but U-238 can not fission to a significant extent. Natural uranium is 99.3 percent U-238 and 0.7 percent U-235.

- Most nuclear power plants today use enriched uranium in which the concentration of U-235 is increased from 0.7 percent U-235 (nowadays) to about 4 - 5 percent U-235.

- In 1993 there were 109 licensed power reactors in the U.S. and about 400 in the world. They generate about 20 percent of the U.S. electricity. (There are also a large number of naval power reactors.) The expansion of nuclear power depends substantially on politics.

- Present reactors that use only the U-235 in natural uranium are very likely good for some hundreds of years. Breeder reactors may be able supply energy for some billions of years.

- A power reactor contains a core with a large number of fuel rods. Each rod is full of pellets of uranium oxide. An atom of U-235 fissions when it absorbs a neutron. The fission produces two fission fragments and other particles that fly off at high velocity. When they stop the kinetic energy is converted to heat - 10 million times as much heat as is produced by burning an atom of coal.

- Besides the fission fragments several neutrons are produced. Most of these neutrons are absorbed by something other than U-235, but in the steady-state operation of the reactor exactly one is absorbed by another U-235 atom causing another fission to occur. The steam withdrawn and run through the turbines controls the power level of the reactor. Control rods that absorb neutrons can also be moved in and out to control the nuclear reaction. The power level that can be used is limited to avoid letting the fuel rods get too hot.

- The heat from the fuel rods is absorbed by water, which is used to generate steam to drive the turbines that generate the electricity.

- After about two years, enough of the U-235 has been converted to fission products and the fission products have built up enough so that the fuel rods must be removed and replaced by new ones.

What to do with the spent fuel rods is what causes most of the fuss concerning nuclear power.

- Besides fission products, spent fuel rods contain some plutonium produced by the U-238 in the reactor absorbing a neutron. This plutonium and leftover uranium can be separated in a reprocessing plant and used as reactor fuel.

- Running a reactor for four years produces enough plutonium to run it for one more year provided the plutonium is extracted and put into new fuel rods.

- After the fuel has been in the reactor for about 18 months, much of the uranium has already fissioned and considerable quantities of fission products have built up in the fuel. Replacing about 1/3 of the fuel rods then refuels the reactor. This generally takes one to two months.

- When fuel rods are removed from the reactor they contain large quantities of highly radioactive fission products and are generating heat at a high rate. They are then put in a large tank of water about the size of a swimming pool. There they become less radioactive as the more highly radioactive isotopes decay and also generate less and less heat. The longer the spent fuel is stored, the easier it will be to handle, but many reactors have been holding spent fuel so long that their tanks are getting full. They must either send the rods off or build more tanks.

- The fission products are then put in a form for long-term storage. A large reactor produces about 1.5 tons of fission products per year. The fission products are originally in a mixture with other substances, so reprocessing is required to get it down to 1.5 tons.

- Breeder reactor design is much more economical in terms of neutrons. Enough U-238 can be converted to plutonium so that after a fuel cycle there is more fissionable material than there was in the original fuel rods in the reactor. Breeder reactors essentially use U-238 as fuel, and there is 140 times as much of it as there is U-235. The billion year estimates for fuel resources depend on breeder reactors. The French built two of them, the U.S. has a small one, the British built one, the Russians built one and the Japanese are building one.

- Breeder reactors seem to be a resource rather than a reserve. They are more expensive than present reactors and won't be economically practical until the price of uranium ore goes up. This is unlikely to be soon, because large uranium reserves have been discovered in recent years.

A.P. Environmental Science Study Guide - Chapter Two  Awesome Guides, Inc.

Are nuclear power plants perfectly safe?

- Nuclear reactors are not bombs. A bomb converts a large part of its U-235 or plutonium into fission fragments in about 10^-8 seconds and then flies apart. This depends on the fact that a bomb is a very compact object, so the neutrons don't have far to go to hit another fissionable atom. A power plant is much too big to convert an important part of its fissionable material before it has generated enough heat to fly apart. This fact is based on the fundamental physics of how fast fission neutrons travel. Therefore, it doesn't depend on the particular design of the plant.

- Power plants can have severe accidents, if not properly designed and operated. The Chernobyl plant reached 150 times its normal power level before its water turned to high-pressure steam and blew the plant apart, thus extinguishing the nuclear reaction. This only took a few seconds.

- In terms of immediate deaths it was a rather small disaster, 31 people died and about 20 square miles of land became uninhabitable for a long period of time.

- Fall-out from the Chernobyl explosion will contribute to the increase of cancer all over Europe; exactly how much of an increase is disputed.

- The Three Mile Island accident destroyed the reactor, but the core itself remained confined. Radioactive gases were vented, but there is no accepted evidence that this harmed the public.

- Possible failures have been generated and studied. However, there could be something not taken into account.

- At the end of 1998 there were 9012 civilian power reactor years of experience throughout the world, and Chernobyl is the only nuclear power plant accident that harmed the public.

- In 1999, Japanese technicians mixing up fuel for an experimental reactor violated the safety procedures and created a critical mass of uranium, which caused an increasing nuclear reaction until the container with the mixture boiled over and stopped the reaction. Three people were hospitalized, two of whom died.

- Nuclear waste consists of the fission products. They are highly radioactive at first, but most of the radioactive isotopes decay very fast. About one cubic meter of waste per year is generated by a power plant. It needs to be kept away from people. After 10 years, the fission products are 1,000 times less radioactive, and after 500 years, the fission products will be less radioactive than the uranium ore they are originally derived from.

Advantages of Nuclear Fission:

1. The fuel supply is potentially larger. However, the uranium supply alone seems to be large enough.
2. Fission products are not produced, although there will be induced radioactivity in the structures of the power plants.
3. No material useful for bombs is produced, for the most part.

Disadvantages of Nuclear Fission:

1. The problem of disposal of nuclear wastes hasn't been solved.

2. It is bad for humanity to have plenty of energy. - *unrelated opinion*.
3. Nuclear reactors produce plutonium.

Radiation from operating nuclear reactors and other activities involved in nuclear energy is dangerous

Nuclear Fusion — is the process that takes place on the sun. Energy is made by combining hydrogen atoms to make helium. The problem of using this source of energy is due to the millions of degrees required to get hydrogen atoms to combine. Hydrogen bombs, by using ordinary nuclear fission, can set off the fusion of the hydrogen isotopes of deuterium and tritium. Power plants using nuclear fusion are a long way off using current technology and knowledge. Fusion power has the following possible advantages if it can be made to work.

Alternative and Renewable Energy Resources

Solar

- **Passive solar** — is an old concept that takes advantage of the sun rather than compete with it. In building design, the position of structures such as windows and solar panels are a very important consideration. Good passive solar design is based upon the position of the sun. For example, the sun faces the south side of a building for most of the day in the northern hemisphere. Thus the south side of a building has the most solar radiation. Placement of solar panels, windows and insulation are all based with this information in mind. South-facing windows and building materials that absorb and slowly release the sun's heat represent a passive solar design. No mechanical means are employed in passive solar heating. Incorporating passive solar designs can reduce heating bills by as much as 50 percent. Passive solar designs can also include natural ventilation for cooling.

- **Active solar** - hot water heaters, for example, use the sun to heat either water or a heat-transfer fluid in collectors. A typical system will reduce the need for conventional water heating by about two-thirds. High-temperature solar water heaters can provide energy-efficient hot water and hot water heat for large commercial and industrial facilities. Since hot water is actively regulated by pumps and thermostats this process is considered active, thus the term active solar.

- **Photovoltaic** - (or PV) systems convert light energy into electricity. The term "photo" is a stem from the Greek "phos," which means "light." "Volt" is named for Alessandro Volta (1745-1827), a pioneer in the study of electricity. "Photo-voltaics," then, could literally mean "light-electricity." Photovoltaic solar cells, which directly convert sunlight into electricity, are made of semi conducting materials. Most commonly known as "solar cells," PV systems are already an important part of our lives. The simplest systems power many of the small calculators and wrist watches we use every day. More complicated systems provide electricity for pumping water, powering communications equipment, and even lighting our homes and running our appliances. In a surprising number of cases, PV power is the cheapest form of electricity for performing these tasks.

A.P. Environmental Science Study Guide – Chapter Two   Awesome Guides, Inc.

Advantages:

1. Little to no environmental damage
2. Nonpolluting
3. Easy to handle, process and transform
4. Saves fossil fuel resources

Disadvantages:

1. Not always available
2. Cannot be stored
3. High initial cost
4. Must have appliances and lamps that run on lower voltage

Wind — energy has been harnessed for hundreds of years. From old Holland to farms in the United States, windmills have been used for pumping water or grinding grain. Modern windmill's use a *wind turbine* and use the wind's energy to generate electricity. The terms "wind energy" or "wind power" describe the process by which the wind is used to generate mechanical power or electricity. Wind turbines convert the kinetic energy in the wind into mechanical power. This mechanical power can be used for specific tasks (such as grinding grain or pumping water) or a generator can convert this mechanical power into electricity to power homes, businesses and schools.

Modern wind generator

Wind turbines, like windmills, are mounted on a tower to capture the most energy. At 100 feet (30 meters) or more aboveground, they can take advantage of the faster and less turbulent wind. Turbines catch the wind's energy with their propeller-like blades. Usually, two or three blades are mounted on a shaft to form a *rotor*.

A blade acts much like an airplane wing. When the wind blows, a pocket of low-pressure air forms on the downwind side of the blade. The low-pressure air pocket then pulls the blade toward it, causing the rotor to turn. This is called *lift*. The force of the lift is actually much stronger than the wind's force against the front side of the blade, which is called *drag*. The combination of lift and drag causes the rotor to spin like a propeller, and the turning shaft spins a generator to make electricity.

Wind turbines can be used as stand-alone applications, or they can be connected to a utility power grid or even combined with a photovoltaic (solar cell) system. Stand-alone wind turbines are typically used for water pumping or communications. However, homeowners or farmers in windy areas can also use wind turbines as a way to cut their electric bills. For utility-scale sources of wind energy, a large number of wind turbines are usually built close together to form a *wind plant*. Several electricity providers today use wind plants to supply power to their customers.

Even though the cost of wind power has decreased dramatically in the past 10 years, the technology requires a higher initial investment than fossil-fueled generators. Roughly 80% of the cost is the machinery, with the balance being the site preparation and installation. However, if wind generating systems are compared with fossil-fueled systems on a "life-cycle" cost basis (counting fuel and operating expenses for the life of the generator), wind costs are much more competitive with other generating technologies because there is no fuel to purchase and minimal operating expenses.

Advantages:

1. Numerous public opinion surveys have consistently shown that the public prefers wind and other renewable energy forms over conventional sources of generation.
2. Wind energy is a free, renewable resource, so no matter how much is used today, there will still be the same supply in the future.
3. Wind energy is also a source of clean, non-polluting, electricity. Unlike conventional power plants, wind plants emit no air pollutants or greenhouse gases. In 1990, California's wind power plants offset the emission of more than 2.5 billion pounds of carbon dioxide, and 15 million pounds of other pollutants that would have otherwise been produced. It would take a forest of 90 million to 175 million trees to provide the same air quality.

Disavantages:

1. Although wind power plants have relatively little impact on the environment compared to other conventional power plants, there is some concern over the noise produced by the rotor blades.
2. Aesthetic (visual) impacts on the landscape.
3. Occasionally, birds are killed by flying into the rotors.
4. It is intermittent and that the wind does not always blow when electricity is needed.
5. Wind cannot be stored (unless batteries are used); and not all winds can be harnessed to meet the timing of electricity demands.
6. Good wind sites are often located in remote locations far from areas of electric power demand (such as cities).
7. Wind resource development may compete with other uses for the land and those alternative uses may be more highly valued than electricity generation. However, wind turbines can be located on land that is also used for grazing or even farming.

Tidal - in coastal areas with large tides, flowing tidal waters contain large amounts of potential energy. The principal of harnessing the energy of the tides dates back to eleventh century England when tides were used to turn waterwheels, producing mechanical power. More recently, rising and falling tides have been used to generate electricity, in much the same manner as hydroelectric power plants.

One of the main barriers to the increased use of tidal energy is the cost of building tidal generating stations. For example, it has been estimated that the construction of the proposed facility on the Severn River in England would have a construction cost of $15 billion. Operating and maintenance costs of tidal power plants are very low because the "fuel" (sea-water), is free; but the overall cost of electricity generated is still very high.

The few studies that have been undertaken to date to identify the environmental impacts of a tidal power scheme have determined that each specific site is different and the impacts depend greatly upon local geography. Local tides changed only slightly due to the La Rance barrage, and the environmental impact has been negligible, but this may not be the case for all other sites. It has been estimated that in the Bay of Fundy, tidal power plants could decrease local tides by 15 cm. This does not seem like much when one considers that natural variations such as winds can change the level of the tides by several meters.

A.P. Environmental Science Study Guide - Chapter Two  Awesome Guides, Inc.

Advantages:

1. Tidal energy is a renewable source of electricity, which does not result in the emission of greenhouse gases responsible for global warming.
2. There is no generation of acid precipitation associated with fossil fuels.
3. Use of tidal energy could also decrease the need for nuclear power, with its associated radiation risks.

Disadvantages:

1. Changing tidal flows by damming a bay or estuary could result in negative impacts on aquatic and shoreline ecosystems, as well as navigation and recreation.
2. Very little is understood about how altering the tides can affect incredibly complex aquatic and shoreline ecosystems. One fear is that enhanced mixing of water could be caused by tidal barrages would potentially stimulate the growth of the "red tide" organism, *Gonyalaux excavata*, which causes paralysis in shellfish.
3. Unfortunately, one of the only methods of increasing our knowledge about how tidal barrages affect ecosystems may be to study the effects of facilities after they have been built.

Biofuels -
are alcohols, ethers, esters, and other chemicals made from cellulosic biomass such as herbaceous and woody plants, agricultural and forestry residues, and a large portion of municipal solid and industrial waste. The term biofuels can refer to fuels for electricity and fuels for transportation. Biofuels that are used for transportation, include bioethanol, biodiesel, biomethanol, and pyrolysis oils. The two most common types of biofuels that are being developed and used in the United States are bioethanol and biodiesel. This is due to several factors including the state and feasibility of feedstock conversion technology, feedstock availability, and fuel usability.

Ethanol is the most widely used biofuel today. More than 1.5 billion gallons are added to gasoline in the U.S. each year to improve vehicle performance and reduce air pollution. Ethanol is an alcohol, and most is made using a process similar to brewing beer where starch crops are converted into sugars, the sugars are fermented into ethanol, and then the ethanol is distilled into its final form. Ethanol made from cellulosic biomass materials instead of traditional feed stocks (starch crops) is called bioethanol.

Ethanol is used to increase octane and improve the emissions quality of gasoline. The Clean Air Act Amendments of 1990 mandated the sale of oxygenated fuels in areas of the country with unhealthy levels of carbon monoxide. Since that time, there has been strong demand for ethanol as an oxygenated blend of gasoline. In some areas of the United States today, ethanol is blended with gasoline to form an E10 blend (10% ethanol and 90% gasoline), but it can be used in higher concentrations such as E85 or in its pure form. All automobile manufacturers that do business in the United States approve the use of certain ethanol/gasoline blends. Fuel ethanol blends are successfully used in all types of vehicles and engines that require gasoline. Approval of ethanol blends is found in the owners' manuals under references to refueling or gasoline.

Unlike ethanol, which is an alcohol, biodiesel is composed of fatty acid alkyl esters. Biodiesel is manufactured from most vegetable oils, animal fats, and recycled greases. Through a process called transesterification, organically derived oils are combined with alcohol (ethanol or methanol) and chemically altered to form fatty esters such as ethyl or methyl ester. The biomass-derived ethyl or methyl esters can be blended with conventional diesel fuel or used as a neat fuel (100% biodiesel).

Biodiesel is typically used as a fuel additive in 20% blends (B20) with petroleum diesel in compression ignition (diesel) engines, although other blend levels can be used depending on the cost of the fuel and the desired benefits. The Energy Policy Act of 1992 (EPAct) as amended in 1998 allows regulated fleets to use 450 gallons of biodiesel per vehicle per year in any blend level for EPAct credit. Biodiesel can help extend the diesel fuel supply much as ethanol has extended the gasoline supply. Biodiesel use in 2000 in the U.S. is nearly 50 million gallons per year and growing. U.S. producers use recycled cooking oils.

The United States produced about 5 million gallons of soy oil. Biodiesel is used in some federal, state, and transit fleets and other equipment. Neat and blended biodiesel is used in marinas, tourist boats, and launches. There is a growing interest in using biodiesel where workers are exposed to diesel exhaust, in aircraft to control local pollution near airports, and in locomotives that face restricted use unless emissions can be reduced.

Advantages:

1. Biofuels are good for the environment because they add fewer emissions to the atmosphere than petroleum fuels and they use wastes that currently no one is utilizing.
2. Unlike petroleum, which is a nonrenewable natural resource, biofuels are renewable and an inexhaustible source of fuel.
3. Because biofuels are grown domestically, they reduce our dependence on foreign oil, help boost the U.S. economy, and help strengthen U.S. energy security.

Disadvantages:

1. Biofuels are not currently developed enough to rely on as a steady source of energy.

Hydrogen - gas (H_2) is being explored for use in combustion engines and fuel-cell electric vehicles. It is a gas at normal temperatures and pressures, which presents greater transportation and storage hurdles than exist for the liquid fuels. Storage systems being developed include compressed hydrogen, liquid hydrogen, and chemical bonding between hydrogen and the storage material (for example, metal hydrides).

While no transportation distribution system currently exists for hydrogen transportation use, the ability to create the fuel from a variety of resources and its clean-burning properties make it a desirable alternative fuel.

Chemical Properties: The simplest and lightest fuel is hydrogen gas (H_2). Hydrogen is in a gaseous state at atmospheric pressure and ambient temperatures. Fuel hydrogen is not pure hydrogen gas. It has small amounts of oxygen and other materials.

Two methods are generally used to produce hydrogen: (1) electrolysis and (2) synthetic gas production from steam reforming or partial oxidation.

Electrolysis uses electrical energy to split water molecules into hydrogen and oxygen. The electrical energy can come from any electricity production sources including renewable fuels.

A.P. Environmental Science Study Guide - Chapter Two

DOE has concluded that electrolysis is unlikely to become the predominant method for large quantities of hydrogen production in the future.

The predominant method for producing synthesis gas is steam reforming of natural gas, although other hydrocarbons can be used as feedstock. For example, biomass and coal can be gasified and used in a steam reforming process to create hydrogen.

A distribution system for hydrogen as a transportation fuel does not exist. While pipeline transportation is generally the most economic means of transporting gaseous fuels, a pipeline system is currently not in place. Transportation of Hydrogen is typically in canisters and tanker trucks.

Advantages:

1. Germany, Japan, Canada, Belgium, and Saudi Arabia took the U.S. invented technology for hydrogen production and have been expanding on it for years. The United States has stubbornly clung to oil. Investing in hydrogen development would keep the U.S. in step with global competition.
2. Relying on the Middle East for energy weakens national strength. The U.S. could be energy self-sufficient with hydrogen.
3. Converting to a hydrogen-based economy would create thousands of permanent scientific and industrial jobs. Building plants, manufacturing parts, selling equipment, and developing technology would all be U.S. investments that stimulate U.S. jobs and growth. Someday, fossil fuels will run dry.
4. Hydrogen is renewable and, therefore, unlimited. Solving energy supply problems today will ensure our nation's stability tomorrow.
5. Pollution from cars and airplanes has created smog clouds across the country. Magnificent scenic vistas like the Grand Canyon are disappearing in toxic haze and valleys like Las Vegas and Reno are becoming smog pits. Hydrogen emits no toxins.
6. U.S. trade balance sheets show that oil imports drain $1 billion from the U.S. economy every week. The government spends billions of taxpayer dollars every year to subsidize oil exploration and to militarily defend access to oil in the Middle East.
7. Huge oil spills like the Exxon Valdez are becoming common, killing countless waterfowl and harming many other species. If hydrogen were spilled, it would evaporate immediately. The only by-product of hydrogen fuel is water.
8. Mass consumption of oil requires continued drilling into pristine wilderness areas, wreaking havoc on some of the world's greatest ecosystems. Hydrogen production leaves no environmental scars.
9. Increasing pollution from cars and airplanes makes people sick. Hydrogen is clean and efficient.

Disadvantages:

1. Hydrogen is not currently developed enough to rely on as a steady source of energy.

Pollution

Types of pollutants

Pesticides — are classified into several groups depending on the level of persistence (how long it takes to break down in the environment), and the type of organism it acts on. Herbicides attack plants, insecticides attack insects. Persistent pesticides are not easily broken down in the environment, thus they affect ecosystems for long periods of time. Non-persistent pesticides DO break down more quickly, thus may not affect ecosystems for long periods of time. Some pesticides are also called broad spectrum, which mean that they kill many different kinds of pests, including beneficial ones.

DDT is a pesticide that was used during the 1940's- the 1960's. It is now banned in developed countries because of its damage to humans and the environment. Developing countries continue to use DDT because it is very cheap and helps in the war on malaria (a disease carried by anopheles mosquitoes and protozoans and causing hundreds of thousand of deaths annually. DDT is very persistent and is a broad-spectrum pesticide. Some mosquitoes have become resistant to DDT creating a new and difficult problem to solve.

The "best" example of biomagnification comes from DDT. This long-lived pesticide (insecticide) has improved human health in many countries by killing insects such as mosquitoes that spread disease. On the other hand, DDT is effective in part because it does not break down in the environment. It is picked up by organisms in the environment and incorporated into their fat. Even here, it does no real damage in many organisms (including humans). In others, however, DDT is deadly or may have more insidious, long-term effects. In birds, for instance, DDT interferes with the deposition of calcium in the shells of the bird's eggs. The eggs laid have very soft shells and are easily broken; so birds afflicted are rarely able to raise young. This causes a decline in their numbers. This was so apparent in the early 1960's that it led the scientist Rachel Carson to postulate a "silent spring" without the sound of birdcalls. Her book "*Silent Spring*" led to the banning of DDT, and a search for pesticides that would not biomagnify. This gave birth to the "modern" environmental movement in the 1960's. Birds such as the bald eagle have made comebacks in response to the banning of DDT in the US. Ironically, many of the pesticides that replaced DDT are more dangerous to humans, and without DDT, disease (primarily in the tropics) would claim more human lives.

Summary:

In order for a pollutant to biomagnify, the following conditions must be met:

1. The pollutant must be long-lived.
2. The producers must concentrate the pollutant.
3. The pollutant must be fat-soluble.

Insecticide Examples:

Compound Class	Examples	Persistence in the Environment
Organochlorides (chlorinated hydrocarbons)	DDT, DDD, aldrin, chlordane, toxaphene, lindane	High — 5 to 15 years
Organophosphates	diazinon, malathion, parathion, chloropyrifos,	Intermediate — 1 week to several weeks
Carbamates	Carbaryl (sevin), matacil, temik, zectran, aminocarb	Low — 2 weeks or less
Pyrethroids	decamethrin, permethrin, bifenthrin	Low - days

A.P. Environmental Science Study Guide - Chapter Two  Awesome Guides, Inc.

Herbicide Examples:

Compound Class	Examples
Triazines	Atrazine, cyanizine, simazine,
Dinitroaniline	oryzalin, triflualin
Phenoxy	2,4-D; 2,4,5, -T; MCPB
Thiocarbamate	butylate, cycloate, EPTC,
Acidamine	alachlor, propachlor

Point and non-point sources — are pollutant classifications used for the purpose of regulation. Point source pollutants are directly put into the environment through sewer pipes or systems, power plant discharge, direct factory discharge and coal / oil operations. The actual source is usually easy to find resulting in a system that is relatively easy to regulate and monitor. Nonpoint source pollutants are difficult to "pin-point" and can be spread over, large areas. They may be far away from the effected area. Examples of possible nonpoint pollutant sources include: storm water runoff, agriculture, pastures and the atmosphere.

Thermal Pollution - There are three major causes of thermal pollution:

1. water as a cooling agent in power generation

2. deforestation of shorelines

3. soil erosion

The most common cause of thermal pollution is water as a cooling agent in nuclear power plants and other industrial facilities. When water has absorbed excess heat from nuclear rods or other machinery it is returned to the environment (usually a river or lake) at temperatures 9 to 20 degrees warmer. Stringent regulations are imposed in the U.S. for release of excess heat. Unfortunately, most of the world's nuclear power plants are located in France and other European nations don't have stringent regulations. That's why we must **THINK GLOBALLLY AND ACT LOCALLY!**

Shoreline deforestation and soil erosion contribute to the problem, although they represent a much smaller percent of the thermal pollution problem. Soil erosion makes the water muddy (darker), which in turn increases light absorption and raises the water temperature. Deforestation of shorelines further contributes to the problem in two ways:

1. it increases soil erosion and

2. it increases the amount of light that strikes the water, both cause an increase in water temperature.

Effects of Thermal Pollution - Higher water temperatures can greatly affect an aquatic ecosystem. Since water temperature is inversely proportional to the amount dissolved oxygen (DO), and an increase of heat will decrease the DO. Higher water temperature may also increase the photosynthesis rate, as aquatic plants like warm temperatures. Intially, this may increase the DO, however as plants die and decompose, they will ultimately remove DO from the water. Less oxygen, and more demand for it, results in a decrease of DO. Since aquatic organisms require DO, then death may be the result for these organisms. Additionally, warmer water increases the metabolic rate of fish. Higher metabolic rates mean that fish will eat more aquatic insects, resulting in a large decrease in insects. As insect populations decline so do all of the organisms that depend on them. Thermal pollution will also increase some fish's sensitivity to toxic waste, resulting in an increase in parasites and other diseases.

Consequences of Pollutions

Greenhouse gases - rising concentrations of water vapor (H_2O), carbon dioxide (CO_2), methane (CH_4), nitrous oxide (N_2O), ozone (O_3), perfluorocarbons (PFCs), hydrofluorocarbons (HFCs), and sulphur hexafluoride (SF6) in the atmosphere are causing a warming of the earth's surface. The result is a destabilizing effect on our climate system. These gases, known as greenhouse gases, absorb and send infrared radiation back to the earth, causing the "greenhouse effect."
Methane (CH_4) and carbon dioxide (CO_2) are two of six greenhouse gases that need to be stabilized in order to mitigate the economic and environmental damages of global warming. Nitrous oxide (N_2O) is another potent greenhouse gas that has both natural and anthropogenic sources. Several classes of halocarbons that contain fluorine and chlorine are also greenhouse gases. Fluorine containing halocarbons include: hydrofluorocarbons (HFCs), perfluorocarbons (PFCs), and sulfur hexafluoride (SF6). Unlike methane, these greenhouse gases are generated exclusively by anthropogenic (human-related) activities. Currently, atmospheric concentrations of these gases are relatively small compared to other greenhouse gases. These compounds, however, have the potential to greatly impact global warming due to their potency and extremely long atmospheric persistance. Because they remain in the atmosphere almost indefinitely, concentrations of these gases will increase as long as their emissions continue.

Ozone — is a layer of gas in the upper atmosphere that screens out harmful ultraviolet (UV) radiation. Many environmental and health effects result from increased exposure to ultraviolet-B (UV-B) radiation caused by stratospheric ozone depletion.

Stratospheric ozone protects the biosphere from potentially damaging doses of (UV-B) radiation. Recent depletion of stratospheric ozone could lead to significant increases in UV-B reaching the earth's surface. UV-B radiation is responsible for a wide range of potentially damaging human and animal health effects, primarily related to the skin, eyes, and immune system. Human exposure to UV-B depends upon an individual's location (latitude and altitude), the duration and timing of outdoor activities (time of day, season of the year), and precautionary behavior (use of sunscreen, sunglasses, or protective clothing). An individual's skin color and age can influence the occurrence and severity of some of the health effects from exposure to UV-B.

Global warming - is the phenomenon of rising global temperatures related to increasing concentrations of greenhouse gases? This warming occurs near surface temperature of the earth and is believed to result from a buildup of so-called greenhouse gases (see previous section), which include water vapor, carbon dioxide (CO_2), methane (CH_4), nitrous oxide (N_2O), and ozone (O_3). Although these gases are naturally occurring, particular human activities (anthropogenic sources) also generate certain greenhouse gases and contribute significantly to global warming.

A.P. Environmental Science Study Guide - Chapter Two  Awesome Guides, Inc.

CFC's Cycle in the Atmosphere

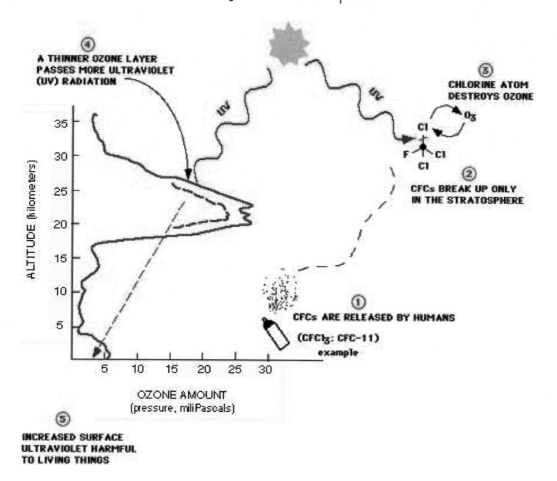

Ultraviolet radiation —occurs on the electromagnetic spectrum with a wavelength of .1 μm, slightly shorter than that of violet light. This invisible electromagnetic radiation is found between visible violet light and X rays. The ultraviolet radiation in sunlight is divided into three bands:

1. UVA (320-400 nanometers), which can cause skin damage and may cause melanoma (skin cancer).

2. UVB (280-320 nanometers), stronger radiation that increases in the summer and is a common cause of sunburn, and the most common skin cause of melanoma.

3. UVC (below 280 nanometers), the strongest and potentially most harmful form.

The shorter electromagnetic wavelengths are more harmful, because energy is inversely proportional to wavelength. Much UVB and most UVC radiation is absorbed by the ozone before it can reach the earth's surface. Depletion of stratospheric ozone increases the amount of ultraviolet radiation that can pass through it, and results in damage to biological tissues. The result is damaged protein and DNA molecules at the surfaces of all living things.

Rising Sea Level - Sea level has risen by 8cm since 1961 and continues to rise at a rate of 2mm per year. Global warming affects this rise by causing thermal expansion of ocean waters, and melting of glaciers and ice fields. Scientists don't agree on the exact rate of sea level rising, however, even the lowest estimates will cause flooding of many coastal areas. Estimates range from 15 to 95 cm (6 to 37 inches) over this century.

Levels and loss of biodiversity – Biodiversity refers to the variety of life. Biodiversity occurs at different levels, 1) ecosystem level 2) species level 3) genetic level. At each level there are a tremendous amount of individual differences. Loss of biodiversity is of great concern because many of our domestic animals and plants come from wild varieties. The introduction of new genes from wild species increases crop yields, and the overall health of these species. If all organisms had the same genetic makeup (NO biodiversity) then any disease, for example, would eliminate the entire species. Additionally, many of our medications come from wild species and with an estimated 13 million species still unidentified; the possibility of loosing future cures for diseases is very probable. Loss in biodiversity occurs for several reasons:

- **Habitat Loss and Fragmentation** - Ecosystems have shrunk dramatically in size over past decades. Human population growth is exponential and resource consumption continues to grow with the higher demands of our technologic society. Ninety-eight percent of the tropical dry forest along Central America's Pacific coast has disappeared. Thailand lost 22 percent of its mangroves between 1981 and 1985, and virtually none of the remainder is undisturbed. In marine ecosystems, high coastal development has wiped out numerous reef and near-shore communities. Tropical rain forests are experiencing tremendous loss of habitat to make room for timber, agriculture, cattle and their increasing human population. Numerous forest, fisheries, and wildlife resources have been overexploited, sometimes to the point of extinction. Some species of animals are so specialized that they require an intact forest for their survival. When an ecosystem is partially deforested (fragmented) those specialized species cannot exist.

  - **Pollution of soil, water, and atmosphere** —puts incredible stress on ecosystems and may reduce or eliminate populations of sensitive species. Pollutants can be biomagnified along the food chains, which means they increase their concentration as they move up trophic levels. Sources of atmospheric pollution include; 1) particulates 2) acid-forming compounds 3) photochemical smog 4) CO_2 5) CFC's 6) nuclear waste and 7) pesticides and herbicides. Sources of water and soil pollution include: 1) toxic chemicals 2) solid waste 3) nutrient oversupply and 4) sediments.

  - **Global climate change** – as discussed earlier, could have serious consequences. Anthropogenic caused increases in greenhouse gases could rise by 1 to 3 degrees Celsius (2 to 5 degrees Fahrenheit) during the next century. Sea levels are also expected to rise over the next century. In the United States rising sea levels may cover entire habitats causing as many as 80 species to become extinct. Many of the world's islands would be completely submerged.

  - **Industrial agriculture and forestry** - Until this century, farmers and ranchers bred and maintained a tremendous biodiversity in their crops and livestock. Today, this biodiversity is dwindling, resulting in monocultures. Monocultures refer to organisms that are genetically identical. The result can be catastrophic. For example, should a particular disease infect a monoculture crop, then the entire harvest could be "wiped-out" because the genetic diversity and resistance to that disease would be lost.

A.P. Environmental Science Study Guide - Chapter Two  Awesome Guides, Inc.

Management of pollutants

Wastewater treatment - Sewage is the wastewater released by residences, businesses and industries in a community. It is 99.94 percent water, with only 0.06 percent of the wastewater as dissolved and suspended solid material. The cloudiness of sewage is caused by suspended particles, which in untreated sewage ranges from 100 to 350 mg/l. A measure of the strength of the wastewater is biochemical oxygen demand, or BOD_5. The BOD_5 measures the amount of oxygen microorganisms require in five days to break down sewage. Untreated sewage has a BOD_5 ranging from 100 mg/l to 300 mg/l. Pathogens or disease-causing organisms are present in sewage. Coliform bacteria are used as an indicator of disease-causing organisms. Sewage also contains nutrients (such as ammonia and phosphorus), minerals and metals. Ammonia can range from 12 to 50 mg/l and phosphorus can range from 6 to 20 mg/l in untreated sewage.

Sewage treatment is a multi-stage process to renovate wastewater before it reenters a body of water or is applied to the land or it is reused. The goal is to reduce or remove organic matter, solids, nutrients, disease-causing organisms and other pollutants from wastewater. Each receiving body of water has limits to the amount of pollutants it can receive without degradation. Therefore, each sewage treatment plant must hold a permit listing the allowable levels of BOD_5, suspended solids, coliform bacteria and other pollutants.

Waste Water Treatment Facility Diagram

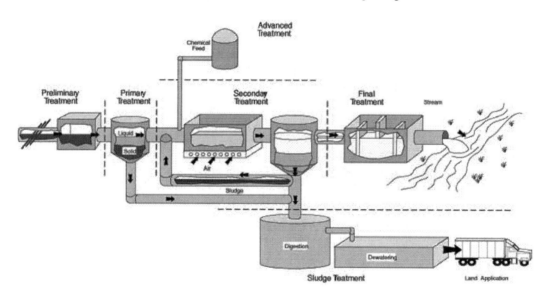

Preliminary Treatment —Preliminary treatment screens out, grinds up, and/or separates debris as the first step in wastewater treatment. Sticks, rags, large food particles, sand, gravel, toys, etc., are removed at this stage to protect the pumping and other equipment in the treatment plant. Treatment equipment such as bar screens, comminutors (a large version of a garbage disposal), and grit chambers are used as the wastewater first enters a treatment plant. The collected debris is usually disposed of in a landfill.

Primary Treatment - Primary treatment is the second step in treatment and separates suspended solids and greases from wastewater. Wastewater is held in a quiet tank for several hours allowing the particles to settle to the bottom and the greases to float to the top. The solids drawn off the bottom

Awesome Guides, Inc. A.P. Environmental Science Study Guide - Chapter Two

and skimmed off the top receive further treatment as sludge. The clarified wastewater flows on to the next stage of wastewater treatment. Clarifiers and septic tanks are usually used to provide primary treatment.

Secondary Treatment - Secondary treatment is a biological treatment process to remove dissolved organic matter from wastewater. Sewage microorganisms are cultivated and added to the wastewater. The microorganisms absorb organic matter from sewage as their food supply. Three approaches are used to accomplish secondary treatment; fixed film, suspended film and lagoon systems.

- Fixed film systems grow microorganisms on substrates such as rocks, sand or plastic. The wastewater is spread over the substrate, allowing the wastewater to flow past the film of microorganisms fixed to the substrate. As organic matter and nutrients are absorbed from the wastewater, the film of microorganisms grows and thickens. Trickling filters, rotating biological contactors, and sand filters are examples of fixed film systems.

- Suspended film systems stir and suspend microorganisms in wastewater. As the microorganisms absorb organic matter and nutrients from the wastewater they grow in size and number. After the microorganisms have been suspended in the wastewater for several hours, they are settled out as sludge. Some of the sludge is pumped back into the incoming wastewater to provide "seed" microorganisms. The remainder is wasted and sent on to a sludge treatment process. Activated sludge, extended aeration, oxidation ditches, and sequential batch reactor systems are all examples of suspended film systems.

- Lagoon systems are shallow basins that hold the wastewater for several months to allow for the natural degradation of sewage. These systems take advantage of natural aeration and microorganisms in the wastewater to renovate sewage.

Final Treatment - Final treatment focuses on removal of disease-causing organisms from wastewater. Treated wastewater can be disinfected by adding chlorine or by using ultraviolet light. High levels of chlorine may be harmful to aquatic life in receiving streams. Treatment systems often add a chlorine-neutralizing chemical to the treated wastewater before stream discharge.

Advanced Treatment - Advanced treatment is necessary in some treatment systems to remove nutrients from wastewater. Chemicals are sometimes added during the treatment process to help settle out or strip out phosphorus or nitrogen. Some examples of nutrient removal systems include coagulant addition for phosphorus removal and air stripping for ammonia removal.

Sludge

- Sludge is generated through the sewage treatment process. Primary sludge, material that settles out during primary treatment, often has a strong odor and requires treatment prior to disposal. Secondary sludge is the extra microorganisms from the biological treatment processes. The goals of sludge treatment are to stabilize the sludge, reduce odors, remove some of the water, reduce volume, decompose some of the organic matter, kill disease-causing organisms and disinfect the sludge.

- Untreated sludge is about 97 percent water. Settling the sludge and decanting off the separated liquid removes some of the water and reduces the sludge volume. Settling can result in sludge with about 96 to 92 percent water. More water can be removed from sludge by using sand drying beds, vacuum filters, filter presses, and centrifuges resulting in sludge with between 50 to 80 percent water. This dried sludge is called a sludge cake. Aerobic and anaerobic digestion are used to

A.P. Environmental Science Study Guide - Chapter Two  Awesome Guides, Inc.

decompose organic matter and reduce volume. Digestion also stabilizes the sludge to reduce odors. Caustic chemicals can be added to sludge or it may be heat treated to kill disease-causing organisms. Following treatment, liquid and cake sludge are usually spread on fields, returning organic matter and nutrients to the soil.

- Wastewater treatment processes require careful management to ensure the protection of the water body that receives the discharge. Trained and certified treatment plant operators measure and monitor the incoming sewage, the treatment process and the final effluent.

Municipal solid waste - The three possible methods to dispose of solid waste are:

Sanitary Landfills - are areas where a large portion if our solid wastes are processed. When solid waste is deposited into a sanitary landfill physical, chemical and biochemical reactions occur. As natural processes degrade the waste material, both methane and leachate are produced. Leachate is a liquid that is formed as a result of rain percolating (soaking) into the wastes, picking up chemicals as it seeps downward. Leachate is significantly affected by the presence of both aerobic and anaerobic bacteria. Additionally, methane gas is produced by the decomposition of wastes and is either vented into the air, or burned off, causing air pollution. Sometimes this gas is trapped and used as an energy source.

- The initial stages of land filling begin with decomposition by aerobic bacteria, which readily metabolize biodegradable organic waste. The by-product produced consists of carbon dioxide, small quantities of water, small molecule fatty acids and heat. During these early stages the leachate strength is relatively low and odor is practically non-existent.

- The next step in processing the wastes depletes aerobic microbes allowing anaerobic microbes to become dominant. This results in a period of facilitative (in other words, the first step helps the second step) microbial activity. Typically, the transition is characterized by a sharp reduction in pH accompanied by an increase in BOD and COD. Usually the high reduction in pH results in the mobilization of metals and their accompanying anions. Leachate at this point has increased levels of hardness, dissolved solids and heavy metals. Usually, iron concentrations are high during this phase. This imbalance results in the emission of a foul odor and a leachate flow that, aside from being thick and dark in color, emits strong foul odor. Generally, fly, insect and pest infestations increase during this period. The wastes are sealed covered and compacted.

Incineration – Wastes of all kinds produced by human societies is increasing in quantity. Many times the solid wastes are incinerated (burned) to reduce their volume. This practice, when used, is controversial due to the lack of air pollution control. Many unknown toxic substances could be put into the atmosphere, because no one monitors exactly what goes into the incinerator. Strong political and industrial measures are urgently needed to change this trend.

- Incinerators reduce the volume of solid waste but they do not make the problem of toxic substances in the waste disappear. Incinerators emit a wide range of pollutants in their stack gases, such as, ashes and other residues, and dioxins. Incineration is the #1 source, about 95% of dioxin production world-wide. The filters used to clean incinerator stack gases also produce solid and liquid toxic wastes.

- Dioxin is a general term that describes a group of hundreds of chemicals that are highly persistent in the environment. The most toxic compound is 2,3,7,8-tetrachlorodibenzo-p-dioxin or

TCDD. The toxicity of other dioxins and chemicals like PCBs that act like dioxin are measured in relation to TCDD. Dioxin is formed as an unintentional by-product of many industrial processes involving chlorine such as waste incineration, chemical and pesticide manufacturing and pulp and paper bleaching. Dioxin was the primary toxic component of Agent Orange(a substance used in the Viet Nam War to defoliate trees and that cause many adverse health effects), was found at Love Canal in Niagara Falls, NY and was the basis for evacuations at Times Beach, MO and Seveso, Italy. Dioxin pollution is also associated with paper mills which use chlorine bleaching in their process and with the production of Polyvinyl Chloride (PVC) plastics.

- After Incineration, Wastes Are Converted to: CO, CO_2, Water and Ash.

- Depending on the composition of the initial waste, compounds containing: halogens, metals, nitrogen, sulfur and dioxin.

Recovery/recycling/composting
Although source reduction, reuse, recycling, and composting can divert large portions of municipal solid waste (MSW) from disposal, some waste still must be placed in landfills. Modern landfills are well-engineered facilities that are located, designed, operated, monitored, closed, cared for after closure, cleaned up when necessary, and financed to insure compliance with federal regulations. The federal regulations were established to protect human health and the environment. In addition, these new landfills can collect potentially harmful landfill gas emissions and convert the gas into energy.

Landfills
A secure landfill is a carefully engineered depression in the ground (or built on top of the ground, resembling a football stadium) into which wastes are put. The aim is to avoid any hydraulic [water-related] connection between the wastes and the surrounding environment, particularly groundwater. Basically, a landfill is a bathtub in the ground; a double-lined landfill is one bathtub inside another. Bathtubs leak two ways: out the bottom or over the top.

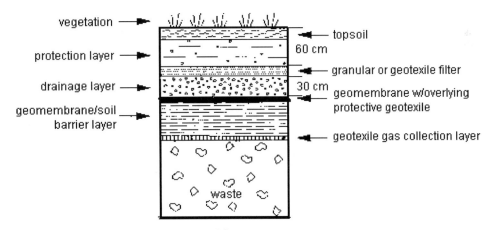

A typical landfill cross section

Landfills have four critical elements: a bottom liner, a leachate collection system, a cover, and the natural hydrogeologic setting. The natural setting can be selected to minimize the possibility of wastes escaping to groundwater beneath a landfill. The three other elements must be engineered and each of these elements is critical to the landfill success.

The Natural Hydrogeologic Setting
You want the geology to do two contradictory things for you. To prevent the wastes from escaping, you want rocks as tight (waterproof) as possible. Yet if leakage

occurs, you want the geology to be as simple as possible so you can easily predict where the wastes will go. Then you can put down wells and capture the escaped wastes by pumping. Fractured bedrock is highly undesirable beneath a landfill because the wastes cannot be located if they escape. Mines and quarries should be avoided because they frequently contact the groundwater.

- **Bottom Liners** - One or more layers of clay or a synthetic flexible membrane (or a combination of these) can effectively create a bathtub liner in the ground. If the bottom liner fails, wastes will migrate directly into the environment. There are three types of liners: clay, plastic and composite.

- **Clay Liners** - Natural clay is often fractured and cracked. A mechanism called diffusion will move organic chemicals like benzene through a three-foot thick clay landfill liner in approximately five years. Some chemicals can degrade clay.

- **Plastic Liners** - The very best landfill liners today are made of a tough plastic film called high-density polyethylene (HDPE). A number of household chemicals will degrade HDPE, permeating it (passing though it), making it lose its strength, softening it, or making it become brittle and crack. Not only will household chemicals, such as moth balls, degrade HDPE, but much more benign things can cause it to develop stress cracks, such as, margarine, vinegar, ethyl alcohol (booze), shoe polish, peppermint oil, to name a few.

- **Composite Liners** - A composite liner is a single liner made of two parts, a plastic liner and compacted soil (usually clay soil). Reports show that all plastic liners (also called Flexible Membrane Liners, or FMLs) will have some leaks. It is important to realize that all materials used as liners are at least slightly permeable to liquids or gases and a certain amount of permeation through liners should be expected. Additional leakage results from defects such as cracks, holes, and faulty seams. Studies show that a 10-acre landfill will have a leak rate somewhere between 0.2 and 10 gallons per day.

Leachate Collection System - Leachate is water that gets badly contaminated by contacting wastes. It seeps to the bottom of a landfill and is collected by a system of pipes. The bottom of the landfill is sloped; pipes laid along the bottom capture contaminated water and other fluid (leachate) as they accumulate. The pumped leachate is treated at a wastewater treatment plant (and the solids removed from the leachate during this step are returned to the landfill, or are sent to some other landfill). If leachate collection pipes clog up and leachate remains in the landfill, fluids can build up in the bathtub. The resulting liquid pressure becomes the main force driving waste out the bottom of the landfill when the bottom liner fails.

Problems with Leachate Collection Systems

Leachate collection systems can clog up in less than a decade. They fail in several known ways:

1. They can clog up from silt or mud.
2. They clog up due to growth of microorganisms in the pipes.
3. Minerals can precipitate in the pipes and cause a clog.

Awesome Guides, Inc. A.P. Environmental Science Study Guide - Chapter Two

4. The pipes become weakened by chemical attack (acids, solvents, oxidizing agents, or corrosion) and may then be crushed by the tons of garbage piled on them.

Cover - A cover or cap is an umbrella over the landfill to keep water out (to prevent leachate formation). It will generally consist of several sloped layers: clay or membrane liner (to prevent rain from intruding), overlain by a very permeable layer of sand or gravel soil (to promote rain runoff), overlain by topsoil in which vegetation can root (to stabilize the underlying layers of the cover). If the cover (cap) is not maintained, rain will enter the landfill resulting in buildup of leachate to the point where the bathtub overflows its sides and wastes enter the environment.

Problems with Covers

1. Covers are vulnerable to attack from at least seven sources:
2. Erosion by natural weathering (rain, hail, snow, freeze-thaw cycles, and wind).
3. Vegetation, such as shrubs and trees that continually compete with grasses for available space, sending down roots that will relentlessly seek to penetrate the cover.
4. Burrowing or soil- dwelling mammals (woodchucks, mice, moles, voles), reptiles (snakes, tortoises), insects (ants, beetles), and worms present constant threats to the integrity of the cover.
5. Sunlight (if any of these other natural agents should succeed in uncovering a portion of the umbrella) will dry out clay (permitting cracks to develop), or destroy membrane liners through the action of ultraviolet radiation.
6. Subsidence--an uneven cave-in of the cap caused by settling of wastes or organic decay of wastes, or by loss of liquids from land filled drums--can result in cracks in clay or tears in membrane liners, or result in ponding on the surface, which can make a clay cap mushy or can subject the cap to freeze-thaw pressures.
7. Rubber tires, which "float" upward in a landfill.
8. Human activities of many kinds.

Reduction and Reuse

Reduction and reuse - During the past 35 years, the amount of waste each person creates has almost doubled from 2.7 to 4.6 pounds per day. The most effective way to stop this trend is by preventing waste in the first place. Waste prevention; also know as "source reduction," is the practice of designing, manufacturing, purchasing, or using materials (such as products and packaging) in ways that reduce the amount or toxicity of trash created. Reusing items is another way to stop waste at the source because it delays or avoids that item's entry in the waste collection and disposal system. Source reduction, including reuse, can help:

- Reduce waste disposal and handling costs, because it avoids the costs of recycling, and municipal composting, land filling, and combustion.

- Conserve resources and reduces pollution, such as greenhouse gases that contribute to global warming.

- Save natural resources. Waste is not just created when consumers throw items away. Throughout the life cycle of a product, from extraction of raw materials, to transportation to the processing and manufacturing facilities to manufacture and use, waste is generated. Reusing items or making them with less material decreases waste dramatically. Ultimately, fewer materials need to be recycled or sent to landfills or waste combustion facilities.

- Reduce toxicity of waste. Selecting nonhazardous or less hazardous items is another important component of source reduction. Using less hazardous alternatives for certain items (e.g., cleaning products and pesticides), sharing products that contain hazardous chemicals instead of throwing out leftovers, reading label directions carefully, and using the smallest amount of a product necessary, are all ways to reduce waste toxicity.

- Reduce costs. The benefits of preventing waste goes beyond reducing reliance on other forms of waste disposal. Preventing waste also can mean economic savings for communities, businesses, schools, and individual consumers.

Toxicology — is the science of poisons, and the studies the harmful effects of chemicals on living organisms. Scientists who study these harmful effects and assess the probability of their occurrence are called toxicologists.

- Toxicology encompasses the study of the adverse effects of chemicals on living organisms.

- Toxicology assesses the probability of hazards caused by such effects.

- Toxicology estimates the results of these effects on animal and human populations.

- Toxicological investigations consider the cause, circumstances, effects and limits of safety of unintended harmful effects of food, food additives, drugs, household and industrial products or wastes.

- Toxicological studies deal with adverse effects ranging from short-term to long-term.

Environmental Laws, Public Policy, and Trade-offs

Environmental Choices

Conservation - practices reduce soil erosion, protect the Nation's ability to produce food and fiber, reduce sedimentation in streams and lakes, improve water quality, establishes wildlife habitat, and enhances forest / wetland resources. It encourages farmers to convert highly erodible cropland or other environmentally sensitive acreage to vegetative cover, such as tame or native grasses, wildlife plantings, trees, filter strips, or riparian (water) buffers. Farmers receive an annual rental payment for the term of the multi-year contract. Cost sharing is provided to establish the vegetative cover practices.

Preservation — is a land ethic that attributes inherent value to both ecological systems and species of organisms. The main idea is that some things are valuable in themselves, not merely for their use in supporting the lives of individual animals or plants. In preservation practices, land is COMPLETELY kept in its natural state. In keeping ecosystems intact, organisms may have a better change of survival. When the number of individuals in a species falls below a certain number, the species may not recover, but will

Awesome Guides, Inc.   A.P. Environmental Science Study Guide - Chapter Two

possibly go extinct. Wild species play the same important roles in ecological systems as people do in a human economy. Just as a human community needs, teachers, farmers, contractors, and doctors; an ecological system needs plants, herbivores, carnivores, and decomposers. The concept of preservation strives to meet these goals.

Development – is idea of using the land without consideration of wild species of organisms, ecosystems, biodiversity, or indigenous people in the area. Examples include, clear-cutting of forests, or putting raw, untreated sewage in a river or stream. Many environmental laws stop or slow down this practice in developed countries, but many developing countries do not control development.

Sustainability – Involves the concept of sustainable development that combines social, cultural, economic and ecological considerations within an ecological standard. Sustainability allows land use for human needs (in contrast to preservation) by making sure that conservation and development do not compete with one another, but rather complements their activities towards the same goals. To implement sustainable development, it is necessary to research and develop systems that maintain the ecological integrity of environmental systems while still being able to use its resources. Sustainable development is defined by United Nations Agenda 21 protocols for the environment. Agreed upon at the 1992 United Nations Conference on the Environment held in Rio de Janeiro, Brazil, they built on earlier conferences in Paris (1968) and Stockholm (1972). Practical and applied models of sustainable development are often used to demonstrate how natural can restore ecosystems. Sustainable development uses scientific knowledge and technology to restore and maintain environmental systems. Theoretically, sustainable development allows the use of the worlds ecosystems indefinitely.

Restoration - is the process by which contaminated sites and facilities are identified, characterized, and existing contamination is contained or removed and disposed of to allow beneficial reuse of the property. Environmental Restoration directs the assessment and cleanup of inactive sites and surplus facilities contaminated from previous defense and non-defense related programs. All cleanup activities must comply with federal, state, Indian Nation, and local laws and regulations. In completing environmental restoration activities, DOE is committed to working with stakeholders to understand technical issues and evaluate alternatives. Two important program goals include stabilizing urgent contamination problems to protect human health, safety, environment, and investing in technology research to solve contamination problems now and in the future. Environmental Restoration activities are categorized as either remedial actions or decommissioning.

Mitigation - is the cornerstone of emergency management. It's the ongoing effort to lessen the impact disasters have on people and property. Mitigation involves keeping homes away from floodplains, engineering bridges to withstand earthquakes, creating and enforcing effective building codes to protect property from hurricanes and other disasters.

Remediation – or "Site Remediation" means environmental cleanup. Many statutes or guidelines are used to determine how the remediation is to be completed. Which statute to use depends on what kind of release there's been (oil? hazardous waste?) and from where (an underground storage tank? an abandoned facility? a working facility?). "Enforcement" is when EPA investigates the identity of, and negotiates with responsible parties to do the cleanup or to recover the costs of a cleanup.

A.P. Environmental Science Study Guide - Chapter Two  Awesome Guides, Inc.

Environmental Laws

Regional - Each state, county and city set their own policies, so there are thousands of regional laws are "on the books", and there are simply too many to include here. Additionally, they only apply to the local region in which they were created.

National

- **The Endangered Species Act (ESA)** - of 1973 passed by Congress, protects both endangered and threatened from killing, trapping, uprooting (plants) or engaging in commerce (world wide) of either parts or species. The Act requires the U.S. Fish and Wildlife Service to draft recovery plans for protected species. Habitats must be mapped and a program for preservation and management of critical habitats must be implemented so that species can rebuild their populations. The ESA was reauthorized in 1988.

- **Lacy Act** — passed by Congress in 1900, forbids interstate commerce to deal in illegally killed wildlife. This made it difficult for hunters to sell their kills.

- **Animal Damage Control (ADC)** — Now called Wildlife Services, removes nuisance animals by trapping, killing, poisoning, and other methods. This service is very controversial.

- **Rivers and Harbors Act** - of 1899, protects national waters to promote commerce.

- **The Clean Water Act** — of 1972, protects waterways from any physical, chemical, and biological activity that lowers water quality. Businesses and individuals must have permits and meet federal standards for any discharge. Billions of dollars were provided for sewage treatment facilities.

- **The Clean Air Act** — of 1970, 1977, and 1990 established ambient standards for four primary pollutants: sulfur dioxide, particulates, carbon monoxide, and nitrogen oxides. Amended from the Air Quality Act of 1967, in 1970, 1977, and 1990, the Clean Air Act (CAA) was originally enacted to protect the quality of the Nation's air resources and the public health and welfare. The second purpose of the CAA is to initiate a research and development program to achieve the prevention and control of air pollution. Third, the act provides means for technical and financial assistance for State and local governments so that they may carry out air pollution prevention and control programs. The final goal of the CAA is to encourage the development of regional air pollution prevention and control programs.

- **The Water Quality Act** - of 1987 adds to the Clean Water Act by providing funding for the construction of treatment plants. It requires communities to address watersheds and nonpoint source pollutions in their development plans.

- **Marine Protection, Research and Sanctuaries Act** — of 1972 prevents improper ocean dumping. Designates the National Wildlife Refuge System (NWRS) and tasks the Fish and Wildlife Service with administration of the NWRS. Acts to enhance the habitat of migratory birds and the habitat of mammals and non-migratory birds in general. Regulates and controls activities such as hunting, fishing, and mining on these lands.

- **Wilderness Act** - Mindful of the increasing populations impact on the amount of remaining wilderness lands, this was created to secure an enduring resource of wild America. The Act establishes a National Wilderness Preservation System. The system is meant to reserve wilderness areas for the use and enjoyment of the American people in such a manner as will leave them unimpaired for future use and enjoyment of wilderness, the protection of these areas, the preservation of their wild character, and for the gathering and dissemination of information regarding their use and enjoyment as wilderness areas.

- **The Federal Land Policy Management Act** - (FLPMA) includes thirteen points of policy declared by Congress which develop the concept of multiple land use. The first is that public lands be retained in Federal ownership unless it is determined that disposal of a particular parcel will serve the national interest. Following this is a call to inventory public lands and project their present and future use through land use planning. This is to be coordinated between Federal and state efforts. The Act provides for review of lands without designated uses to be considered. The lands designated as public must be managed in a manner that will protect various ecological and educational values. Further, the act addresses areas of critical environmental concern by requiring regulations and plans for such areas to be promptly developed.

- **Toxic Substances Control Act** - (ToSCA) is to develop adequate data with respect to the effect of chemical substances on health and the environment. Economic considerations were intended to be considered as well, as authority over chemical substances should not impede unduly or create unnecessary economic barriers to technological innovation. The risks that a chemical poses are intended to be understood before that chemical is introduced into commerce.

- **The Federal Insecticide, Fungicide, and Rodenticide Act** - (FIFRA) supplies the legal requirements to have pesticides registered, classified, labeled, distributed, and properly used. FIFRA was written to protect humans and the environment from the possible adverse effects of insecticides, fungicides, and rodenticides.

- **Safe Drinking Water Act** - of 1974 was enacted with the general intent to protect the quality of drinking water the public receives from public water systems. To accomplish this, the SDWA focuses on two approaches. 1.) to assure the quality of drinking water coming from the tap and 2.) to prevent the contamination of groundwater that may be a source for drinking water.

- **National Environmental Policy Act** - (NEPA) was signed into law in 1970 by President Nixon. NEPA acts as a stop and think statute for projects that may affect the environment. NEPA requires that Federal agencies stop and consider the potential effects of actions that might adversely affect the environment, and consider possible alternative courses of action to reduce these impacts, before approving the project.

- **Fish and Wildlife Coordination Act** - provides for wildlife conservation by entrusting the Secretary of the Interior with certain duties. One of these is to provide assistance to, and cooperation with, Federal, state, and public or private agencies and organizations to provide that wildlife conservation receive equal consideration and be coordinated with other features of water-resource development programs. The Act was also written to lend ways to conduct surveys and investigations of wildlife in the public domain.

A.P. Environmental Science Study Guide - Chapter Two 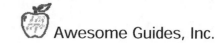 Awesome Guides, Inc.

- **Estuary Protection Act** - strikes a balance between the national need of conserving the beauty of the nation's estuaries and the need to develop these estuaries to further growth and development. States are given much of the responsibility of protecting, conserving, and restoring estuary areas.

- **Surface Mining Control and Reclamation Act** - of 1977 states a need for balance between protection of the environment and agricultural productivity and the nation's need for coal as an essential source of energy. Some provisions include:

    1. Prime farmland cannot be mined unless it can be restored to an equivalent or higher level of yield.
    2. Return land to approximate original contour and land must be restored to a condition capable of supporting the pre-mining land use or a higher or better use.
    3. Each state is to assume primary authority for the program. They must establish a mechanism for declaring lands unsuitable for mining if their reclamation is not technologically or economically feasible, contrary to local land use plans, or if the mining affects fragile or historic lands.

- **Ocean Dumping Ban** - of 1988, makes it unlawful for any person to dump, or transport for the purpose of dumping, sewage sludge or industrial waste into ocean waters after December 31, 1991.

- **Resource Conservation and Recovery Act** – RCRA (pronounced "rick-rah") gave EPA the authority to control hazardous waste from the "cradle-to-grave." This includes the generation, transportation, treatment, storage, and disposal of hazardous waste. RCRA also set forth a framework for the management of non-hazardous wastes.

- **Comprehensive Environmental Response, Compensation and Liability Act** – CERCLA (pronounced SIR-cla) provides a Federal "Superfund" to clean up uncontrolled or abandoned hazardous-waste sites as well as accidents, spills, and other emergency releases of pollutants and contaminants into the environment. Through this Act, EPA was given power to seek out those parties responsible for any release and assure their cooperation in the cleanup.

- **Food Quality Protection Act** – (FQPA) of 1996 amended the Federal Insecticide, Fungicide, and Rodenticide Act (FIFRA) and the Federal Food Drug, and Cosmetic Act (FFDCA). These amendments fundamentally changed the way EPA regulates pesticides. The requirements included a new safety standard-reasonable certainty of no harm-that must be applied to all pesticides used on foods.

- **Nuclear Waste Policy Act** —provides for the development of repositories for the disposal of high-level radioactive waste and spent nuclear fuel. It also established a program of research, development, and demonstration regarding the disposal of high-level radioactive waste and spent nuclear fuel.

- **Low Level Radioactive Policy Act** - of 1980 Radioactive Waste Policy Act. This legislation gives states the responsibility to provide for disposal of commercial low-level radioactive waste and encourages states to form interstate agreements, or compacts, to cooperatively implement the law. The federal legislation of 1980, and the subsequent Low-Level Radioactive Waste Policy Amendments Act of 1985, was endorsed by the Governors of the 50 states.

Awesome Guides, Inc. A.P. Environmental Science Study Guide - Chapter Two

International

- **Agenda 21** - A program designed to promote sustainable development, with a definite plan, that was a result of the 1992 Earth Summit in Rio de Janeriro, Brazil. The 21 refers to the 21st. century.

- **Montreal Protocol** —of 1987 was intended to scale back CFC production 50% by the year 2000. The agreement was signed by 140 countries. The Montreal Protocol, as amended in 1990, 1992, is signed by 93 countries (as of November, 1992), with the goal of protecting the ozone layer by taking "precautionary measures to control equitably total global emissions of substances that deplete it, with the ultimate objective of their elimination. . ., taking into account technical and economic considerations, and bearing in mind the developmental needs of developing countries."

- **Kyoto Protocol** – of 1997 was intended to reduce emissions of six greenhouse gases below 1990 levels. Thirty-eight industrialized countries signed this agreement.

- **Convention on International Trade in Endangered Species of Wild Flora and Fauna**— (CITES) is an international agreement between governments. Its aim is to ensure that international trade in specimens of wild animals and plants does not threaten their survival. CITES is an international agreement to which States (countries) adhere voluntarily. States that have agreed to be bound by the Convention ('joined' CITES) are known as Parties. Although CITES is legally binding on the Parties - in other words they have to implement the Convention - it does not take the place of national laws. Rather it provides a framework to be respected by each Party, which has to adopt its own domestic legislation to make sure that CITES is implemented at the national level. Not one species protected by CITES has become extinct as a result of trade since the Convention entered into force and, for many years, CITES has been among the largest conservation agreements in existence, with now over 150 Parties.

Benefit to Cost Ratio

Many times decision making in the field of Environmental Science involves "trade-offs". That is to say, the costs of a project should always be weighed against the potential benefits to society. For example, let's say that it costs $10.00 to treat a certain amount of raw sewage, and that 93% or the organic solids are removed for that cost. Let's also say, that by using another treatment process, 99% of organic solids are removed, but the cost is now $20.00 to treat the same amount of raw sewage. The Environmental Scientist must weigh the benefit gained to the community, the environment, future benefits, and anticipate many other possible factors to justify the treatment of an additional 6% removal or organic solids. This process is sometimes very complicated and involves many different disciplines.

Environmental Decisions

Ethics – is about doing the right thing; doing GOOD things. Environmental ethics is about doing the right thing to or for the environment. Ethical questions arise such as:

- Do humans have the right to deny future generations of the same or better resources than exist at the present time?
- Do we have the right to take the resources from the indigenous peoples in other countries?
- What moral duties do we have towards future generations?

A.P. Environmental Science Study Guide - Chapter Two  Awesome Guides, Inc.

Governments must be encouraged to support ethics. Environmental Ethics is based upon, and can be debated using several concepts:

1. Moral principles and moral rules
2. There must be some proof or back-up reason for preserving the world's ecosystems. This concept should be reinforced by using sound science standards.
3. Present specific cases or site examples of why protecting ecosystems is beneficial for everyone of the planet.

Morals- Rules or habits of conduct, concerned with the judgment of the goodness or badness of human action and character. We should be teaching and exhibiting goodness or correctness of character and behavior through our ecological actions. Conforming to standards of what is right or just in behavior; virtuous. Morals arise from conscience and the sense of right from wrong. Sometimes doing what's best for the environment has psychological rather than physical or tangible effects. We should let the lessons and principles contained in our past be a voice for future decisions.

Aesthetics – is concerned with natural beauty. What criteria are considered aesthetic is a broad question. However some ideas about aesthetics involve:

1. Location of dump sites, or the NIMBY (not in my back yard) principle
2. Deforestation
3. Toxic waste dumps
4. Trash
5. Smell
6. Noise

Cultural Importance - Environmental decisions can be made purely on ethical values. There is no financial value put on this, but it involves the right that humans have to have equal access to resources. One justification to save ecosystems is to take into account the indigenous people in an area.

The proper design and maintenance of landfills is a crucial part of today's society.

Chapter 3
AP Environment Science Laboratory Review

Hint! Read chapter 2 before reviewing your laboratory assignments, it will save you from going back and forth to look up information. By doing this, you will find that you already know many of the laboratory skills and won't spend as much time going over the same information twice.

There are 18 major subject areas that you should have some experience with before taking the A.P. Environmental Science Exam. All of these subject areas are purely hands-on practice of the "topics outline" from the previous section (chapter 2), as well as a test of your vocabulary application (chapter 1). **If a subject is covered completely in the "topics outline" or vocabulary tune-up then you will be referred to that section rather than repeating the same information over again.** Remember that this is a review guide, and it is not intended to replace field trips, actual laboratory skills and data collection. It should be used as a tune-up to help you recall skills and subjects you have already covered. Some of the labs your teacher assigned to you may differ somewhat from those given in this chapter. Environmental science is incredibly varied from situation to situation however; the type and level of activities should be similar. Non-the-less, the laboratory skills will help you review the major concepts and will reinforce your environmental science knowledge. Read each laboratory concept carefully. Since the labs are a review of the A.P. Environmental Science course curriculum, refer to chapters 1 and 2 for information that you don't understand.

It is not necessary to memorize every fact you will see in this laboratory section; that would drive you crazy. However, you should have a solid understanding of the concepts these facts are implying. Major concepts relating to energy use, wastewater treatment, acid precipitation, and others, as well as their connection with their source, their environmental effects, the laws relating to their use, and techniques or alternatives to slow down their use, are important and should be understood and committed to memory. You should understand what is taking place in these processes, and the major goals of each process without memorizing the exact figures.

1. Ecosystem Ecology - collecting and recording environmental data

a. You should have some experience with an ecosystem in the area that you live, or even on your school campus.
b. Measure and/or list abiotic factors for your selected study area. (See chapters 1 and 2)
c. Be familiar with instruments that are used to measure abiotic conditions, such as temperature (thermometer), atmospheric pressure (barometer), DO (if a lake or stream is present, done with a kit or meter), humidity (hygrometer), and historical weather patterns (climate), etc.
d. Describe the biotic components of the selected ecosystem. (See chapters 1 and 2)
e. Propose a hypothesis that shows how anthropogenic actions have affected some aspect, such as an organism, of your ecosystem.
f. Remember that a hypothesis is an <u>educated</u> guess, NOT just a guess. You must have some background information, such as the data you have collected on your ecosystem, to back up your hypothesis.
g. Be very specific in the statement of your hypothesis, and remember that a hypothesis MUST BE TESTABLE, through experimentation.

A.P. Environmental Science Study Guide - Chapter Three  Awesome Guides, Inc.

h. A hypothesis is sometimes stated, but not always, as an if/ then statement.

2. Earth Science - plate tectonics and its relation to volcanism and earthquakes

a. Be able to read a seismogram (S & P waves). Below is a description of an S (shear) wave and a P (compressional) wave. Notice that the S wave is up and down and the P wave is side to side.

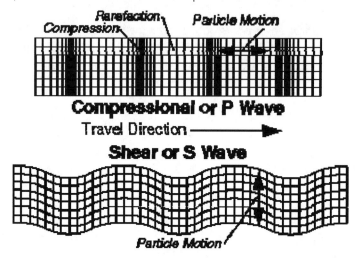

The seismogram below shows a tremor that occurred on June 26, 1994. There were three small earthquakes located in Berkeley, California, which were recorded by the BDSN station MHC at a distance of 86 km from the epicenter. The first event registered a local magnitude of 3.2 and was followed 5 minutes later by a 2.5 earthquake. Seven minutes after that, a 4.2 earthquake rattled the residents of the East Bay. The magnitude 3.2 and 4.2 events are clearly visible on this image; the 2.5 event is a very low-amplitude squiggle.

b. Understand how volcanic eruptions affect weather patterns.

- During volcanic eruptions large amounts of pyroclastic material explode into the atmosphere. Ash, also generated, can stay up in the atmosphere for, weeks, months, or even years.

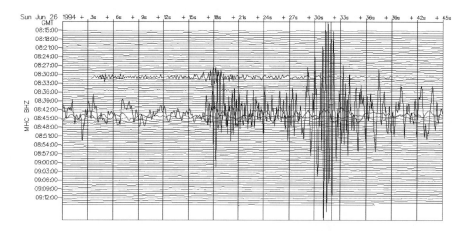

Typical seismogram showing both S and P waves.

Obviously areas close to the volcano will have a higher level of ash in the air than areas that are further away. The wind direction helps determine the area that will receive ash from a volcanic eruption.
- If the wind direction was to change so would the area affected by ash fall.
- Large amounts of volcanic ash in the atmosphere will darken the sky during the day. This may result in temperature changes as much as 5 to 10 C cooler than normal.

c. Relate the diversity of organisms to the theory of evolution, and explain what role plate tectonics has in this process.

- According to the theory of plate tectonics, 225 million years ago the continents were together in one large mass called Pangaea. As the continents slowly separated, due to continental drift, habitats also changed. These changing habitats made way for a large variety of organisms that adapted to their new habitats, thus providing the earth with tremendous biodiversity.
- Plate tectonics also created other changes on earth through earthquakes, and volcanoes, further separating organisms from each other, and changing habitats once again. Each of these adds to the world's diversity in plants and animals.

3. Earth Science - soil structure and the rock cycle

a. Understand the process of weathering, both chemical and mechanical (See Chapter 2).
b. Understand how soil is formed through weathering (See Chapter 2).
c. Be able to point out examples of weathering in an ecosystem around your community.

4. Earth Science - geotechnical science

a. Be able to determine the slope in an ecosystem. This may be done in several ways. Many geotechnical (soil) engineering use a "dumpy" level or other high tech instruments to find the slope. Without having these instruments, slope can still be estimated by first marking a 100' straight line somewhere in your ecosystem. Work with a partner and have him/her at one end and, and you at the other end of your 100' marks. Using a clipboard or similar device, hold it at eye level and see where it falls on your partner. Now switch sides and do the same thing on the other side. If there is any slope you should see the difference as to where the eye level view falls on your partner. For example, lets say you view the clipboard level at your partner's head at one side and his/her chest on the other side. In many cases, depending on the size of your partner, this might be around 2 feet. Two feet over 100' is equal to a 2% slope.
b. Know the horizons in a soil profile (See chapter 2).
c. Understand what kinds of soils hold water (See chapter 2).
d. Understand the chemical components of soil (See chapter 2).
e. Be able to cite alternative uses of land that create an economical, ecological, uncontaminated and sustainable environment. (See chapter 2).

5. Population Ecology - effects of environmental factors on the distribution of organisms

a. You should be able to set up an experimental ecosystem and understand what abiotic or biotic conditions will cause organisms to partition (separate) or be attracted to these varied conditions.

A.P. Environmental Science Study Guide - Chapter Three  Awesome Guides, Inc.

b. It is very important to remember that in any experiment that you must include a control ecosystem and only change one variable at a time to have valid data.

c. When studying an organism you should learn as much about that organism, (its life history - which includes: reproduction, habitat needs, nutritional needs, behaviors etc.) before conducting your experiment.

d. Be a careful observer and compare the control results with the experimental results.

e. In many cases researchers observe the LD 50 rule where, an experimental treatment is stopped if 50% of the organisms die.

6. Population Ecology - calculating population data from given data

Look at the population chart below and be able to answer the following questions:

Population Chart

	Projected Population (millions) 2025	Projected Population (millions) 2050	Infant Mortality Rate	Total Fertility Rate	Percentage of Population of Age <15
WORLD	7,818	9,036	56	2.8	30
Developed Countries	1,248	1,242	8	1.6	18
Developing Countries	6,570	7,794	61	3.2	33
Developing Countries (Excl. China)	5,139	6,425	67	3.6	36

a. Make a graph using the above data that compares the world population with both developed and undeveloped countries. Include information on infant mortality, fertility rate, and percent of population under the age of 15.

  From your graph answer these questions:
  1. How is age structure important in determining the growth of a population?
  2. What is the impact of infant mortality on the growth of a population?
  3. How do developed countries compare to developing countries in their population growth?
  4. How important is fertility rate to the growth of a population?

b. Understand the consequences of uncontrolled population growth (such as famine, loss of biodiversity, loss of ecosystems that support populations etc.).

c. Know that populations have a certain carrying capacity, which is a certain number of organisms that a population can sustain.

d. Understand that there are limiting factors that control an environment, and that it only takes one limiting factor, such as oxygen, to control the health of an ecosystem, regardless of how many other resources are available even if the quantities are unlimited.

Awesome Guides, Inc. A.P. Environmental Science Study Guide - Chapter Three

7. Population Ecology - Sampling techniques and data collection

a. In an ecosystem be able to find the population of a group of organisms by using the quadrant and/or transect methods.

- In an ecosystem, it is not practical to study all of the populations of an area due to time constraints, physical barriers, etc. so environmental scientists often take a sample of a population or "cross-section" of an area and use those samples to estimate the population of the entire ecosystem. Two methods used are quadrant and transect methods.
- Quadrants represent square sample areas where all of the populations of each quadrant are counted.
- Transects represent straight-line sample areas, where all of the populations along the line are counted, several feet on either side of that line.

b. Determine the doubling time of a population. This is very easy and simple using the rule of 70, which is 70 divided by the percent of growth.

c. You should know how to determine the various stages of ecological succession in an area (See chp 2).

d. Be able to make a food chain and food web for the organisms in your sample ecosystem (See chp 2).

8. Population Ecology - Human Demographics

a. You should be able to determine the growth rate of a population given the population #'s over a given time period. This simply involves finding a percent increase or decrease by dividing one population size into another. For example, lets say that the population has, 2,253,291 in January of 2000, and 2,264,617 in January of 2001, then 2,253,291/2,264,617 = .995% growth rate in one year.

b. Be able to use interpret age structure histograms. (See chapter 2).

c. Understand how age structure, birth rates, death rates and male to female ratios affect human populations.

d. Determine the impact that human growth rate, currently increasing exponentially, has had of the world's resources (See chapter 2).

9. Energy - calculating consumption

Compare energy use data for several different types of fuel:

- ### OIL - 1999

Oil Consumption in million tons:
USA - 882.8 million tons (25.5% share of world total usage)
Total North America - 1047.1 million tons (30.2% share of world total usage)
Total Europe - 755.2 million tons (21.8% share of world total usage)
Asia Pacific - 928.7 million tons (26.9% of world total usage)
Total World - 3462.4 million tons
USA - oil consumption in quadrillion BTU - 37.706 (share of world total usage = 25.5%)

A.P. Environmental Science Study Guide - Chapter Three  Awesome Guides, Inc.

Oil Consumption in thousand barrels daily
USA - 18490 thousand barrels daily
Europe - 15990 thousand barrels daily
Asia Pacific - 19920 thousand barrels daily
Total World - 73215 thousand barrels daily
OECD share of world total = 62.7%

- **NATURAL GAS - 1999**

USA - Natural gas consumption in quadrillion BTU - 22.096 (share of world total usage = 26.9%)

Natural Gas Consumption in million tons oil equivalent:
USA - 555.3 million tons oil equivalent (26.9% of world total usage)
North America - 651.5 (31.6% of world total usage)
Europe - 399.6 (19.4% of world total usage)
Asia Pacific - 241.7 11.7% of world total usage)
Total World - 2063.9
OECD share of world total = 54.7%

Natural Gas Consumption in billion cubic meters:
USA - 617 billion cubic meters
North America - 723.9
Europe - 443.9
Asia Pacific - 268.2
Total World - 2292.6

Natural Gas Consumption in billion cubic feet per day:
USA - 59.7 billion cubic feet per day
No. America - 70
Europe - 43.3
Asia Pacific - 25.9
Total World - 222.2

- **COAL - 1999**

USA - coal consumption in quadrillion BTU - 21.698 (share of world total usage = 25.5%)

Coal Consumption in million tons oil equivalent:

USA - 543.3 million tons oil equivalent (25.5% of world total usage)
North America - 581.2 (27.3% of world total usage)
Europe - 348 (16.5% of world total)
Asia Pacific - 912.5 (42.9% of world total)
World Total - 2129.5

FOSSIL FUELS - 1999

USA - fossil fuel consumption in quadrillion BTU - 81.557

NUCLEAR ENERGY - 1999

USA - Nuclear energy consumption in quadrillion BTU - 7.733

Nuclear Energy Consumption - Million tons oil equivalent:

USA - 197.7 million tons oil equivalent (30.4% of world total usage)
North America - 219.3 (33.7%% of world total usage)
Europe - 246.1 (37.8% of world total usage)
Asia Pacific - 125.9 (19.3% of world total usage)
World total - 650.8
OECD share of world total = 86.7%

HYDROELECTRIC - 1999

USA - Hydroelectric consumption in quadrillion BTU - 3.417

Hydroelectricity Consumption in million tons oil equivalent:

USA - 25.8 million tons oil equivalent (11.4% of world total usage)
North America - 58.2 (25.6% of world total)
Europe - 51.5 (22.8% of world total)
Asia Pacific - 46.2 (20.3% of world total)
Total World - 226.8
OECD share of world total = 51.7%

GEOTHERMAL ENERGY - 1999

USA - Geothermal Consumption in quadrillion BTU - .327

WOOD AND WASTE - 1999

USA - Wood and waste consumption in quadrillion BTU - 3.514

SOLAR - 1999

USA - Solar Consumption in quadrillion BTU - .076

A.P. Environmental Science Study Guide - Chapter Three  Awesome Guides, Inc.

- **WIND - 1999**

USA - Wind Consumption in quadrillion BTU - .038

- **TOTAL RENEWABLE ENERGY - 1999**

USA - Renewable Energy Consumption in quadrillion BTU - 7.373

a. Be prepared to calculate energy use by month and year.

If you want a general estimate of how much electricity your home appliances consume, you can refer to the list below, which provides the energy consumption (wattage) of some typical home appliances. If you have appliances that are not listed in the table, or desire a more exact figure based on a specific appliance in your home, use the following formula to estimate the amount of energy a specific appliance consumes:

<u>Wattage Hours Used Per Day</u> = Daily Kilowatt-hour (kWh) consumption (1 kilowatt (kW) = 1,000 Watts)
      1000

Multiply this by the number of days you use the appliance during the year for the annual consumption. You can then calculate the annual cost to run an appliance by multiplying the kWh per year by your local utility's rate per kWh consumed.

Here are some examples of the range of nameplate wattages for various household appliances:

APPLIANCE	WATTS
Aquarium	50-1210
Clock radio	10
Coffee maker	900-1200
Clothes washer	350-500
Clothes dryer	1800-5000
Dishwasher	1200-2400
(using the drying feature greatly increases energy consumption)	
Dehumidifier	785
Electric blanket *Single/Double*	60 / 100
Monitor — awake / asleep	150 / 30 or less
Laptop	50
Radio *(stereo)*	400
Refrigerator *(frostfree, 16 cubic feet)*	725
Televisions (color):19"	110
27"	113
36"	133
53"-61" Projection	170

APPLIANCE	WATTS
Fans: Ceiling	65-175
Window	55-250
Furnace	750
Whole house	240-750
Hair dryer	1200-1875
Heater *(portable)*	750-1500
Clothes Iron	1000-1800
Microwave oven	750-1100
Personal Computer: CPU - awake / asleep	120 / 30 or less
Flat Screen	120
Toaster	800-1400
Toaster Oven	1225
VCR/DVD	17-21 /20-25
Vacuum cleaner	1000-1440
Water heater *(40 gallon)*	4500-5500
Water pump *(deep well)*	250-1100
Water bed *(w/ heater, no cover)*	120-380

Awesome Guides, Inc. A.P. Environmental Science Study Guide - Chapter Three

Example Computations:

1. Window fan:

$\frac{200 \text{ Watts} \times 4 \text{ hours/day} \times 120 \text{ days/year}}{1000} = 96$ kWh × 8.5 Cents/kWh = $8.16 /year

2. Personal Computer and Monitor:

$\frac{(120+150) \text{ Watts} \times 4 \text{ hours/day} \times 365 \text{ days/year}}{1000} = 394$ kWh × 8.5 Cents/kWh = $33.51/year

You can usually find the wattage of most appliances stamped on the bottom or back of the appliance, or on its "nameplate." The wattage listed is the maximum power drawn by the appliance. Since many appliances have a range of settings (for example, the volume on a radio), the actual amount of power consumed depends on the setting used at any one time.

b. Know renewable and nonrenewable resources (See chapter 2).

c. Understand the concept of how to conserve and preserve energy resources, such as reducing energy use, energy efficient devices, developing alternate renewable resources, etc. (see chapter 2).

10. Pollution - Atmospheric

a. Know what particulate matter is and how to collect it. Collection of air quality particulate matter involves equipment that you may not have at your school. However, an easy way to collect and examine particulate matter in an ecosystem is to take several microscope slides and put Vaseline on them. Place them strategically around a study area and after a day or two, collect these and examine them under a microscope. You will collect things other than particulate matter, such as pollen (depending on the time of year), flower parts, leaves etc. Particulate matter is usually dark.

b. Between the years 1900 and 1970, the emission of six principal pollutants increased significantly, also called criteria pollutants. They are: particulate matter, sulfur dioxide, carbon monoxide, nitrogen dioxide, ozone, and lead. In 1970, the Clean Air Act (CAA) was signed into law, setting ambient air quality standards, they are shown in the chart on the next page.

c. Compare EPA National Ambient Air Quality Standards with those in your area.

d. Know the major air pollutants and their sources and the effect on human health:

National Ambient Air Quality Standards

Carbon Monoxide (CO)

8-hour Average	9 ppm	(10 mg/m^3)	Primary
1-hour Average	35 ppm	(40 mg/m^3)	Primary

Nitrogen Dioxide (NO2)

Annual Arithmetic Mean	0.053 ppm	(100 µg/m^3)	Primary & Secondary

Ozone (O3)

1-hour Average	0.12 ppm	(235 µg/m^3)	Primary & Secondary
8-hour Average	0.08 ppm	(157 µg/m^3)	Primary & Secondary

Lead (Pb)

Quarterly Average	1.5 µg/m^3	Primary & Secondary

Particulate (PM 10) — Particles with diameters of 10 micrometers or less

Annual Arithmetic Mean	50 µg/m^3	Primary & Secondary
24-hour Average	150 µg/m^3	Primary & Secondary

Particulate (PM 2.5) — Particles with diameters of 2.5 micrometers or less

Annual Arithmetic Mean	15 µg/m^3	Primary & Secondary
24-hour Average	65 µg/m^3	Primary & Secondary

Sulfur Dioxide (SO2)

Annual Arithmetic Mean	0.03 ppm	(80 µg/m^3)	Primary
24-hour Average	0.14 ppm	(365 µg/m^3)	Primary
3-hour Average	0.50 ppm	(1300 µg/m^3)	Secondary

Awesome Guides, Inc. A.P. Environmental Science Study Guide - Chapter Three

POLLUTANT	HEALTH EFFECTS	EXAMPLES OF SOURCES
Particulate Matter (PM10: less than or equal to 10 microns)	• Increased respiratory disease • Lung damage • Premature death	• Cars and trucks, especially diesels • Fireplaces, woodstoves • Windblown dust, from roadways, agriculture and construction
Ozone (O3)	• Breathing difficulties • Lung damage	• Formed by chemical reactions of air pollutants in the presence of sunlight. Common sources: motor vehicles, industries, and consumer products
Carbon Monoxide (CO)	• Chest pain in heart patients • Headaches, nausea • Reduced mental alertness • Death at very high levels	• Any source that burns fuel such as cars, trucks, construction and farming equipment, and residential heaters and stoves
Nitrogen Dioxide (NO2)	• Lung damage	• See Carbon Monoxide sources
Toxic Air Contaminants	• Cancer • Chronic eye, lung, or skin irritation • Neurological and reproductive disorders	• Cars and trucks, especially diesels • Industrial sources such as chrome platers • Neighborhood businesses, such as dry cleaners and service stations • Building materials and products

11. Toxicology - assaying an ecosystem

a. You should have some experience measuring (assaying) toxic material in a laboratory situation. There are literally thousands of possibilities, some involve simple tests, some "high tech" and some very complex. This might include examining heavy metals (such as lead or mercury), or pesticide concentrations, etc.

b. Know that the LD 50 rule refers to a lethal dose of a chemical that can kill 50% of a population. In determining this value in a laboratory situation, a toxic substance is added slowly over a period of time until ½ of the organisms die. The dose is recorded and that figure is the LD 50 for that particular chemical and organism under study.

12. Aquatic Ecology - testing water quality

a. You should be familiar with testing that determines fecal coliform, dissolved oxygen (DO) and biological oxygen demand (BOD).

Fecal coliform - If coliform bacteria are present in a body of water, then the water may be contaminated with sewage or other decomposing waste. Coliform bacteria are found in greater abundance on the surface or in the bottom sediments. Fecal coliform is found in the lower intestines of humans and other warm-blooded animals. The presence of fecal coliform in a water supply is a good indication that sewage is present. Testing can be done for fecal coliform specifically or for total coliform bacteria, which includes all coliform bacteria strains. Results are represented by number of colonies per 100ml sample of water. The presence of coliform bacteria may be an indication that the water is polluted. However, further tests would be necessary in order to identify the specific bacteria present and the level of contamination.

Fecal coliform bacteria counts are considered safe for different activities are:

1. Drinking water - 0 colonies per 100ml sample of water.
2. Swimming - less than 200 colonies per 100 mL sample of water.
3. Boating/Fishing - less than 1000 colonies per 100 mL sample of water.

Dissolved oxygen - or (DO) is essential to healthy streams and lakes. The dissolved oxygen level can be an indication of how polluted the water is and how well the water can support aquatic plant and animal life. Generally, when dissolved oxygen level is high, the water quality is better. If dissolved oxygen levels are too low, some organisms may not be able to survive. Dissolved oxygen in water comes from atmospheric O2, and from the photosynthesis of aquatic plants. On sunny days, high DO levels are higher due to higher rates of photosynthesis. Rapidly moving streams have higher DO levels because air is in contact with moving water and the oxygen in the air dissolves in the water.

Water temperature also affects DO levels. Dissolved oxygen is inversely proportionally to temperature, thus, cold water can hold more oxygen warm water. There is usually a difference in DO levels at test site if water is tested early in the morning and then in the afternoon. First, the water is cooler in the morning, in some regions, and less photosynthesis is occurring. There are also seasonal DO changes for those same reasons. Depth of the water also affects DO levels. Species such as sludge worms, black fly larvae, catfish, and leeches are more tolerant of the low dissolved oxygen levels in warm waters. Species that require high levels of dissolved oxygen include northern pike, trout, bass, salmon, mayfly nymphs, stonefly nymphs and caddisfly larvae.

Low DO levels often occur where organic material, such as dead plant and animal matter or bacteria are decaying. This decomposition requires oxygen and thus, depletes the water of oxygen. Areas near raw sewage discharge may have low DO for that reason. DO levels will also be low in warmer months and in stagnant water. Dissolved oxygen levels can be measured in either parts per million (ppm) or percent of saturation. Percent of saturation measures the amount of oxygen dissolved in the water sample compared to the maximum amount of oxygen that could be present at the same temperature. For example, water is said to be 100 % saturated if it contains the maximum amount of oxygen that it can hold at that temperature. A water sample that is 50 % saturated only has half the amount of oxygen that it could potentially hold at that temperature.

Awesome Guides, Inc. A.P. Environmental Science Study Guide - Chapter Three

Testing for DO is done by several techniques, either by using a test kit, where reagents are mixed with collected water samples, or by an instrument that gives a direct reading. Direct reading instruments are much more accurate and efficient, but do require the researcher to calibrate the DO sensor from time to time. Typical readings for DO are:

- 9ppm to 10ppm are considered very good; usually clean water.
- 3.5ppm or below are considered deadly to many organisms (such as trout, bass, mayflies, etc.).
- Below 3.5 many organisms can still survive (such as leeches, some catfish, gizzard shad, etc.). Therefore the expression dead lake, does not apply to many situations of low DO. However, as DO drops, organism diversity changes.
- For percent of saturation: 80 —110% is considered excellent. 55% or lower is considered poor water quality.

Biological oxygen demand - or (BOD) is a measure of the oxygen used by microorganisms to decompose waste. The more waste, the higher the BOD value. Nitrates and phosphates in water can cause BOD levels to increase. When BOD levels are high, dissolved oxygen (DO) levels decrease.

It takes 5 days to test BOD. The BOD level is determined by measuring the DO level of a water sample, then placing that sample in a dark incubated location and measuring the final DO after 5 days. This is sometimes called the BOD5. The difference between the two DO levels represents the amount of oxygen used by microorganisms. The BOD level is determined by subtracting the Day 5 reading from the Day 1 reading in ppm. Typical BOD readings are:

* BOD of 1 ppm-2 ppm is considered very good; clean water.
* BOD of 3-5 is considered moderately clean water.
* BOD of 6-9 is considered somewhat polluted water.
* BOD above 10 is considered very polluted water.

The Environmental Protection Agency (EPA) sets water quality standards for various bodies of water for varying uses. Standards are set for both environmental water quality and for drinking (potable) water quality. A water quality criterion was developed to protect both aquatic life and human health. In addition to DO and BOD, the EPA currently sets aquatic life criteria for copper, silver, lead, cadmium, iron and selenium and is developing new aquatic life criteria for atrazine, diazinon, nonylphenol, methyl tertiary-butyl ether (MtBE), manganese and saltwater dissolved oxygen.

13. Environmental Engineering - potable and wastewater treatment

a. Be familiar with the operation and flow chart of a wastewater treatment plant (See chapter 2).
b. Explain each step of the wastewater treatment process (See chapter 2).
c. Compare the levels of nitrogen, phosphorus, dissolved suspended solids, suspended solids, BOD levels and toxic substances.

Total Suspended Solids (TSS)	200-300 mg/L
5-day Biochemical Oxidation Demand (BOD)	200-250 mg/L
Chemical Oxidation Demand (COD)	350-450 mg/L
Total Nitrogen as N	25-60 mg/L
Total Phosphorus as P	5-10 mg/L
Oil and Grease	80-120 mg/L

A.P. Environmental Science Study Guide - Chapter Three  Awesome Guides, Inc.

WASTEWATER COMPOSITION

Domestic sewage is a significant contributor to water pollution. Domestic sewage originates mostly from households, public facilities and businesses. Wastes from communities where most homes and businesses have piped water, typical pollutant composition of domestic sewage is as follows:

SEWAGE TREATMENT GOALS

The primary purpose of sewage treatment is to remove pollutants from wastewater streams before disposal into receiving waters including:

Pathogens - These organisms are harmful to humans and cause many illnesses and deaths each year in developing countries. Pathogens commonly found in raw sewage include hepatitis, pathogenic enteric viruses, Klebsiella pneumonia, Shigella, Salmonella, Leptospira, Vibrio cholerae, typhoid bacillus bacteria, pathogenic protozoa such as Entamoeba histolitica and Giardia lambda, and parasitic organisms such as Schistosoma, Ascaris lumbricoides, and hookworm.

TYPICAL INDUSTRIAL WASTEWATER POLLUTANT CHARACTERISTICS

Industry	BOD Concentration (mg/L)	TSS Concentration (mg/L)	Oil & Grease Concentration (mg/L)	Metals Present	Volatile Compounds Present	Refractory Organics Concentration (mg/L)
Oil Refinery	100 to 300	100 to 250	200 to 3,000	Arsenic, Iron	Sulphides	Phenols 0 to 270
Tanneries	1000-3000	4000-6000	50-850	Chromium 300-1000	Sulphides Ammonia 100-200	
Bottling Plant	200 to 6,000	0 to 3,500				
Distillery, Molasses, or Sugar Factory	600 to 32,000	200 to 30,000			Ammonia 5 to 400	
Food Processing	100 to 7,000	30 to 7,000				
Paper Factory	250 to 15,000	500 to 100,000		Selenium, Zinc		Phenols 0 to 800
Chemical Plant	500 to 20,000	1,000 to 170,000	0 to 2,000	Arsenic, Barium, Cadmium		Phenols 0 to 5,000

Organic and other oxygen demanding materials - Organic materials are a major pollutant in sewage. The common measure of the organic content of sewage is the Biochemical Oxygen Demand (BOD) test. BOD is a measure of the oxygen needed to degrade organic and inorganic compounds in the waste stream. It is called "Biochemical Oxygen Demand" because bacteria in the sample are the primary catalysts for conversion of organic materials and consumption of oxygen in the sample. High BOD levels in natural waters cause a drop in dissolved oxygen (DO) concentration, often killing aquatic life. The chemical oxygen demand (COD) test is a simple laboratory analysis in which all of the oxidizable material in the sample is oxidized by potassium dichromate. The COD test measures the combined oxygen demand of biochemically reducible contaminants and non-biochemically degradable reduced contaminants. Fats, greases, and lignins are biochemically degradable. However, the rate of oxidation is very slow and they have little effect on the 5 day BOD test. These are measured by the COD test.

Total suspended solids (TSS) - High levels of suspended solids can be damaging to benthic habitats and cause anaerobic conditions on the bottoms of lakes, rivers and seas due to the breakdown of volatile materials in the solids.

Nutrients - An excess of the nutrients nitrogen and phosphorus may cause eutrophication in natural waters (a state of excessive nutrient concentration). Eutrophication begins with algal blooms, followed by high BOD levels (when the algae die) and low DO concentrations.

PARAMETERS AND STANDARDS FOR DOMESTIC AND INDUSTRIAL WASTEWATER DISCHARGES IN THE WCR

Parameter	Standard for Non-Sensitive Waters	Standard for Sensitive Waters
Total Suspended Solids	100 mg/L	30 mg/La
Biochemical Oxygen Demand (5 day)	150 mg/L	30 mg/L
COD	300 mg/L	150 mg/L
Fecal Coliform	No standard established	43 MPN/100 mL in shellfish harvesting areas 200 MPN/100 mL in all other areas
Total Inorganic Nitrogen	No standard established	10 mg/L in nutrient sensitive waters
Soluble Phosphorus	No standard established	1 mg/L in nutrient sensitive waters
pH	6 to 10	6 to 10
Fats, Oils, And Greases	50 mg/L	2 mg/L
Ammonia as N	No standard established	5 mg/L
Total Chlorine Residual	No standard established	0.1 mg/L
Floatables	No visible floatables	No visible floatables

A.P. Environmental Science Study Guide - Chapter Three  Awesome Guides, Inc.

Fats, oil and grease (FOG) - Fats, oil and grease float on the surface of receiving waters. FOG interfere with natural reaeration, can be toxic to certain species of fish and aquatic life, can create a fire hazard when present in sufficient quantity, destroy vegetation along the shoreline which can lead to increased erosion, and create an unsightly film on the surface of the water which can reduce recreational uses.

- **Preliminary / Primary treatment:** 50-60% of total suspended solids and up to 50% of pathogens and toxic contaminants are removed.

- **Secondary treatment:** Secondary treatment raises the level of pollution removal to over 85%.

- **Disinfection:** After passing through primary and secondary treatment, wastewater is disinfected with sodium hypochlorite to kill bacteria. in which the effluent is mixed with sodium hypochlorite. Finally, sodium bisulfite is added to dechlorinate the water, so that chlorine levels in the ultimate discharge will not threaten marine organisms. After disinfection and dechlorination, the effluent is ready to be discharged.

14. Environmental Engineering - solid wastes

a. Know what kinds of wastes are generated in a typical household in your neighborhood.

Municipal Solid Wastes (MSW), more commonly known as trash or garbage, consists of everyday items such as product packaging, grass clippings, furniture, clothing, bottles, food scraps, newspapers, appliances, paint and batteries.

In 1999, U.S. residents, businesses and institutions produced more than 230 million tons of MSW, which is approximately 4.6 pounds of waste per person per day, up from 2.7 pounds per day in 1999.

Trends in MSW Generation: 1960-1999

The rate by which per capita generation of waste (in pounds per person per day) and total waste generation (in million tons) has increased from 1960 to 1999. In 1960, the per capita generation of waste was 2.7 pounds per person per day, and total waste generation was 88.1 million tons. In 1970, the per capita generation of waste was 3.3 pounds per person per day, and total waste generation was 121.1 million tons. In 1980, the per capita generation of waste was 3.7 pounds per person per day, and total waste generation was 151.6 million tons. In 1990, the per capita generation of waste was 4.5 pounds per person per day, and total waste generation was 205.2 million tons. In 1999, the per capita generation of waste was 4.6 pounds per person per day, and total waste generation was 229.9 million tons.

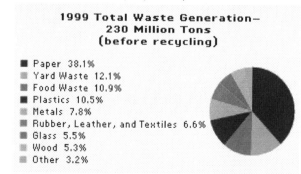

Waste Recycling Rates: 1960-1999

Waste recycling rates in the U.S. from 1960 to 1999, both in percentage and tons. In 1960, the recycling rate was 6.4%, and 5.6 million tons of materials were recycled. In 1970, the recycling rate was 6.6%, and 8 million tons of materials were recycled. In 1980, the recycling rate was 9.6%, and 14.5 million tons of materials were recycled. In 1990, the recycling rate was 16.2%, and 33.2 million tons of materials were recycled. In 1999, the recycling rate was 27.8%, and 63.9 million tons of materials were recycled.

The following figures depict the recycling rates of selected materials in 1999.

1999 Recycling Rates

Auto batteries: 93.8%	Steel Cans: 56.1%
Aluminum Packaging: 54.5%	Yard Waste: 45.3%
Paper and Paperboard: 41.6%	Plastic Soft Drink Containers: 40.0%
Glass Containers: 26.6%	Tires: 26.5%

b. Be able to describe a typical solid waste sanitary landfill (See chapter 2).
Although source reduction, reuse, recycling and composting can divert large portions of municipal solid waste (MSW) from disposal, some waste still must be placed in landfills. Modern landfills are well-engineered facilities that are located, designed, operated, monitored, closed, cared for after closure, cleaned up when necessary, and financed to insure compliance with federal regulations. The federal regulations were established to protect human health and the environment. In addition, these new landfills can collect potentially harmful landfill gas emissions and convert the gas into energy.

Federal Landfill Standards

- **Location restrictions** ensure that landfills are built in suitable geological areas away from faults, wetlands, flood plains, or other restricted areas.
- **Liners** are geomembranes or plastic sheets reinforced with two feet of clay on the bottom and sides of landfills.
- **Operating practices** such as compacting and covering waste frequently with several inches of soil help reduce odor; control litter, insects, and rodents; and protect public health.
- **Groundwater monitoring** requires testing groundwater wells to determine whether waste materials have escaped from the landfill.
- **Closure and postclosure care** include covering landfills and providing long-term care of closed landfills.
- **Corrective action** controls and cleans up landfill releases and achieves groundwater protection standards.
- **Financial assurance** provides funding for environmental protection during and after landfill closure (i.e., closure and postclosure care).

c. Be able to cite types of waste disposal alternatives.

- Source reduction can be a successful method of reducing waste generation. Practices such as grass recycling, backyard composting, two-sided copying of paper and transport packaging reduction by industry have yielded substantial benefits through source reduction. Source reduction has many environmental benefits. It prevents emissions of many greenhouse gases,

reduces pollutants, saves energy, conserves resources and reduces the need for new landfills and combustors.
- Recycling (including composting), diverted 64 million tons of material away from landfills and incinerators in 1999, up from 34 million tons in 1990. Typical materials that are recycled include batteries, recycled at a rate of 96.9%, paper and paperboard at 41.9% and yard trimmings at 45.3%. These materials and others may be recycled through curbside programs, drop-off centers, buy-back programs and deposit systems.
- Recycling prevents the emission of many greenhouse gases and water pollutants, saves energy, supplies valuable raw materials to industry, creates jobs, stimulates the development of greener technologies, conserves resources for our children's future, and reduces the need for new landfills and combustors. Recycling also helps reduce greenhouse gas emissions that affect global climate. In 1996, recycling of solid waste in the United States prevented the release of 33 million tons of carbon into the air - roughly the amount emitted annually by 25 million cars.
- Combustion / Incineration (burning of MSW) can generate energy while reducing the amount of waste by up to 90 percent in volume and 75 percent in weight.

15. Field testing and preparing reports - the greenhouse effect

a. Understand the greenhouse effect (See chapter 2).
b. Know the typical greenhouse gases (See chapter 2).
c. Be able to determine the effect of global warming (See chapter 2).
d. Cite ways to reduce greenhouse gases (See chapter 2).

16. Field testing and preparing reports - acid deposition
a. Be able to test water for acidity using a pH meter.

Acid rain is measured using a scale called "pH." The lower a substance's pH, the more acidic it is. Pure water has a pH of 7.0. Normal rain is slightly acidic because carbon dioxide dissolves into it, so it has a pH of about 5.5. As of the year 2000, the most acidic rain falling in the US has a pH of about 4.3.

b. Know how to reduce pollutants that effect a body or waters pH

Acid rain causes acidification of lakes and streams and contributes to damage of trees at high elevations (for example, red spruce trees above 2,000 feet) and many sensitive forest soils. In addition, acid rain accelerates the decay of building materials and paints, including irreplaceable buildings, statues and sculptures that are part of our nation's cultural heritage. Prior to falling to the earth, SO_2 and NOx gases and their particulate matter derivatives (sulfates and nitrates), contribute to visible degradation and harm public health.

To solve the acid rain problem, people need to understand how acid rain causes damage to the environment. They also need to understand what changes could be made to the air pollution sources that cause the problem. The answers to these questions help leaders make better decisions about how to control air pollution and therefore how to reduce, or even eliminate acid rain. Since there are many solutions to the acid rain problem, leaders have a choice of options, or combinations of options are best. The major sources and solutions for acid deposition are listed below:

- Almost all of the electricity that powers modern life comes from burning fossil fuels like: coal, natural gas and oil. Two pollutants that are released into the atmosphere, or emitted, when these fuels are burned, cause acid deposition: sulfur dioxide (SO_2) and nitrogen oxides (NOx).

- Coal accounts for most U.S. sulfur dioxide (SO_2) emissions and a large portion of NOx emissions. Sulfur is present in coal as an impurity, and it reacts with air when the coal is burned to form SO_2. In contrast, NOx is formed when any fossil fuel is burned.
- There are several options for reducing SO_2 emissions, including: using coal containing less sulfur, washing the coal, and using devices called scrubbers to chemically remove the SO_2 from the gases leaving the smokestack. Power plants can also switch fuels; for example, burning natural gas creates much less SO_2 than burning coal. Certain approaches will also have additional benefits of reducing other pollutants such as mercury and carbon dioxide. Understanding these "co-benefits" has become important in seeking cost-effective air pollution reduction strategies. Finally, power plants can use technologies that don't burn fossil fuels. Each of these options has it's own costs and benefits. However; there is no single universal solution.
- Similar to scrubbers on power plants, catalytic converters reduce NOx emissions from cars. These devices have been required for over twenty years in the U.S., and it is important to keep them working properly. Tailpipe restrictions have been tightened recently and the EPA has also made, and continues to make, changes to gasoline that allow it to burn cleaner.
- There are other sources of electricity besides fossil fuels. They include: nuclear power, hydropower, wind energy, geothermal energy and solar energy. Of these, nuclear and hydropower are used most widely; in this country. Wind, solar and geothermal energy have not yet been harnessed on a large scale.
- There are also alternative energies available to power automobiles, including: natural gas powered vehicles, battery-powered cars, fuel cell, and combinations of alternative and gasoline powered vehicles.

All sources of energy have environmental costs as well as benefits. Some types of energy are more expensive to produce than others, which means that not all Americans can afford all types of energy. Nuclear power, hydropower and coal are the cheapest forms today, but changes in technologies and environmental regulations may shift that in the future. All of these factors must be weighed when deciding which energy source to use today and which to invest in for tomorrow.

Acid deposition penetrates deeply into the fabric of an ecosystem, changing the chemistry of the soil as well as the chemistry of the streams and narrowing, sometimes to nothing, the space where certain plants and animals can survive. Because there are so many changes, it takes many years for ecosystems to recover from acid deposition, even after emissions are reduced and the rain becomes normal again. For example, while the visibility might improve within days, and small or episodic chemical changes in streams improve within months, chronically acidified lakes, streams, forests, and soils can take years to decades or even centuries (in the case of soils) to heal.

Individuals can contribute directly by conserving energy, since energy production causes the largest portion of the acid deposition problem. For example, you can:

1. Turn off lights, computers, and other appliances when you're not using them.
2. Use energy efficient appliances: lighting, air conditioners, heaters, refrigerators, washing machines, etc.
3. Only use electric appliances when you need them.
4. Keep your thermostat at 68 F in the winter and 72 F in the summer. You can turn it even lower in the winter and higher in the summer when you are away from home.
5. Insulate your home as best you can.

6. Carpool, use public transportation, or better yet, walk or bicycle whenever possible.
7. Buy vehicles with low NOx emissions, and maintain all vehicles well.
8. Be well informed.

    c. Determine how weather patterns affect acid precipitation.

Weather patterns can move waste material from factories and power plants over great distances away from the original source of generation. Weather phenomena such a thermal or temperature inversions (where warm air is at a higher elevation than cold air in the troposphere, in other words, warm air at altitude sits on top of cooler air at the ground level below) can trap pollutants in like a lid over a pan. The diagram shows a typical pattern of air pollution movement in the atmosphere.

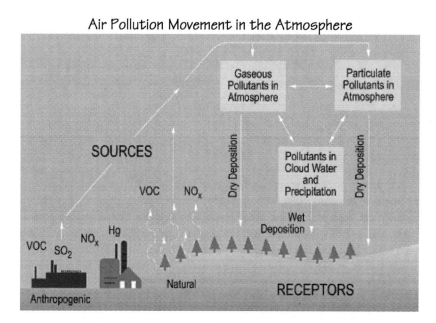

17. Field testing and preparing reports - radiation and growth factor
    a. Understand the effects that radiation has on the growth of plants.
    b. Know how irradiated organisms are affected by both dose and time of exposure.

- With the increasing interest about the impact of human activities on the ecology, environmental protection against ionizing radiation is getting attention. There is, however, only limited information about radiation effects on environmental organisms such as plants. In field studies of a nuclear accident, deleterious effects such as poor growth and genetic damages were observed in plants after a large dose of irradiation. On the other hand, some reports have shown that a low dose of irradiation could stimulate plant growth. The below study is a biological model plant, arabidopsis, to elucidate the radiation effects on plants.

- The seeds of arabidopsis (var. Columbia) were surface sterilized and soaked in water at 4° C for 2 days, before being cultured on the medium containing 0.8% agar under light in a controlled environment chamber. The plants were irradiated with X rays (0.5 20 Gy, 1 Gy/min) or gamma rays (50 Gy 1000 Gy, 10 Gy/min) at various growth stages. When young plant seedlings were irradiated, their root elongation was inhibited at doses more than 100 Gy, although elongation of the hypocotyls was not affected even at 1000 Gy. This indicates that the inhibition of growth by a high dose of irradiation varies with tissues, and the root is relatively sensitive to irradiation.

- Irradiation of seeds did not affect their germination when they were cultured at the cultural temperature of 23° C. However, when the seeds were cultured at 8° C, which is almost the lower limit for germination, the irradiated seeds germinated faster than the non-irradiated seeds. The effect of seed irradiation could be observed at a dose as low as 0.5 Gy. The acceleration of germination by seed irradiation was observed not only under the chilling stress, but also under the stress induced by a chemical agent. When seeds were grown at 23° C on medium containing methyl viologen, a biological radical generator, pre-irradiation of seeds reduced the methyl viologen-induced retardation of germination. This suggests that irradiation of seeds could enhance anti-oxidant systems that enable seeds to germinate promptly under stress.

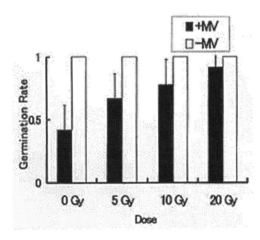

Reduction of methyl viologen (MV) - induced retardation of se germination by X-ray pretreatment.

18. Designing a professional environmental impact study
   a. Be able to describe a local environmental issue.
   b. Design a method to study this issue.
   c. Be able to list and describe equipment to study this issue.
   d. Use local, state, and national laws and regulations to that apply to your issue (See chp 2).
   e. Cite possible solutions to the problem.

Awesome Guides, Inc. A.P. Environmental Science Study Guide – Chapter Four

Chapter 4
A.P. Environmental Science Practice Test #1

The A.P. Environmental Science Exam will have two sections; 1) multiple choice and 2) free response (essay) questions. You will have 90 minutes to complete each section. It's a good idea to time yourself when you take the following test and see how close you come to the actual time limit of 90 minutes. The multiple-choice section accounts for 60% of your grade. Before taking this test, check out the testing hints at the front of your guide. This will help you understand the "nuts and bolts" of taking this exam. Use the provided answer sheet to complete the test. **Good luck!**

After taking the test, use the test key to check your answers. Read the justification section below each answer to learn about the reasoning behind the questions. In addition, write down the question numbers that you missed to compare them with the subject index, and see what areas you are weak in and should focus your studies on.

The number of questions in each subject area is not an indication of how many you will have on your AP Environmental Science Exam; no one knows this for sure. However, the questions are spread out by the approximate percentage of topics that the AP College Board wants you to know.

USE THE ANSWER SHEET IN THE APPENDIX AT THE BACK OF YOUR STUDY GUIDE!

A.P. Environmental Science Practice Test #1

1. Which of the following factors contribute to urban blight?
    a. declining tax revenue resulting from lower property values
    b. reductions in local services like garbage collection, police and fire protection and public
    c. increased tax rate
    d. businesses close and properties deteriorate
    e. all of the above

2. Which of the following provide rationale for keeping forests sustainable?
    a. conservation of biodiversity
    b. moderate regional climatic conditions such as temperature and rainfall
    c. prevent mineral loss through erosion
    d. are a source of oxygen, store carbon, and remove carbon dioxide
    e. all of the above

3. Which population profile below best describes a developing country?
    a. the population profile has a small base
    b. the profile would show a decline of the older population and a reduction in the number of children and young people
    c. the population profile shows a high fertility rate
    d. the population profile shows a low fertility rate
    e. the profile would show a decrease in the number of children and young people

4. According to the energy flow of ecosystems the conversion of light to organic matter by photosynthesis has an efficiency of:
    a. 100%
    b. 87%
    c. 50%
    d. less than 10%
    e. variable rate 10%-87%

5. The "tragedy of the commons" refers to:
    a. a resource that is owned or not owned and used by many people in common
    b. restricting deforestation of rainforests by private individuals
    c. a population of common species exceeding their carrying capacity
    d. the restricting of cattle from grazing on federally owned grasslands
    e. both b and d are correct

6. The gradual movement of tectonic plates on the Earth's surface may cause
    a. volcanism and earthquakes
    b. formation of mountains and oceanic ridges
    c. continental drift
    d. both a and b are correct
    e. all of the above

Awesome Guides, Inc. A.P. Environmental Science Study Guide - Chapter Four

7. The sustainability of societies begins with individuals. Which of the following activities would meet these goals?
   a. becoming involved in local governmental decision making
   b. supporting environmental organizations
   c. reducing your energy use, water use, and solid waste production
   d. encouraging businesses to produce products that are reusable
   e. all of the above

8. Examples of adaptations in organisms include:
   a. coping with abiotic factors
   b. extensive root systems for absorbing water and nutrients
   c. antlers on deer species for attracting mates
   d. escaping predation
   e. all of the above

9. If a population is growing at a constant rate of 4.5% per year then it will double in about
   a. 15 years
   b. 25 years
   c. 30 years
   d. 45 years
   e. 50 years

10. If the fertility rate of a developing country is reduced by 5%, the population would
    a. continue to grow for a few years, then decline
    b. continue to grow for many decades, but gradually stabilize
    c. continue to grow until a much higher reduction of fertility takes place
    d. begin to decrease immediately
    e. none of the above

11. Among the hazardous chemicals found in urban areas, which of the following are associated with both air and water pollution?
    a. heavy metals
    b. hydrocarbons and volatile organic compounds
    c. particulate matter
    d. ozone
    e. PAN's

12. The half-life of a substance such as plutonium is:
    a. half of the amount of radioactivity available for use in nuclear fusion
    b. the measure of the rate of radioactive decay of stable isotopes
    c. the time for half of the amount of a radioactive isotope to decay
    d. 24,000 years
    e. both c and d

13. The sum of all genes of all individuals of a particular species is that species':
    a. gene pool
    b. level of genetic differences in each population of a community
    c. variations over many generations
    d. a and b
    e. none of the above

14. Within an ecosystem, consumers may represent which of the following:
    a. photosynthetic green plants
    b. photosynthetic bacteria
    c. parasites associated with plants and animals
    d. chemosynthetic bacteria
    e. a, b and c are all correct

15. A calorie is defined in terms of a certain amount of:
    a. food.
    b. weight in milligrams.
    c. heat.
    d. fat.
    e. carbohydrate.

16. Factors that greatly constitute environmental resistance to human population growth in developing countries include:
    a. war
    b. famine
    c. disease
    d. all of the above
    e. none of the above

17. The phenomena known as coral bleaching is
    a. the loss of the coral's zooxanthellae algae
    b. the illegal harvesting of coral
    c. caused by the cooling down of tropical oceans due to polar ice melting
    d. a direct result of touching the coral polyps
    e. the greenhouse effect

18. Salinization refers to:
    a. the amount of salt in marine ecosystems
    b. the accumulation of salts in soil, restricting plant growth
    c. the excessive irrigation of soil allowing salts to build up
    d. the irrigation of crops using diluted water from the oceans
    e. both b and c are correct

19. Breeder reactors:
    a. use only fissionable fuel in the main reactor
    b. breeds more air pollution into the atmosphere
    c. uses nonfissionable uranium 238
    d. start their process with plutonium 239
    e. uses fissionable 235 only

20. Consumption of fossil fuels can be decreased by
    a. making cars with greater fuel efficiency
    b. lowering the speed limit
    c. providing better insulation in buildings
    d. designing appliances with greater energy efficiency
    e. all of the above

21. To be considered a pest an organism must
    a. be an insect
    b. always be an animal
    c. only affect agricultural crops
    d. all of the above
    e. none of the above

22. The minimum number of individuals needed to sustain a breeding population is called the:
    a. critical factor principle
    b. zero number
    c. population base number
    d. maximum support number
    e. critical number of a species

23. A population can change in size by all of the following factors, EXCEPT:
    a. biotic potential
    b. environmental resistance
    c. herbivore/carnivore principle
    d. disease
    e. ability to cope with adverse conditions

24. All of the following contribute to the decline of biodiversity EXCEPT:
    a. controlled hunting of duck species
    b. physical alteration of habitats such as conversion and fragmentation
    c. exotic species
    d. pollution
    e. all of the above contribute to decline of biodiversity

25. Which of the following are considered to be sources of humus:
    a. peat
    b. shredded newspaper
    c. manures
    d. compost
    e. all of the above

26. Strictly anthropogenic process(es) that put carbon dioxide into the atmosphere is/are
    a. forest fires started by lightening
    b. volcanic eruptions
    c. internal combustion
    d. aerobic respiration
    e. decomposition of leaf litter

27. The Endangered Species Act
    a. has saved all endangered and threatened species since its inception
    b. has saved at least all species previously listed as endangered
    c. is criticized by both environmentalists and developers
    d. receives bipartisan support in Congress
    e. has expired and is no longer in effect

28. Costs of pollution control may show a better cost-benefit ratio by:
    a. using materials generated from recycling former waste products
    b. providing jobs generated in the pollution control industry
    c. development of new production techniques which are more efficient as well as less polluting
    d. less time lost from job as a consequence of worker illnesses
    e. all of the above

29. Which statement is NOT true about replacement fertility rate?
    a. it is the average fertility rate that doubles the population in one generation
    b. it is the average fertility rate that just replaces the parents
    c. it is slightly greater than 2.0
    d. it is slightly higher in developing countries than in developed countries
    e. all of the above statements are true

30. To be considered sustainable, a society might:
    a. place annual quotas on fish harvests
    b. place size limits on fish that can be harvested
    c. release hatchery raised fish to augment wild populations
    d. use sound science and stewardship in decision making
    e. all of the above

Awesome Guides, Inc. A.P. Environmental Science Study Guide – Chapter Four

31. One of the major factors resulting in "urban sprawl" is:
    a. automobiles
    b. mass transit in large cities
    c. large immigration of people and industry into the cities
    d. lack of natural resources in the inner city
    e. all of the above

32. Atmosphere pollutions have the greatest effect on:
    a. stratosphere
    b. troposphere
    c. mesosphere
    d. all of the above
    e. only a and b are correct

33. A typical soil profile has horizons in which order from top to bottom?
    a. A, B, C, E, O
    b. O, E, C, B, A
    c. A, C, B, O, E
    d. O, A, E, B, C
    e. A, E, O, C, B

34. In the United States, the environmental movement
    a. began in the late 1800s
    b. was initiated in part over concern that many areas of the country were inhabited
    c. gained momentum over concerns about air and water quality
    d. became a public issue with the publication of Rachel Carson's Silent Spring in 1962
    e. all of the above

35. If the relative humidity of an air mass is 100% and the temperature is 85 degrees, what will happen if the temperature cools to 65 degrees?
    a. condensation occurs
    b. there will be an decrease in the humidity
    c. there will be an increase in the humidity
    d. the barometric pressure will decrease
    e. none of the above

36. What type of biome would you expect to find in a region where temperatures are about 78 degrees and where significant precipitation occurs year round?
    a. tundra
    b. tropical rainforest
    c. temperate deciduous forest
    d. desert
    e. savanna

37. The path of primary and secondary sewage treatment follows in which order?
    a. raw sewage, primary clarifier, aeration tank, secondary clarifier, disinfection, grit chamber and release
    b. raw sewage, primary clarifier, grit chamber, aeration tank, secondary clarifier, disinfection and release
    c. raw sewage, grit chamber, primary clarifier, aeration tank, secondary clarifier, disinfection and release
    d. raw sewage, grit chamber, primary clarifier, secondary clarifier, aeration tank, disinfection and release
    e. raw sewage, grit chamber, disinfection, primary clarifier, aeration tank, secondary clarifier and release

38. Removing groundwater and the developing of natural recharge areas can result in:
    a. lowered water tables
    b. land subsidence
    c. wells going dry
    d. water shortages
    e. all of the above

39. The major natural ecosystem of Central North America and subequatorial Africa is:
    a. coniferous forest
    b. deciduous forest
    c. desert
    d. grassland
    e. tundra

40. In the U.S., most sewage now receives
    a. preliminary treatment, but no more
    b. preliminary and primary treatment, but no more
    c. preliminary, primary, and secondary treatment, but no more
    d. preliminary, primary, secondary and advanced treatments
    e. it goes untreated

41. Selective pressures in ecosystems that result in a direct response to:
    a. organisms
    b. community
    c. entire populations
    d. resources
    e. all of the above

42. Biomes exist in different regions of the world due mainly to:
    a. geographical location
    b. soil characteristics
    c. light amount
    d. habitat destruction
    e. temperature and rainfall

43. Which of the following statements is a direct result of environmental law?
    a. In the U.S., the first sewage treatment plants were constructed around the turn of this century.
    b. In the 1970s many cities were still discharging raw sewage into natural waterways causing severe pollution problems.
    c. The Clean Water Act of 1972 provided funding for building and upgrading sewage treatment plants.
    d. Currently, waterways are more polluted than ever with sewage.
    e. all of the above apply

44. The world's worst nuclear power plant disaster to date occurred at:
    a. Chernobyl, Ukraine
    b. Grenoble, France
    c. Love Canal
    d. Berlin, Germany
    e. Three-Mile Island, PA

45. Our spread-out-suburban living pattern (urban sprawl) we have created since WW II has caused:
    a. more energy consumption and consequent energy problems
    b. air pollution, especially "smog"
    c. more consumption of iron, rubber, and other resources
    d. development of valuable farm and park land
    e. all of the above

46. Causes of cultural entrophication include:
    a. excess organic wastes from waste treatment facilities
    b. excess nutrients, such as fertilizers
    c. human activities
    d. all of the above
    e. only b and c

47. At this point in time, experts feel the most practical way to deal with the depletion of the ozone is to:
    a. stop fossil fuel use
    b. stop production of CFCs and find substitutes
    c. use more solar energy
    d. use more hydroelectric energy
    e. all of the above

48. Waste to energy facilities:
    a. separate most recyclables prior to combustion
    b. burn rubbish to produce heat energy which produces electricity
    c. generate ash that is usually placed in landfills
    d. are also known as WTE
    e. all of the above

49. Tapping into oil shale and tar sands as sources of petroleum will solve the problem of crude oil shortages because:
    a. oil shales and tar sands are too expensive to exploit unless the price of oil goes up considerably
    b. oil shales and tar sands can't provide enough energy to meet current needs
    c. the technology to extract these resources doesn't exist at present
    d. a and b only
    e. a, b, and c only

50. In natural populations, only a small percentage of the offspring survive and reproduce another generation. The adaptive features that develop in organisms include:
    a. As organisms grow, they become larger and more aggressive
    b. become smaller and less conspicuous
    c. develop any combination of traits that enhance the organism's ability to survive and reproduce
    d. eventually become extinct as population numbers decline
    e. none of the above

51. Water pollutants include:
    a. sediments
    b. toxic chemicals
    c. solid wastes
    d. nutrients
    e. all of the above

52. When groundwater is depleted faster than it is replenished, lowering the water table, the following may occur:
    a. the streams flow rate may decrease
    b. in coastal cities, saltwater may intrude and contaminate groundwater supplies
    c. agricultural lands that rely on irrigation become unproductive
    d. property values decline
    e. all of the above

53. We receive some radiation from:
    a. X-rays and microwaves
    b. rock and stone building materials
    c. cosmic rays
    d. radon and uranium gas
    e. all of the above

54. Which of the following is not found in storm water runoff?
    a. fertilizer
    b. pesticides
    c. bacterial waste and oil
    d. activated sludge
    e. leaves and sticks

55. World food production has been negatively affected by all of the following EXCEPT:
    a. desertification
    b. high-yield varieties
    c. depletion of water resources
    d. increased demand for meat and dairy products
    e. Tragedy of the Commons

56. Consequences of global warming may include:
    a. changes in the major ocean currents
    b. melting of polar ice caps and glaciers
    c. rise of sea level
    d. thermal expansion of the oceans
    e. all of the above

57. The gross national product (GNP) is a measure of:
    a. nation's wealth
    b. the sum of all goods and services produced in a country per unit time
    c. does not factor the loss or decline of a nation's valuable natural resources
    d. all of the above
    e. only a and b

58. The earliest pesticides, such as DDT:
    a. are called first generation pesticides
    b. included heavy metals such as lead, arsenic and mercury
    c. accumulate in soils and are resistant to breakdown in the environment
    d. did and still do save lives
    e. all of the above

59. A species is best defined as:
    a. any individual plant, animal, or microbe
    b. any group of plants, animals, or microbes
    c. the total population of a kind of plant, animal, or microbe all the members of which do or potentially can interbreed and produce fertile offspring
    d. an ecosystems organisms
    e. all of the above

60. Acid precipitation is:
    a. any precipitation which is more acidic than 7.0
    b. any precipitation which is more acidic than normal
    c. precipitation which is strongly acidic, below 3.7
    d. irrigation with line compounds
    e. precipitation which can cause gully erosion

61. Suburbs developed in the 1950s and 1960s. As populations moved out of the cities, which groups remained:
    a. poor and homeless people
    b. European immigrants and other minorities
    c. the handicapped and elderly
    d. all of the above
    e. None of the above. Moving is a personal choice, not affected by the suburbs

62. The Cuyahoga River which flows through Cleveland Ohio:
    a. once caught on fire
    b. has high biodiversity
    c. has high DO levels due to the inflow of underwater streams
    d. has no nonpoint pollution
    e. b, c and d are correct

63. Secondary sewage treatment involves the:
    a. removal of all organic material and pathogens in the water
    b. removal of 90% plus of organic material and all pathogens
    c. removal of 90% plus of organic material and little to no pathogens
    d. removal of organic material and is ready to be released into the
    e. none of the above

64. The daily measure of a region's temperature and precipitation is that region's:
    a. ecotype
    b. weather
    c. climate
    d. ecology
    e. ecotone

65. Carbon dioxide is returned to the atmosphere through all of these processes except:
    a. volcanoes
    b. forest fires
    c. internal combustion
    d. aerobic respiration
    e. photosynthesis

66. Soil bacteria play (an) important role(s) in:
    a. the water cycle
    b. the carbon cycle
    c. the nitrogen cycle
    d. the phosphorus cycle
    e. all of the above

67. County governments raise money for the services that run a city's infrastructure through:
   a. property taxes
   b. federal income taxes
   c. gasoline taxes
   d. state lotteries
   e. direct billing of intangible taxes

68. The Magnuson Act of 1976 allows additional jurisdiction to the U.S. up to _____ offshore.
   a. 5 mile international limit
   b. 12 mile international limit
   c. 200 miles
   d. 500 miles, but only for whaling disputes
   e. unlimited miles depending on what governmental division is involved

69. The "New Forestry" management plans emphasize:
   a. removal of all debris and leaf litter
   b. sustainability
   c. clear cutting techniques
   d. limiting control burns
   e. none of the above

70. The following practices reduce desertification:
   a. increased irrigation techniques
   b. deforestation projects
   c. reduced livestock grazing intensity
   d. tilling of crop land
   e. all of the above

71. The reason forests are being cut down faster than they are being regenerated is:
   a. developing countries use wood as fuel for heating and cooking
   b. wood is burned to make charcoal and sold
   c. developing countries convert forests to agricultural land for food production
   d. no laws or penalties exist to prevent deforestation in developing countries
   e. all of the above

72. The Highway Trust Fund Act does not:
   a. collect funds generated by the gas tax
   b. take into any account the preservation of open space and agricultural land
   c. designate funds for building new highways
   d. grow proportionately as commuting increases
   e. allow modifications after 2000

73. If rabbits are selectively bred for thinner hair, then:
    a. genes for thinner hair become more abundant in the normal breeding population
    b. genes for thicker hair are completely lost
    c. genes for thinner hair are more abundant and genes for thicker hair are less abundant in the breeding population
    d. mutations for thinner hair are eliminated
    e. changing hair is not possible due to the genome

74. Selective pressure that influences evolution of a species includes all of the following except:
    a. climate
    b. resource availability
    c. predation and parasitism
    d. principle of the limits
    e. immigration of organisms of the same species

75. Organic wastes have the potential to:
    a. cause pollution
    b. contain pathogens found in fecal material
    c. include food wastes
    d. a and b only
    e. all of the above

76. Which of the following statements about the use of DDT is/are FALSE?
    a. DDT saved millions of lives
    b. ecologists have always recognized the environmental problems with DDT
    c. Paul Muller was awarded a Nobel prize for his discovery of DDT
    d. DDT is inexpensive
    e. Crop production increased dramatically as a result of DDT use

77. Which is NOT considered a renewable resource?
    a. the sun
    b. fossil fuels
    c. wind energy
    d. hydroelectric power
    e. thermal power

78. Conventional cars can use all of these fuels except:
    a. gasoline
    b. petroleum
    c. hydrogen gas
    d. gasohol
    e. sugar compound

79. Primary treatment of sewage water includes:
    a. screening large pieces and debris in a grit chamber
    b. settling of colloidal material
    c. pathogen removal
    d. biological treatment and nutrient removal
    e. a & c are correct

80. The Clean Air Act of 1990 includes all of these statements EXCEPT:
    a. sulfur reduction by 50%
    b. adding alcohol to some gasolines
    c. better emission control on automobiles
    d. mandatory radon testing for businesses
    e. development of maximum achievable control technology standards for 189 toxic pollutants

81. Passive solar heating systems are considered more beneficial than active solar systems because:
    a. they are more efficient
    b. they are quiet to operate
    c. they are easier to operate
    d. they are less costly to install and maintain
    e. only a, b and c are correct

82. People in developed countries:
    a. have the same biotic potential as those in developing countries
    b. have lower fertility rates than humans in developing countries
    c. have a higher standard of living than humans in developing countries
    d. have greater access to education than humans in developing countries
    e. all of the above

83. Disadvantages of solar energy include all of the following EXCEPT:
    a. it needs to be in one area to work and provide useful energy
    b. it is available only intermittently
    c. using it may upset the overall electromagnetic spectrum of the biosphere
    d. it can not be stored
    e. it does not provide enough energy for our modern technology

84. Which of the following has **NOT** been a significant factor in increased world food production over the last 50 years?
    a. increased irrigation
    b. increased fertilizers
    c. genetically engineered plants
    d. global warming
    e. increased crop hectares worldwide

85. The transitional zone between an ecosystem with an adjacent ecosystem is called the
    a. community
    b. biome
    c. ecotone
    d. optimum
    e. zone of tolerance

86. When the mass of the atom is less than the mass of the reactant atom and which process produces energy:
    a. nuclear fusion
    b. nuclear fission power
    c. nuclear acceleration
    d. hydrogen fusion
    e. hydrogenation

87. If two lakes are close to each other and receive the same amount of acidic precipitation, and one lake has turned acidic in recent years while the other lake is still neutral, then the following may have occurred:
    a. the acid was neutralized by a spring
    b. acidification eutrophies differently in different water columns
    c. difference in buffering capacity of the two lakes
    d. wind patterns moving over hills and mountains
    e. it is impossible to determine from the above data

88. The human population is growing by
    a. 100 million per year
    b. 10 million per year
    c. 1 million per year
    d. 0.1% and leveling off
    e. 1.0% and leveling off among the poor and elderly

89. The environmental effects of urban sprawl can best be described by:
    a. depletion of fossil fuel resources
    b. more air & water pollution
    c. more solid wastes
    d. loss of natural ecosystems and biodiversity
    e. all of the above

90. The most significant factor in reducing sulfur dioxide in the troposphere include:
    a. catalytic burners
    b. banning refuse incineration
    c. building coal-burning power plants with tall smokestacks
    d. increased recycling of toxic wastes
    e. all of the above

Awesome Guides, Inc. A.P. Environmental Science Study Guide - Chapter Four

91. The ecological process that converts atmospheric nitrogen (N2) to forms useable by living things is called:
    a. photosynthesis
    b. aerobic respiration
    c. nitrogen fixation
    d. denitrification
    e. fermentation

92. Nuclear power plants differ significantly from coal-fired power plants in that nuclear power plants:
    a. are clean burning with little to no air pollution
    b. produce acid precipitation
    c. contribute greatly to global warming
    d. cost of energy is much more expensive
    e. all of the above

93. A species with high biotic potential would:
    a. invade new environments
    b. produce large numbers of offspring, and have a little protection of their young
    c. migrate long distances
    d. tolerate many types of abiotic conditions
    e. all of the above

94. One third of the world's population, approximately 1.5 billion people:
    a. live in absolute poverty and are illiterate
    b. have no clean water
    c. suffer from malnutrition
    d. all of the above
    e. none of the above

95. DDT can be best described by all of the following except:
    a. it's a broad spectrum pesticide
    b. it is a persistent pesticide
    c. it's currently banned in the u.s.
    d. it is very expensive but very effective
    e. it's relatively non-toxic to humans

96. Halo generated hydrocarbons describe what type of material?
    a. heavy metals
    b. organic pesticides
    c. HHC pesticides
    d. synthetic nonbiodegradable organic compounds
    e. organic biodegradable pesticides

97. Geothermal Energy may be used from the Earth's interior through:
    a. drilling into naturally hot groundwater aquifers and allowing the escaping steam to drive generators
    b. heating water heaters
    c. harnessing energy from geysers
    d. using the Earth's magnetic field
    e. both a and b

98. Poor nations usually suffer from a rapidly increasing population because:
    a. there is increased competition for available resources
    b. economic gains are wiped out by population growth
    c. there is not enough capital to create jobs leading to high unemployment
    d. they have a relatively small portion of the population that is economically active
    e. all of the above

99. Problem(s) associated with storing solid waste in landfills is/are
    a. cell liners rupturing
    b. leachate moving toward groundwater
    c. surface subsidence
    d. the venting of methane gas
    e. all of the above

100. The first trophic level in an ecosystem refers to:
    a. carnivores
    b. consumers
    c. cherbivores
    d. all autotrophs
    e. both a and b are correct

Go to Free Response Questions after a 10 minute break.........

A.P. Environmental Science Practice Test #1
Free Response Questions

You will be answering 4 free response questions on your AP Environmental Science Exam. Many of the questions will have multiple sections. Be sure to answer all sections. You may **NOT** use a calculator. Read each question very carefully. For every essay question, you are awarded 10 points, equaling 40 % of your grade. In addition to the testing hints given at the beginning of your study guide, the following suggestions may further help you in completing the free response questions. **Good luck!**

- Read ALL of the questions first, before attempting to solve or write down your answers. After reading the questions, go to the ones that you feel you are most prepared for, and answer those first. Many times, you recall concepts while answering other questions.

- You can receive partial credit for answers that may not be completely correct. Therefore, be sure to show all of your work, and attempt to answer all sections of each of the free response questions, to the best of your ability, even if you don't know the answer to some sections. Sometimes the part before another is related to the previous section, such as part b, may be related to part c. You may receive some partial credit for answering another related part even though you were not familiar with the previous section.

- Organize your answers and make sure that you write legible and clearly, so that the grader will understand what you are trying to say. If you complete work that you think is incorrect, put an "X" through it.

- Show the steps you used to solve the question.

- Pay attention to units you use in your calculations.

- Your exam booklet will have an insert containing the questions, but no answer sheet. Remove this and use it as a reference; however no credit is given for answers written on this insert. Only answer questions on the official space provided.

- Don't simply jot down a bunch of erroneous or "bogus" answers hoping that they might be correct. Try to focus on the questions asked, and then write down all of the RELATED information about that subject. Graders may actually deduct points for extraneous or incorrect information.

ANSWER THE FOLLOWING QUESTIONS ON YOUR OWN PAPER!

1. Lake Silver is located in Orlando, Florida on the campus of Edgewater High School. Once a month the APES students monitor the water quality and trophic status of this lake. During the month of May, the students discover an algae bloom while collecting the water samples.
   a. Describe the meaning of algae bloom.
   b. Identify the possible point and nonpoint sources that would account for the change in water quality.
   c. Suggest what further testing would be necessary to determine if the lake is safe to swim in.
   d. What are the long-term consequences of this phenomenon?
   e. Develop a plan to remediate the lake. Give the water quality parameters that would meet the goals of your plan.
   f. Cite the governmental regulations that might be used to control additional widespread pollution problems of this type.

2. Sewage (Wastewater) Treatment policies require local utilities to treat their wastewater before it is discharged into the environment. Below is a flow diagram of a typical wastewater treatment facility.

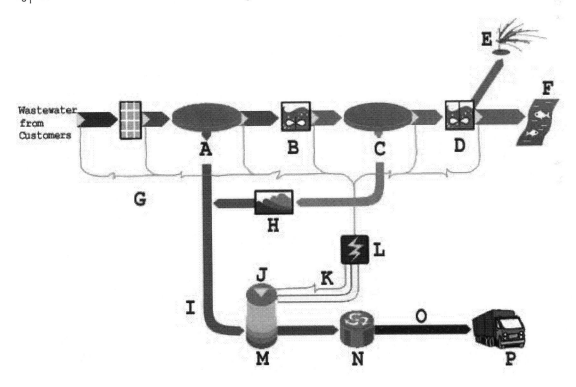

   a. Identify and describe the components in the diagram. Include a description and function of each component. Explain each treatment process in terms of:
   - BOD before and after each process
   - percent removal of organic solids

A.P. Environmental Science Study Guide – Chapter Four  Awesome Guides, Inc.

    b. Explain possible uses for the materials produced as a result of the treatment process.
    c. Cite and explain two environmental policies that would affect wastewater treatment facilities.

3. Energy —A large municipal landfill that serves a population of 2 million people receives 5000 tones of MSW per day. Assume that the facility charges an average of $50.00 per ton as a disposal fee. Also assume that 65% of the MSW is used for energy and that 20% is recovered and 15% is land filled.
    a. If 10,000 BTU's are required to generate 1 KW-hour of electricity and 1 ton of MSW produces 1,000,000 BTU's of electricity how many KW-hours of electricity are generated each day, in mega-watt hours.
    b. If a megawatt-hour sells for $100.00 on the open market, and 25% of the process goes towards operating costs, what is the daily profit generated by the power plant?
    c. Discuss the advantages and disadvantages of using the waste to produce energy.
    d. If aluminum accounts for 5% of the recovered material and sells for $10.00 per ton and 100% can be recovered, how much profit is made from selling and recycling this material?
    e. What problems are associated with the material that is land filled?

4. In Glacier Bay, southeastern Alaska, the glaciers have been retreating northward at a very rapid rate. Approximately 100 kilometers have disappeared since 1750. As the glaciers of ice retreat they leave the bare minerals or soil, also known as a moraine. Typical types of vegetation found in the area consist of alders, dryas and sitka spruce.

PH	Successional Stage
8-8.5	bare rock
6.2	20 years / alders
7.7	20 years / dryas
5	35 years / alders
7.1	35 years / dryas

    a. What assumptions about the moraines can be made when comparing older moraines (southern) with newer (northern) moraines?
    b. What does this assumption imply about the steps of ecological succession?

Using the chart on the right to answer the following questions:
    c. How has the soil changed over time with respect to the dryas species and alders species?
    d. How does this change affect ecological succession?
    e. What might happen to the soil pH in 45 years? For the alders? For the dryas?

Use the data below to answer the following questions:

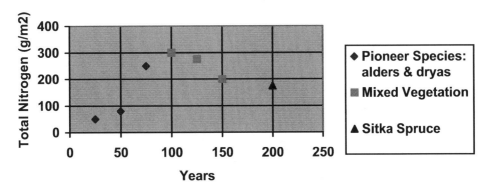

f. What effect do sitka spruce have on the total nitrogen levels of the soil?

g. Do sitka spruce fix nitrogen? Explain.

h. Considering all of the above data, is the process from pioneer species to sitka spruce facilitative, inhibitive or a tolerant process? Explain your reasoning.

A.P. Environmental Science Study Guide - Chapter Five  Awesome Guides, Inc.

Chapter 5
A. P. Environmental Science Practice Test #2

On your exam you may encounter multiple-choice questions that include graphs, diagrams, data, matching etc. The following practice test includes examples of this type of question; they will be incorporated into the multiple-choice section of 100 questions. The first 50 sample questions are of this type. Use the answer sheet to mark your answers and the answer key to check your answers, and review the concepts that you missed. USE THE ANSWER SHEET IN THE APPENDIX AT THE BACK OF YOUR STUDY GUIDE! Good luck!

Use the terms below to answer questions 1-4: a) population   b) ecosystem   c) species   d) biome

1. All the members of a particular organism that interact and produce fertile offspring.
2. A defined area that includes the abiotic and biotic components of that specific region.
3. A very large area where the temperature, soil and rainfall are similar.
4. All members of a particular organism in a given area.

For questions 5-8 choose the most appropriate tropic level:

a) primary consumers   b) secondary consumers   c) autotrophs   d) secondary carnivores

5. Level one
6. Level two
7. Level three
8. Level four

For questions 9-14, select the biome that best describes the below descriptions: (you may use some choices more than once).

a) tropical rain forest   b) coniferous forest   c) grasslands   d) deserts   e) temperate forest

9. Hot days, cool nights, thorny bushes, rodents and lizards
10. Seasonal rainfall (10-60 inches), frequent fires
11. Large grazing mammals
12. 28 degrees C average temperature, very high diversity, soil poor in nutrients
13. Seasonal weather, broad-leaved deciduous trees, Western and Central Europe, Eastern Asia, Eastern North America
14. Seasonal weather, evergreen trees, important nesting area for neotropical birds

Use the letters on the graph to answer questions 15-19:

15. Environmental resistance is greater than biotic potential
16. Occurs if an exotic species populates a new ecosystem
17. Lag phase
18. Represents the carrying capacity
19. Population held in balance by environmental resistance

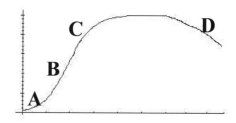

Copyrighted material – do not duplicate!   132   www.awesomeguides.com

Certain organisms are able to adapt to changing environmental conditions. If all organisms were grouped into two categories, a) vulnerable species and b) highly adaptive species, then select the factors below that would pertain to each. Use the choices a) vulnerable or b) highly adaptive species to match each question 20-24.

20. wide distribution
21. small size
22. long generation time
23. limited genetic variation
24. ability to migrate

Use the population histograms below to answer questions 25-28.

25. Diagram A represents:
    a. the world population projection
    b. the age structure in a developing country
    c. the age structure in a developed country
    d. age structure of India
    e. the population of a developing country that is changing into a developed country

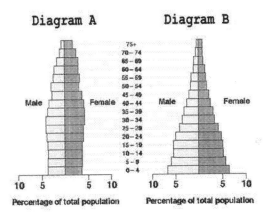

26. Diagram B represents:
    a. the world population projection
    b. the age structure in a developing country
    c. the age structure in a developed country
    d. age structure of India
    e. the population of a developing country that probably will be a developed country in the future

27. Referring to Diagram B, in 25 years:
    a. there will be a large number of elderly people
    b. there will be a small number of elderly people trends with only one graph
    c. there will be a large number of new borns
    d. it is impossible to determine which population is rapidly expanding
    e. there will be the greatest number of middle age people

28. Referring to Diagram B, in 25 years:
    a. there will be a decrease in the population
    b. there will be a decrease only in the younger population
    c. the population is expanding and represents a typical developing country
    d. there will be little to no change in the population
    e. it is impossible to determine population trends with only one graph

A.P. Environmental Science Study Guide – Chapter Five   Awesome Guides, Inc.

Refer to the chart below to answer questions 29-32

29. Considering the available resources in Eastern Europe, which technology would you recommend to generate electricity?

    a. natural gas
    b. petroleum
    c. coal
    d. nuclear fusion
    e. nuclear fission

	Petroleum (billions of barrels)	Natural Gas (trillion Ft3)	Coal (billion tons)
North America	75.7	291.4	285.2
South and Central America	89.5	219.1	23.8
Western Europe	18.9	161.5	99.7
Eastern Europe & Former USSR	58.9	1,999.4	288.4
Middle East	673.6	1,749.5	0.2
Africa	75.4	361.1	67.7
Far East and Oceania	43	359.6	322.3
World Use (1998)	26.6	83	5.04

30. Since one billion barrels of petroleum yields 5.7×10^{15} BTU's or 5.7 quadrillion BTU's, then how many quadrillion BTU's could be used in the Far East and Oceania before the supply runs out?

    a. 245.10 quadrillion BTU's
    b. 2451.00 quadrillion BTU's
    c. 2049.72 quadrillion BTU's
    d. 204972.00 quadrillion BTU's
    e. 724.90 quadrillion BTU's

31. Which country has the largest supply of fossil fuels?

    a. North America
    b. Western Europe
    c. Middle East
    d. Africa
    e. Eastern Europe and former USSR

32. Which country has the smallest supply of fossil fuels?

    a. North America
    b. Far East and Oceania
    c. Western Europe
    d. South and Central America
    e. Africa

For questions 33-37 match the environmental incidence with the proper place that it occurred (you may use some choices more than once).

    a) Chernobyl, Ukraine   b) Love Canal   c) 3 Mile Island   d) Cuyahoga River

33. Toxic waste dump where homes were built and then bought back by the government.
34. Partial meltdown due to human and equipment errors.
35. Over 135,000 people were evacuated.
36. The worst nuclear power accident.
37. Due to excessive dumping of chemicals this body of water caught on fire

Match the following Federal regulations to the current description for questions 38-42 (you may use some choices more than once).

a. Clean Air Act
b. Clean Water Act
c. Safe Drinking Water Act
d. Endangered Species Act
e. Toxic Substances Act

38. Calls for settling ambient standards of particulates, sulfur dioxide, carbon monoxide and nitrogen oxides.
39. Requires industry to have a discharge permit, for waterways and report all toxic chemicals.
40. Requires manufacturing to submit a premanufacturing report to the EPA, for environmental impact assessment.
41. Requires a 50% reduction of current acid-causing emissions.
42. Provides protection from killing, trapping or uprooting protected species.

Use the power plant schematic diagram for questions 43-50 and identify the structures and/or functions from the nuclear power plant diagram below (you may use some letters more than once). For answer choices with two or more letters, mark all of the letters on the same line for that question. For example: 41. ABC

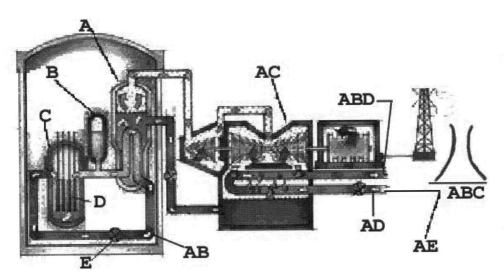

43. Which letter(s) represent the location of the nuclear reactor, where the chain reaction takes place?
44. Which letter(s) represent the steam generator, where the turbine's energy is turned into electricity?
45. Which letter(s) represent the water pump?
46. Which letter(s) represent the cooling towers for elimination of waste heat?
47. Which letter(s) represent the reactor vessel?
48. Which letter(s) represent the control rods?
49. Which letter(s) represent the containment-building, a place where a melt down may occur?
50. Which letter(s) represent a cold water cycle?

51. The major emphasis of the Cairo Conference was to:
    a. Address the world's population growth concerns
    b. Draft a treaty to ban whaling worldwide
    c. Discuss the reduction of Greenhouse gases
    d. Reduce the use of DDT worldwide
    e. Sign a treaty that reduces air pollution

52. Among the soil classes, which of the following represents fertile, dark soils found in temperate grassland biomes?
    a. Oxisols
    b. Aridisols
    c. Alfisols
    d. Mollisols
    e. Spodisols

53. A preying mantis would hold what trophic level of the food chain?
    a. First
    b. Second
    c. Third
    d. Fourth
    e. Top

54. If you were arguing the value of saving a rainforest to a congressional panel which major points prove the spending of millions of dollars to achieve this goal?

    I. Sources of Medicine   III. Recreational, Aesthetic
    II. Genetic Bank   IV. Intrinsic

    a. I and II only
    b. III and IV only
    c. I, II, and III
    d. I, II, and IV
    e. I, II, III, IV

55. Biodiversity shows the greatest in which biome?
    a. Temperate rain forest
    b. Desert
    c. Coral reefs
    d. Taiga
    e. Grasslands

56. The Chernobyl incidence that occurred an April 29, 1986, can be best described as:
    a. A complete meltdown of a nuclear reactor caused by human error
    b. A partial meltdown caused by too much coolant water escaping into the atmosphere
    c. An example of how redundancy issued to prevent nuclear accidents
    d. How safety features of nuclear reactors can prevent serious radioactive fallout
    e. A problem that exits with most nuclear reactors

57. The flow diagram of a typical activated sludge sewage treatment facility can be best followed by:
    a. Removal of particulate organic materials...Removal of debris and girt...Removal of colloidal and dissolved material...Disinfection
    b. Removal of debris and girt ...Removal of particulate organic materials......Removal of colloidal and dissolved material...Disinfection
    c. Disinfection...Removal of particulate organic materials...Removal of debris and girt...Removal of colloidal and dissolved material
    d. Removal of organic materials...Removal of debris and girt... Disinfection ...Removal of colloidal and dissolved material
    e. Removal of colloidal and dissolved ...Removal of organic materials...Removal of debris and girt... material...Disinfection

58. One of the proven ways to curtail urban blight is to:
    a. provide a means to give residents ownership in their homes and within the community
    b. use government funds to build more housing developments to encourage growth
    c. give resident a large tax credit or large sums of money to buy goods and services
    d. encourage volunteers to repair the city's infrastructure
    e. make new policy's that prevent urban blight from happening in the first place

59. To be assimilated by higher plants, nitrogen must be present as _____ or _____ ions:
    a. nitrogen, nitrite
    b. ammonium, nitrite
    c. nitrate, nitrite
    d. nitrogen fixation, nitrifying
    e. ammonia, nitrifying

60. A group of plants is grown in an environment without nitrogen fixing bacteria. All of the plants showed poor growth. From this experiment you could conclude that:
    a. Nitrogen fixing bacteria is necessary for the growth of plants
    b. Nitrogen fixing bacteria is not the only factor that slows down plant growth
    c. Nothing can be concluded because no controls were used
    d. The environment should be tested as well to see if that has a similar effect as the lack of nitrogen fixing bacteria
    e. All plants require nitrogen fixing bacteria for growth.

61. Carbon can be removed from the environment/ecosystem by which methods(s)
    a. photosynthesis and oceans
    b. animal respiration
    c. both plant and animal respiration
    d. decomposers such as funguses
    e. carbon fixation

62. Many species of American warblers reduce competition among themselves by feeding at divergent levels and on different parts of trees. This concept may best described as:
    a. habitat selection
    b. survival of the fittest
    c. symbiosis
    d. Optimum zones
    e. resource partitioning

63. You are an environmental scientist studying a particular ecosystem. The study site has variable salinity, and at times is seasonally dry. The area has very high level of nutrients and thick organic sediments. Of the many organisms present, you find that the predominant biota is salt-marsh grass, mangrove swamps, shellfish, crustaceans, and wading birds. The ecosystem you are MOST likely studying is:
    a. Coastal Ocean
    b. Lake or pond
    c. Estuary
    d. Inland wetland
    e. Open Ocean

64. Refer to this diagram and choose the explanation the best describes it's components

    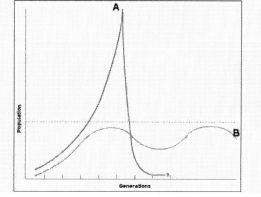

    a. Curve A demonstrates population growth under optimal conditions, while curve B shows a population at equilibrium
    b. Curve B demonstrates population growth under optimal conditions, while curve A shows a population at equilibrium
    c. Both curves show a population explosion under optimal conditions
    d. Both curves show a population at equilibrium
    e. the carrying capacity is different for each population shown.

65. Which of the following factors would be reprehensive of a population that is most likely declining?
    a. ability to cope with adverse conditions
    b. adverse weather conditions
    c. reproduction rate
    d. ability to invade new habitats
    e. ability to migrate or disperse

66. Epiphytic plants such as bromeliads grow on the branches of trees to gain access to sunlight, this symbiotic relationship is considered:
    a. parasitic
    b. competitive
    c. mutualistic
    d. host specific
    e. predator-prey

67. Which of the following is NOT part of the basic principle of ecosystem sustainability:
    a. the size of consumer populations in an ecosystem is maintained such that overgrazing and other forms of overuse do not occur.
    b. Ecosystems show resilience when subject to disturbance
    c. Ecosystems depend on biodiversity
    d. Ecosystems use sunlight as their source of energy
    e. Ecosystems keep waste material and replenish nutrients by recycling all elements

68. Among the following concepts, which is NOT necessary for survival and reproduction:
    a. adaptations for coping with climatic and other abiotic factors
    b. adaptations for obtaining food and water (animals) or nutrients, energy and water (plants)
    c. adaptations for finding and attracting mates (animals) or pollinating and setting seed (plants)
    d. adaptations for staying in the same habitat (animals) or the congregation seeds (plants)
    e. adaptations to deter predators

69. Age structure diagrams of the United States shows that:
    a. deaths before age 60 are relatively high
    b. birth rates were high in the early 1930's due to the Great Depression
    c. birth rates were high after 1946 when veterans returns and started families with relatively large numbers.
    d. population rates minus immigration is increasing at a rate of 3.5
    e. the total fertility rate in the 1990's is about 1.2.

70. Loam textured soils tend to have which of the following characteristics:
    a. 40% sand, 40% silt, 20% clay
    b. 33.3% sand, 33.3% silt, 33.3% clay
    c. 50% sand, 50% silt
    d. 20% sand, 40% silt, 40% clay
    e. 50% sand, 50% clay

71. In a soil profile the O horizon consists of:
    a. topsoil (mixed humus and leached mineral soil)
    b. subsoil (accumulation of leached minerals like iron and aluminum)
    c. weathered parent material (partly broken-down minerals)
    d. Humus (surface litter, decomposing plant material)
    e. Zone of leaching (less humus, minerals resistant to leaching)

A.P. Environmental Science Study Guide - Chapter Five   Awesome Guides, Inc.

72. Which of the following characteristics are necessary to support a soils ecosystem
   i. good supply of nutrients
   ii. good water holding capacity so that little or no infiltration occurs
   iii. low aeration
   iv. pH around 8.5

   a. all of the choices are necessary for a healthy soil ecosystem
   b. i., ii, iv only
   c. i. ii. only
   d. i., iv only
   e. i, only

73. Humus provides all of the following attributes to soil except:
   a. high water holding capacity
   b. high nutrient holding capacity
   c. mineralization
   d. aeration
   e. water infiltration

74. Which of the following is not considered a natural service typically performed by ecosystems?
   a. production of pollutants, as in the natural decomposition processes
   b. erosion control and topsoil building
   c. the control of the earth's climate
   d. maintaining of biogeochemical cycles
   e. regulation of global carbon dioxide

75. The efficiency ratio of the conversion of coal energy to electrical energy is typically about percent?
   a. 5-10%
   b. 15-25%
   c. 30-40%
   d. 50%
   e. 60-75%

76. Most nuclear power plants use _____ fuel as the primary energy source?
   a. 235 U
   b. 238 U
   c. plutonium 239
   d. uranium ore
   e. 239 U

77. What subatomic particles are always released during a nuclear reaction
   a. protons
   b. neutrons
   c. electrons
   d. quarks
   e. plutonium

78. A first generation pesticide is one that:
    a. affects the early development of the target organism
    b. are 100% synthetic
    c. are the most common and safest chemicals used by consumers
    d. are inorganic chemicals such as heavy metals
    e. is the first step in integrated pest management

79. Using sterile males to control insect populations is an example of:
    a. chemical attractants or pheromones that attack insects during reproductive cycles.
    b. how genetically engineered infertile males to control insect populations
    c. effective biological control, since many female insects breed only once in their live time
    d. a biological control that has not proven to be effective
    e. how bacteria's cause sterility in male insects

80. A water quality test in a local lake reveals a somewhat higher than usual level of coliform bacteria. The most probable consequence of the water's quality would be that:
    a. the water is still safe since coliform bacteria is a naturally occurring nonpathogenic bacteria
    b. the water may contain fecal coliform, which is pathogenic
    c. chemical treatment is necessary to prevent a massive fish kill
    d. the water is safe to swim in, but not safe to drink
    e. a lowered biological oxygen demand, BOD

81. An major environmental setback of landfills is that:
    a. dangers associated with methane production
    b. the possibility of groundwater contamination
    c. settling of the compacted materials
    d. sighting new locales that are conducive for landfill construction
    e. all of the above

82. Superfund of 1980 was created to:
    a. clean up abandoned or hazarders waste sites
    b. pay insurance claims to people that are victims of accidental hazardous wastes spills
    c. clean up military nuclear waste sites
    d. fund research into alternative disposal methods for hazardous
    e. clean up waterways that are affected by hazardous wastes

83. According to the provisions of the Resource Conservation and Recovery Act
    a. all states must provide funds for their own toxic waste clean-up
    b. records must be supplied to the federal government concerning the creation, transfer, and disposal of hazardous
    c. all toxic chemicals must be non persistent, recyclable, and pose not immediate threat to human life
    d. any business must obtain the proper license to release toxic chemicals into the environment.
    e. the federal government must provide funds to clean up toxic wastes that are approved by the FDA

84. The U.S. EPA characterizes hazardous wastes on the basis of:
    a. toxicity, carcinogenicity, persistence, and reactivity
    b. molecular weight
    c. ignitability, corrosivity, reactivity, and toxicity
    d. ignitability, corrosivity, reactivity, and environmental persistence
    e. molecular weight and persistence

85. Which of the following atmospheric components is not considered a greenhouse gas
    a. nitrogen oxide
    b. carbon dioxide
    c. methane
    d. water vapor
    e. ozone

86. In 1987, the United Nations convened a conference in Canada to address the problem of ozone depletion. At the conference, affiliate nations reached an agreement to scale back CFC production. This accord is know as the?
    a. Montreal Protocol
    b. Vancouver Principle
    c. CFC UN alliance
    d. Kyoto Agreement
    e. CFC Proscribe Protocol

87. Fluids such as gasoline, paint solvents, and organic cleaning solutions are known to release
    a. nitrogen oxides compounds
    b. sulfur oxides compounds
    c. carbon monoxide
    d. volatile organic compounds
    e. particulate matter

88. Among the following air pollutants, which one has shown the greatest decline in recent years during the 1990's
    a. sulfur dioxide
    b. carbon monoxide
    c. nitrogen oxides
    d. particulates
    e. lead

89. Benefit-cost analysis compares the
    a. estimated costs of a project with the benefits that will be achieved
    b. merits of one project with those of another
    c. tangible with the intangible costs of a project
    d. estimated costs of a project with the expected revenues of the project.
    e. estimated costs of the project with the total life expectancy of the project

90. Which of the following considerations is NOT characteristic of cities with a high degree of livability
    a. high population density
    b. high emphasis on the human dimension in layout and design
    c. high heterogeneity of residences, businesses, stores, and shops
    d. high proportion of land devoted to uses associated with automobiles
    e. high degree of mobility by foot, bicycle, and mass transit

91. The principal adverse environmental impacts of urban sprawl include:
    a. loss of agricultural land
    b. overpopulation, excessive violence, and poor human health
    c. competition for precious land, for instance for waste disposal sites and industrial development
    d. alteration of land, increased energy consumption, and impaired air and water quality
    e. increased commuting time, leading to excessive air pollution and reduced productivity

92. The cause of saltwater intrusion along coastal cities is
    a. replacement of natural dunes with seawalls
    b. excessive irrigation of crops with diluted water
    c. excessive removal of water for the aquifer that open into the ocean
    d. overuse of desalination plants
    e. overuse of cisterns

93. One of the first wildlife protection laws in the United States was the
    a. Muir Condition
    b. Lacey Act
    c. Endangered Species Act
    d. Wildlife Protection Act
    e. Biodiversity Conservation Act

94. A species whose role is absolutely vital for the survival of many other species in an ecosystem is called a(n)
    a. crucial species
    b. key player species
    c. prized species
    d. keystone species
    e. critical species

95. An international agreement that focuses on trade in wildlife and wildlife parts is known as the:
    a. CITES
    b. EPA
    c. NASDAQ
    d. IATWP
    e. GFFC

96. The single largest reason for the current decline in biodiversity worldwide is
   a. pollution
   b. poaching
   c. introduction of exotic species
   d. alteration of habitat
   e. modern technology

97. Forest fragmentation has the **greatest** affect on
   a. specialized species
   b. all species equally
   c. generalist species
   d. mammals
   e. exotic species

98. The Convention on Biological Diversity (CBD) as a result of the 1992 Earth Summit in Rio de Janeiro drafted the subsequent requirements as part of a treaty from all of the nations that participated. Which of the following is NOT part of that treaty:
   a. Adopt specific national biodiversity action plans and strategies
   b. Establish a system of protected areas and ecosystems within a country
   c. Protect threatened species
   d. Restore habitat that has been degraded
   e. Concentrate efforts strictly on naturally occurring organisms other than humans

99. Referring to the idea of maximum sustainable yield (MSY):
   a. once the MSY is reached, the carrying capacity has been passed
   b. a populations rate of sustainable increase at it's maximum level
   c. a populations rate of sustainable increase is at it's minimum level
   d. no system can withstand MSY abuse in terms of pollution
   e. yield is reduced by decreased population

100. The Tragedy of the Commons refers to:
   a. the result of surpassing the optimal population
   b. one person or entity who owns all of the common pool resources
   c. the exploitation of common pool resources
   d. urban sprawl in inner cities communities
   e. a reduced crop yield due to competition

Go to Free Response Questions after a 10 minute break.........

Awesome Guides, Inc.   A.P. Environmental Science Study Guide - Chapter Five

A.P. Environmental Science Practice Test #2
Free Response Questions

You will be answering 4 free response questions on your AP Environmental Science Exam. Many of the questions will have multiple sections. Be sure to answer all sections. You may **NOT** use a calculator. Read each question very carefully. For every essay question, you are awarded 10 points, equaling 40 % of your grade. In addition to the testing hints given at the beginning of your study guide, the following suggestions may further help you in completing the free response questions. **Good luck!**

- Read ALL of the questions first, before attempting to solve or write down your answers. After reading the questions, go to the ones that you feel you are most prepared for, and answer those first. Many times, you recall concepts while answering other questions.

- You can receive partial credit for answers that may not be completely correct. Therefore, be sure to show all of your work, and attempt to answer all sections of each of the free response questions, to the best of your ability, even if you don't know the answer to some sections. Sometimes the part before another is related to the previous section, such as part b, may be related to part c. You may receive some partial credit for answering another related part even though you were not familiar with the previous section.

- Organize your answers and make sure that you write legible and clearly, so that the grader will understand what you are trying to say. If you complete work that you think is incorrect, put an "X" through it.

- Show the steps you used to solve the question.

- Pay attention to units you use in your calculations.

- Your exam booklet will have an insert containing the questions, but no answer sheet. Remove this and use it as a reference; however no credit is given for answers written on this insert. Only answer questions on the official space provided.

- Don't simply jot down a bunch of erroneous or "bogus" answers hoping that they might be correct. Try to focus on the questions asked, and then write down all of the RELATED information about that subject. Graders may actually deduct points for extraneous or incorrect information.

ANSWER THE FOLLOWING QUESTIONS ON YOUR OWN PAPER!

A.P. Environmental Science Study Guide - Chapter Five  Awesome Guides, Inc.

1. Read the article below and answer the questions that follow:

> **Disney Halts Pigeons' Show As Sitting Ducks For Hungry Hawks**
> Call it the circle of life- hungry hawks swooping in and devouring the pigeons released in a flourish at shows and weddings throughout Disney World. This pigeons, used in shows such as Cinderella's Surprise Celebration and at the Magic Kingdom, have become sitting ducks when red-tailed hawks figured out they could count on an easy meal at the same time everyday. But disturbed by the thought of sending birds to almost certain death, Disney this week stopped releasing the homing pigeons- ending a tradition that began 30 years ago.

   (a) Diagram a food chain based on the information above. Describe the flow of energy through that food chain, interrelationships, biotic potential, environmental resistance, and predator-prey relationships.
   (b) Humans have both positive and negative effects on ecosystems. Describe a strategy that Disney World could employ to make a positive environmental impact in-lieu of the situation of banning the release of homing pigeons?
   (c) Homing pigeons are an exotic species to Central Florida, where Disney World is located. Clearly explain what an exotic species is, and environmental problems associated with these organisms.

2. Worldwide, sea levels are rising, and there is no end in site. Making matters even worse, coastal dunes and beaches are being pounded by hurricanes/typhoons, and monster storms, that are larger and more powerful than any in the past known recent history.

   (a) What impacts might these storms have on coastal ecosystems?
   (b) Suggest the cause to the rise in sea level and a solution that would slow the progression.
   (c) Back-up your solution to part (b) using regulations or laws that would support your conclusion.

3. Use the graphs below to answer the questions that follow.

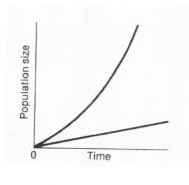

Diagram A

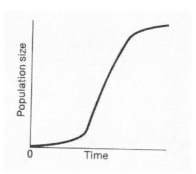

Diagram B

Awesome Guides, Inc.   A.P. Environmental Science Study Guide - Chapter Six

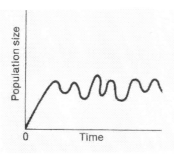

Diagram C   Diagram D

(a) Describe each of the four graphs in terms of their population growth curves.
(b) Using the rule of 70, calculate how many years it will take for a population in diagram to double if the growth rate is 20% per year.
(c) Which population curve would represent a population in equilibrium? Explain your answer.
(d) Which population curve would represent a population of exotic species introduced to a habitable ecosystem? Explain your answer.

4. Answer the questions below regarding an ecosystem study conducted using the quadrant method, in a redwood forest. Assume the following:
   - The ecosystem being studied has 100 hectares (ha), where one hectare equals a 100meter x 100meter square
   - The quadrant method is 90% accurate.
   - Ten random quadrants were investigated of 1 hectare each.
   - Each quadrant averaged the same 20 plant species and 10 animal species.
   - Each quadrant sampling averaged a total of 200 redwood trees, 15 small mammals, 100 invertebrates, and 300 birds.

   (a) Discuss the idea of species diversity in this ecosystem.
   (b) How many <u>actual</u> redwood trees, small mammals, invertebrates, and birds would be expected in this ecosystem?
   (c) Suggest a reason of why so many birds were present in comparison to other animals. Would this be a violation to the 10% rule of energy transfer in ecosystems?
   (d) Why do environmental scientists often use the quadrant method?

A.P. Environmental Science Study Guide - Chapter Six  Awesome Guides, Inc.

Chapter 6
A.P. Environmental Science Practice Test #3

1. Agenda 21 is:
   a. is 21st document based on a static plan of environmental action
   b. an environmental plan adopted by 21 different countries
   c. promotes a plan for sustainable development, globally into the 21st century
   d. is a global agreement addressing 21 major environmental issues
   e. is a plan slated to use early technologies that have been proven successful in the past.

2. The major components of ecosystem structure are:
   a. producers, carnivores, and herbivores
   b. producers, consumers, and decomposers
   c. abiotic and biotic factors
   d. soil, water, minerals, air
   e. food chains, food webs, decomposers, and detritivores

3. Nitrogen fixation refers to:
   a. repairing broken nitrogen molecules
   b. adding fertilizer to plants
   c. releasing nitrogen gas into the atmosphere
   d. converting nitrogen gas to forms plants can use
   e. converting nitrogen gas to forms animals can use

4. Utilities are turning away form nuclear power because of:
   a. government constraints
   b. adverse public opinion
   c. increased costs
   d. concern for the environment
   e. to study alternative energy development and resources

5. The major drawback that geothermal energy, tidal, and wave power all have in common is:
   a. the number of megawatts of electricity produced is too low to sustain a large city.
   b. the technology required for this type of energy conversion is not yet cost effective
   c. the level of environmental damage is too great
   d. the limitations on long tem dependency are uncertain
   e. it promotes dependence of energy from other countries

6. Which of the following is not a **direct** usage of solar power?
   a. conversion to electrical power
   b. passive heating
   c. production of flammable gas
   d. production of biomass to flammable liquids
   e. photovoltaics

7. Hydroelectric power cannot be considered as a power source to a large portion of the population. This is because:
   a. concerns of water pollution
   b. concerns of acid rain deposition
   c. limited geographic distribution
   d. concerns of thermal pollution
   e. high initial and maintenance expense

8. The Dust Bowl of the 1930's was most likely the result of:
   a. Lack of knowledge in practicing modern farming techniques combined with excessive topsoil erosion from runoff.
   b. A large population explosion in he Midwestern states
   c. Technological achievements following World War I, when wheat fields failed to hold soil in place, combined with a drought, causing the loss of large amounts of topsoil
   d. The overgrazing of cattle
   e. A combination of population explosion and overgrazing of cattle.

9. An ecosystem contains which of the following components:
   a. Biotic factors only
   b. Abiotic factors only
   c. Both biotic an abiotic factors
   d. Flora and Fauna
   e. Fauna only

10. The Clean Air Act of 1970 calls for setting ambient standards for which four primary pollutants:
    a. Ozone, particulates, sulfur dioxide, and carbon dioxide
    b. Ozone, particulates, sulfur dioxide, and carbon monoxide
    c. Ozone, particulates, sulfur dioxide, and nitrogen oxides
    d. Particulates, sulfur dioxide, carbon monoxide, and nitrogen oxides
    e. PM10, sulfur dioxide, carbon monoxide, and lead

11. The major factor that has contributed to suburban growth and is blamed for urban sprawl is:
    a. that many farmers sold land to developers
    b. the decline of many services within the central city
    c. the large number of people that own cars
    d. pressure put on farmers to sell land for a profit
    e. groups a noise simply forced residents to leave the city life

12. Of the many types of renewable energy the one that would be most practical for the majority of large cities is:
    a. Wind power
    b. Hydroelectric
    c. Waste to energy/Biogas
    d. Geothermal
    e. Photovoltaic

13. Of the pollutants that adversely affect the air and water resources, the ones that environmental scientists are MOST concerned about that cause global changes are:
    a. toxic chemicals and CFC's
    b. Nutrient oversupply and Pesticides
    c. Acid-forming compounds and Nuclear waste
    d. CFC's and CO2
    e. Nutrient oversupply and Nuclear wastes

14. For a passive solar house to operate with the maximum beneficial affects in reducing energy costs in the Northeastern United States:
    a. Solar collection panels should be places on the roof facing the north exposure
    b. Solar collection panels should be placed on the roof facing the west exposure
    c. Deciduous trees should be planted on the south side of the house
    d. Conifer/evergreen trees should be planted on the south side of the house
    e. Photovoltaic cells could be positioned on the south and west exposures

15. The Highway Trust Fund was developed to:
    a. promote the development of parks and other natural area
    b. benefit both central city and suburban residents
    c. bring people and commerce closer together
    d. aid the inner rural residents, but only disrupts existing communities
    e. build and manage new road project

16. Nitrogen and ammonia return to the atmosphere as nitrogen gas by which of the following processes:
    a. nitrogen fixation
    b. nitrogenation
    c. denitrification
    d. ammonification
    e. nitrogen conversion process (NCP)

17. Environmental Science like other sciences is based on:
    a. one-time events
    b. an idea that tends to give answers to all questions
    c. strives to test value judgments
    d. a slow process that answers questions while at the same time generates more questions
    e. the use of instruments rather than observation

18. In the phosphorus cycle, soil phosphate first enters the ecosystem through:
    a. herbivores
    b. carnivores
    c. green plants
    d. decomposers
    e. third level consumers

19. Trophic levels in an ecosystem may be shown as a pyramid. This is because
    a. Pyramids are very stable and unchanging, like ecosystems
    b. The pyramids shape represents the triangle theory of ecosystem structure
    c. Each point of the pyramid corresponds to the trophic levels in an ecosystem
    d. segments of the pyramid show relative amounts of biomass at each trophic level
    e. Pyramids are NEVER used to represent ecosystems

20. Refer to the survival curve in the diagram and select the correct answer from the chooses below:
    a. The optimal range for an organisms survival is shown by the letter B
    b. The optimum range of survival is shown at each letter C
    c. The range of tolerance is shown at A
    d. The range of tolerance is shown at each letter C
    e. The optimal range for an organisms survival is shown by the letter A

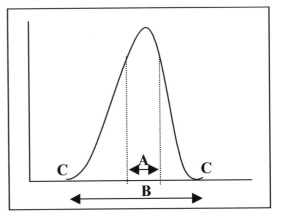

21. On observations of nutrients in certain plant species, Justus von Liebig observed that any one factor outside of the optimal range will cause stress and limited growth, reproduction, and even the survival of a population. We know this concept more commonly as:
    a. the survival of the fittest
    b. the law of limiting factors
    c. the law of optimal ranges
    d. the principle of stress factors
    e. Liebig's Law

22. Among the following forms of energy, choose the list that contains only potential energy sources
    a. battery, gasoline, explosives, electrical power
    b. light and other forms of energy
    c. heat and electrical power
    d. explosives, firewood, gasoline, battery
    e. electrical power, firewood

23. The best example of balanced herbivory could be described as:
    a. the growth of a single species over a wide area
    b. the balance among multiple competing plant populations being maintained by herbivores feeding on them
    c. the balance among herbivore populations that lowers competition and keeps the population in check
    d. the host specific relationship among herbivores
    e. a unified plant population with each species having an equal change of survival.

24. Erosion often leads to desertification. Desertification is BEST described by:
    a. formation and expansion of degraded areas of soil and vegetation cover in semiarid and seasonally dry areas. caused by climatic variations and human activities
    b. the formation of desert pavement which increases the erosion rate by 50%
    c. a consequence of agricultural and ranching, even when good conservations techniques are practices
    d. an ecological process that is part of the normal stages of primary succession
    e. an ecological process that is part of the normal stages of secondary succession.

25. The major reason some farmers practice no-till agriculture is that:
    a. it permits continuous cropping, yet minimizes soil erosion
    b. it is more cost effect that other methods
    c. it is not necessary to control weeds with herbicides
    d. it eliminates the need to make crop furrows
    e. it is mandated by federal law

26. Salinization of soils:
    a. often leaves behind nutrients in the soil that provide plants additional fertilizer
    b. is the process of using weak solutions seawater to irrigate crops
    c. may even be caused by using the freshest irrigation water
    d. is a direct result of soils with a high drainage capacities
    e. is caused by the addition of NaCl alone to soil ecosystems.

27. According to the Hadley cell model that resides over the equator to the subtropics:
    a. raising moist air absorbs moisture as it ascends
    b. dry air absorbs moisture and it descends
    c. trade winds cause horizontal and vertical paths of the cell to flow in south and north directions
    d. the cell is unaffected by trade winds
    e. the cell is unaffected by the earth's rotation

28. The major environmental result of creating power through nuclear fuels is:
    a. sulfer oxide emissions
    b. acid rain
    c. global warming
    d. nitrogen oxide emissions
    e. storing of wastes

29. Nuclear breeder reactors convert:
    a. nonfissable 238U into plutonium
    b. fissionable 235U into 238U
    c. plutonium 239 into 238U
    d. plutonium 239 into 235U
    e. fissionable 235U into plutonium

30. Hydrogen fuel is often considered to solve our energy needs well into the future. Which of the following represents a negative effect of hydrogen power?
    a. it is currently too costly to be considered practical
    b. there is fear that it would disrupt the hydrological cycle
    c. operating temperatures are too high to safely contain waste heat
    d. a primary energy source for refueling hydrogen is not available
    e. it's resources are limited to only a few countries

31. Integrated pest management is the concept that:
    a. all insects can be controlled by using a natural biological or other natural controls.
    b. to have effective pest management, many species of insects must be targeted and controlled at the same time
    c. all nations must control insect populations to have completely effective pest management
    d. uses broad spectrum pesticides is control pests
    e. uses first-generation pesticides

32. One of the most effective classes of modern non-persistent pesticides that are not persistent and have low toxicity to mammals are the:
    a. chlorinated hydrocarbons
    b. organophosphates
    c. trioxins
    d. pyrethroids
    e. chlordanes

33. Benthos organisms are very susceptible to water pollution. These organisms:
    a. represent the microorganisms in a body of water
    b. include both the green and blue-green(cyanobacteria) alga
    c. are found living or rooted on the lakes bottom
    d. live within the photo zone
    e. lack the proper immune systems to filter pollutants

34. Bodies of water that are eutrophic or hypereutrophic typically exhibit:
    a. high nutrients and low visibility
    b. low nutrients and high visibility
    c. oligotrophic characteristics
    d. a low level of primary and secondary productivity
    e. are considered "dead" lakes

35. Chlorine is often added to wastewater for disinfection before effluent discharge. A potential problem with this procedure is that:
    a. chlorine is dangerous to these handling it as well as a potentially hazardous during transport
    b. chlorine is expensive and not very effective
    c. chlorine causes toxic hydrocarbons to be formed
    d. chlorine is a major air pollutant leading to global warming
    e. chlorine is an now renewable resource thus supplies are finite

36. One impediment to the use of treated sludge as agricultural fertilizer is
    a. in some cases, sludge contains toxic metals
    b. sludge contains high levels of bacteria
    c. that there is probability of ground water contamination
    d. excess nitrogen may eutrophy nearby bodies of water
    e. human waste is low in nutrients

37. The largest single component of municipal solid waste (MSW) is:
    a. paper and paper products
    b. plastics
    c. food waste
    d. year waste
    e. disposable diapers

38. The average American generates approximately _____ pound(s) of solid waste daily.
    a. ½ pound
    b. 4 pounds
    c. 14 pounds
    d. 24 pounds
    e. 44 pounds

A.P. Environmental Science Study Guide - Chapter Six  Awesome Guides, Inc.

39. The federal program created in 1980 known as the superfund goes by the acromymn:
    a. SARA
    b. FIFRA
    c. CERCLA
    d. TSCA
    e. RCRA

40. Releases of toxic chemicals to the air are about _____ imes _____ than those to water
    a. 10 and lower
    b. 10 and higher
    c. 2 and lower
    d. 2 and higher
    e. 4 and lower

41. A the EPA's definition of a "brownfield" site is one that:
    a. is abandoned, idled, or under-used industrial and commercial facilities where expansion or redevelopment is complicated by real or perceived environmental contamination
    b. is an abandoned oil field where the land is rendered unsuitable for habitation
    c. is a tract of farmland that has been battered severely by fungus blight where no products may be sold for a period of 1 year.
    d. is an abandoned coal mine
    e. is an abandoned waste water treatment facility

42. What is the shortest wavelength of light visible to reach the human eye?
    a. red
    b. orange
    c. yellow
    d. violet
    e. green

43. The lowest layer of the atmosphere, extending up to 10 miles in the tropics, is referred to as the:
    a. aesthenosphere
    b. troposphere
    c. stratosphere
    d. tropopause
    e. first tropic layer

44. "Where there are threats of serious or irreversible damage, lack of full scientific certainty shall not be used as a reason for postponing cost-effective measures to prevent environmental degradation" This statement is known as the :
    a. Pollution Pervention Principle
    b. Environmental All or Nothing Percausion
    c. Percautionary Principle
    d. Environmental Cost is not a Consideration Principle
    e. The Three C's

45. Which of the following statements would not be a consequence of depletion of the stratospheric ozone layer?
    a. amplified occurrence of severe sun burns
    b. increased occurrence of cataracts
    c. amplified rates of melanoma
    d. increased incidence of premature skin aging
    e. increased rates of lung cancer

46. Among the following air pollutants, which has shown the least decline during the 1990's?
    a. nitrogen oxides
    b. sulfur dioxide
    c. carbon monoxide
    d. lead
    e. particulates

47. Which of the subsequent chemicals has been able to effect the formation of acids in the atmosphere?
    a. carbon monoxide and lead
    b. volatile organic compounds and radon
    c. nitrogen oxides and sulfur oxides
    d. benzene and vinyl chloride
    e. CFC's and asbestos

48. Over the past fifty years, the principal influence on urban planning has been
    a. isolation of residential, commercial, and industrial development
    b. architectural colossal structures such as the Sears Tower
    c. adjustments for an automobile-based lifestyle
    d. larger, more comfortable residential housing
    e. planning for the provision of larger green space within cities

49. Technology is available for the desalination of seawater by reverse osmosis or microfiltration. Why are there methods not used more frequently since our planet is covered with seawater?
    a. there is fear that ocean levels may drop
    b. models show that global climate will be affected
    c. it is three to six times more expensive that using ground or other surface waters
    d. removing large quantities if seawater will adversely affect marine organisms
    e. removal is too much seawater could cause an increase in the sea's salinity

50. Of the arguments against the use of transgenic crops and animals, the one that may have the greatest negative environmental impact is:
    a. the spreading of genetically mutated organisms, or GMO's to other non target organisms
    b. that it may cause a second "Green Revolution" increasing birth rates to critical levels
    c. food produced will not have the proper nutrients thus leading to malnutrition
    d. loss of biodiversity in wild species
    e. transgenic organism have no role in modern food production

51. Loss of the once common passenger pigeons that clouded the skies during the 18th and 19th centuries is a result of:
    a. massive habitat destruction
    b. relentless hunting with little to no restrictions
    c. introduction of exotic species
    d. introduced disease
    e. climatic changes

52. The benefit of a species' existence or its use to another entity, often humans, gives the species a(n)
    a. economic value
    b. intrinsic value
    c. instrumental value
    d. biological value
    e. anthropomorphic value

53. Among vertebrate groups in the United States, the group with the largest number of endangered species is what?
    a. amphibians
    b. birds
    c. reptiles
    d. mammals
    e. fishes

54. In general, it can be said that forests are:
    a. declining in hectares worldwide
    b. increasing in hectares worldwide
    c. increasing in hectares the developing countries only
    d. declining in hectares in only the most populated regions
    e. declining in developing countries and increasing in developed countries

55. Whales found in the open ocean have been heavily depleted by overexploitation. In 1974 this practice was halted by the International Whaling Commission (IWC) by a moratorium. Still, more than 18,000 whales have died since the moratorium. This is due to:
    a. excessive ocean pollution
    b. habitat destruction
    c. global warming
    d. continued harvesting by Japan, Norway and indigenous peoples of some northern countries
    e. disease and strikes by large ships

56. In 1997-98, El Nino brought record high temperature to many tropical regions. The event caused:
    a. the death of zooxanthellae algae, leading to coral bleaching
    b. a lessening effect of global warming
    c. major animal migrations to new habitats
    d. redistribution of native plant species
    e. a more lush rainforest habitat

Awesome Guides, Inc. A.P. Environmental Science Study Guide - Chapter Six

57. The forest service allows multiple use of public lands. Multiple use means that the land may be used for:
   a. recreation only
   b. recreation, and protection of watersheds
   c. protection of watersheds, wildlife, and recreation
   d. protection of resources, organisms, recreation, plus activities such as grazing, logging and mining
   e. preservation only

58-61 Refer to the diagrams A and B below to answer the following questions:

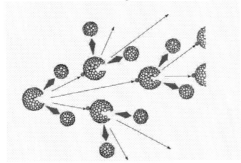
Diagram A

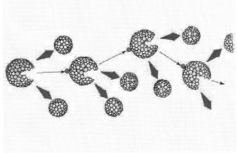
Diagram B

   a. self-amplifying chain reaction
   b. sustaining chain reaction
   c. nuclear explosion
   d. neutrons to be acted upon by control rods
   e. chain reaction

58. Diagram A represents a _____
59. Diagram B represents a _____
60. Diagram A may cause_____
61. Diagram B may cause_____

62. The core of a nuclear reactor is:
   a. large mass of uranium set in adjacent tubes
   b. moderate red by plutonium
   c. is controlled by neutron-releasing rods
   d. uses only heavy water as a moderator
   e. amplifies the normal chain reaction

63. Among the major disadvantages of wind power is:
   a. relativity low level of electricity produced
   b. high level of environmental damage
   c. size/space limitations of the turbines
   d. large maintenance cost
   e. migratory and local bird species

64. A major disadvantage of hydrogen production by solar technology is that:
   a. many oil companies will be out of business, thus crippling the economy
   b. handling of hazardous wastes is too precarious
   c. production of free hydrogen atoms
   d. disruption of the hydrological cycle
   e. cost-effectiveness

65. Estimates of world population growth put the number of people on earth at _____ by 2054:
    a. 20 billion
    b. 30 billion
    c. 9 billion
    d. 30 million
    e. 20 million

66. The decline of biodiversity may be attributed to many factors. Choose the factors that MOST represent this decline?

    I. Habitat destruction
    II. Fragmentation
    III. Erosion Control
    IV. Keystone species introduction

    a. I, and II only are correct
    b. I, II, and IV only are correct
    c. II, III, and IV only are correct
    d. I, II, III only are correct
    e. All are correct

67. Among the main issues concerning greenhouse gases, especially CO2, are
    a. Increased soil erosion in tropical regions
    b. Major changes in global climate
    c. Lower temperatures within the troposphere
    d. Energy strategies that have greater dependence on nuclear fuels
    e. A 2% increase in carbon dioxide in the troposphere

68. To make nuclear fuel, uranium ore is mined. Purified into uranium dioxide and enriched. The reason that best describes this enrichment is that:
    a. Nuclear fuel must be completely free of contaminants before using in a reaction
    b. 99.3% of uranium ore is non-fissionable 238U.
    c. 238U is separated from 235U so that 238U can be used in breeder reactors
    d. Impurities in the fuel may cause a meltdown in the reactor
    e. Uranium ore contains explosive gases that make transport dangerous

69. The widespread use of DDT has:
    a. Saved millions of lives in developing countries
    b. Caused a lower biomagnification level among most species
    c. Tends to thicken egg shells in many bird of prey species
    d. Made it necessary to ban its use worldwide
    e. Had the greatest effects on the lower trophic levels where it is primarily used.

70. Examples of non-point resources are:
    a. Cropland
    b. Wastewater treatment discharge
    c. Factory discharges
    d. Any discharge directly into a body of water
    e. Any discharge where the original source is easy to identify

71. The higher the level of BOD the greater likelihood of:
    a. Higher DO levels and lower fish kills
    b. Aerobic conditions in the body of water
    c. Pathogens entering the water
    d. Oxygen depletion
    e. Inorganic chemicals

72. An major environmental consequence of urban sprawl is:
    a. depletion of energy sources
    b. air, water and soil pollution
    c. the Greenhouse effect
    d. loss of agriculture land
    e. Decline of song birds populations within the inner cities.

73. Grass in typical neighborhood lawns tends to be greener after a thunderstorm because:
    a. The water taken up by root hairs is necessary to produce chlorophyll.
    b. the plant would wilt, turn brown and die with out water
    c. the dust that forms around rain droplets is a natural fertilizer
    d. lightning is able to break the triple covalent bond in atmospheric nitrogen gas later forming into nitrate which the plants uptake
    e. it causes natural fertilizer in the soil to dissolve

74. Theories are:
    a. tested in much the same way as a hypothesis
    b. are not subject to change
    c. do not use if-than reasoning
    d. difficult to change due to the many fact that support them
    e. are rarely revised

75. Among the biogeochemical cycles in the ecosystem all are recycled except:
    a. nitrogen
    b. phosphorus
    c. carbon
    d. energy
    e. biota

76. Suppose that a section of eastern deciduous forest were cleared for agriculture and later abandoned. In what order sequential order would new ecosystems be produced?
    a. grasses, hardwood trees, pine trees, small perennials
    b. grasses, small perennials, pine trees, hardwood trees
    c. Hardwood trees, pine trees, small perennials, grasses
    d. grasses, pine trees, small perennials, hardwood trees
    e. grasses, crabgrass's, hardwood trees, pine trees

77. Synergistic effects on organisms are best described as:
    a. A single environmental factor that affects an organism change or survival.
    b. only biotic factors that affect an organisms growth
    c. only abiotic factors that affect an organisms growth
    d. Two or more factors that affect an organism's growth are interacting together and combined, have a much greater effect combines than each of the two acting separately.
    e. The increasing stress from the optimal range that determines the range of tolerance and the limits of tolerance of any one particular organism.

78. During a field study, an environmental scientist makes the following observations:
    I. Climate and Soil: non seasonal, average temperatures of 28° C soils thin and poor in nutrients
    II. Flora and Fauna: high diversity of broad-leafed trees, dense canopy, epiphytes, little under story, numerous colorful insects.
    The scientist is MOST likely in which biome:
    a. Tropical Rainforest
    b. Temperate Forest
    c. Coniferous Forest
    d. Grasslands
    e. Chaparral

79. In 1859 rabbits were introduced to Australia from England, and used for sport hunting. The most probable direct result of this introduction is that:
    a. many hunters were attracted to the area, increasing human population which in turn wiped our many other species
    b. rabbits were not able to adapt to the new harsh environment of Australia and most died
    c. the rabbit population increased rapidly due to lack of predators, leading to overgrazing of rangeland
    d. many rabbits died, but among those that survived, a superior breed emerged whose populations were kept in check by the hunters
    e. rabbit populations reached there carrying capacity and remain stable according the laws of nature.

80. To ecologists, a forest fire in an ecosystem
    a. represents a destructive force that kills many plants and animals
    b. is absolutely necessary to the survival of many ecosystems
    c. is not necessary because fungus and soil bacteria handle most of an ecosystems recycling needs
    d. is usually the result of arsonists
    e. should never be controlled

81. Speciation among individual populations of organisms occurs when:
    a. there is a lack of physical barriers that separate one organism for another
    b. consistent environmental conditions exist
    c. reproduction isolation along with different environmental conditions exist
    d. genes on DNA have the same alleles
    e. organisms produce clone populations

82. Tectonic plates are:
    a. stationary
    b. the cause of continental drift
    c. form convergent plates at mid-ocean ridges
    d. form divergent plates producing a subduction zone
    e. form transform faults when plates move horizontally past each other

83. The main distinction between developing and developed countries is that:
    a. developing countries have a much higher fertility rate
    b. developed countries have a much higher fertility rate
    c. developed countries have a higher gross national product
    d. developing countries have a higher gross national product
    e. developing countries have a lower per capita birth rate.

84. Negative consequences that may be a result of a population explosion among human populations include (Choose the best answer from the selections below):

    i.   over cultivation
    ii. poaching of wildlife
    iii. mitigation
    iv. loss of biodiversity
    v.   antibiotic resistant strains of malaria, STD's etc.

    a. all of the above are results of human populations explosion
    b. i.. ii., and iv are all correct
    c. i. and iv only are correct
    d. i., ii., iv., v. are all correct
    e. i., iii., iv. and v. are all correct

85. Soils characterized as having the most "workability", that is the ease of cultivation for crop are:
    a. those with high water holding capacity such as clays
    b. those with high permeability, such a sands
    c. those with high pH
    d. those with low pH
    e. clayey-loams

86. The smallest percent of total land area of the Earth falls into in which of the following land types?
    a. croplands
    b. grass lands and savannas
    c. desert and tudras
    d. forest and woodlands
    e.

87. Which of the following whale species is thought to be the most serious in terms of being in danger of extinction?
    a. humpback
    b. sperm
    c. blue gray
    d. minke
    e. blue

88. Which of the following practices would allow exploitation of forest resources without forest destruction?
    a. sustainable logging
    b. ecotourism
    c. cacao and rubber plantations
    d. extractive reserves
    e. all of the above

89. A nations power grid is
    a. a network of all major power lines that is sold to power suppliers on the open market
    b. the sum of available resources of a particular type of fossil fuel
    c. the sum of all the power generated by a power plant
    d. a schematic showing the location of power plants
    e. is the sum of all power generated by alternative energy sources

90. In the United States as well as other developed countries, typical indoor air pollutions include:
    a. asbestos
    b. animal wastes
    c. pesticides
    d. parasites
    e. all of the above

91. Pesticides such as DDT have been banned in the United States because
    a. many insects have grown resistant "super" strains that cause more severe disease
    b. it is persistent in the ecosystem
    c. it causes air pollution that directly destroys ozone
    d. all NATO countries have chosen also chosen to stop it use
    e. it has a history or causing death or genetic disease among human populations

92. Biological oxygen demand or BOD is a measure of the:
    a. total oxygen used by organisms in an ecosystem
    b. total oxygen needed by a particular organism
    c. oxygen using potential of water, wastewater, or other organic substances
    d. ideal oxygen level needed for an organism to reach its optimum range
    e. range of tolerance that organisms can exist in low oxygen environments

93. The ideal modern sewage treatment facility is one that:
    a. everyone handles there own waste on site by means of a septic system
    b. all sewage and storm water are collected together and used for irrigation
    c. sewage and storm water are collected treated together
    d. sewage and storm water are collected and treated separately
    e. all treatment of storm water and sewage are treated by tertiary methods

94. Primary sewage treatment involves the :
    a. treatment of CFC's before they enter the ecosystem
    b. use biological treatment through microorganisms
    c. removal suspended organic matter and particulates
    d. removal nitrates and phosphates
    e. fist step in disinfection of disease causing bacteria

Awesome Guides, Inc. A.P. Environmental Science Study Guide - Chapter Six

95. Among the many materials that can be reused, which of the following components of municipal solid wastes can be recycled?
    a. paper
    b. some plastics
    c. metals
    d. glass
    e. all of the above

96. Which of the following statements does not apply to the use of municipal solid waste (MSW) waste-to-energy (WTE) facilities?
    a. WTE facilities use almost 99% of the MSW waste, therefore eliminating the need to landfill
    b. WTE facilities are able to make large amounts of energy
    c. WTE facilities generate little to NO air pollution
    d. WTE facilities do not typically use materials that are normally recycled
    e. WTE facilities significantly reduce material that is placed in a sanitary landfill.

97. Toxic synthetic organic compounds frequently found in chemical waste dumps have been shown to cause:
    a. liver disease
    b. birth defects
    c. nervous system disorders
    d. cancer
    e. all of the above

98. Environmental issues surrounding the Love Canal are still of concern today. The Love Canal was a:
    a. sanitary landfill that leaked wastes into the Love Canal
    b. a chemical dump site located in a suburban neighborhood and school
    c. a chemical dump site that accidentally discarded toxic waste into the Love Canal, later affecting the adjoining estuary
    d. a government testing site left abandoned, lower property values, and dangerous living conditions to the neighboring communities
    e. a water way, so polluted, that it caught on fire

99. Where carcinogens are concerned, EPA generally
    a. believes that current levels are low enough and does not require regulation
    b. assumes that high levels can be tolerated if exposure is brief
    c. takes a zero-dose, zero-response approach
    d. assumes that a threshold level exists
    e. requires warning labels, but does not prevent their use.

100. Which of the following greenhouse gas is entirely anthropogenic in origin?
    a. methane gas
    b. halogenated hydrocarbons
    c. water vapor
    d. carbon dioxide
    e. nitrogen oxides

Go to Free Response Questions after a 10 minute break.........

A.P. Environmental Science Study Guide - Chapter Six  Awesome Guides, Inc.

A.P. Environmental Science Practice Test #3 Free Response Questions

You will be answering 4 free response questions on your AP Environmental Science Exam. Many of the questions will have multiple sections. Be sure to answer all sections. You may NOT use a calculator. Read each question very carefully. For every essay question, you are awarded 10 points, equaling 40 % of your grade. In addition to the testing hints given at the beginning of your study guide, the following suggestions may further help you in completing the free response questions. **Good luck!**

- Read ALL of the questions first, before attempting to solve or write down your answers. After reading the questions, go to the ones that you feel you are most prepared for, and answer those first. Many times, you recall concepts while answering other questions.

- You can receive partial credit for answers that may not be completely correct. Therefore, be sure to show all of your work, and attempt to answer all sections of each of the free response questions, to the best of your ability, even if you don't know the answer to some sections. Sometimes the part before another is related to the previous section, such as part b, may be related to part c. You may receive some partial credit for answering another related part even though you were not familiar with the previous section.

- Organize your answers and make sure that you write legible and clearly, so that the grader will understand what you are trying to say. If you complete work that you think is incorrect, put an "X" through it.

- Show the steps you used to solve the question.

- Pay attention to units you use in your calculations.

- Your exam booklet will have an insert containing the questions, but no answer sheet. Remove this and use it as a reference; however no credit is given for answers written on this insert. Only answer questions on the official space provided.

- Don't simply jot down a bunch of erroneous or "bogus" answers hoping that they might be correct. Try to focus on the questions asked, and then write down all of the RELATED information about that subject. Graders may actually deduct points for extraneous or incorrect information.

ANSWER THE FOLLOWING QUESTIONS ON YOUR OWN PAPER!

Awesome Guides, Inc. A.P. Environmental Science Study Guide - Chapter Six

1. Nuclear power plants currently generate about 20% of electric power in the United States. There were 104 plants in operation, down from 112, at the latter part of 2000. Worldwide, there are 433 operating nuclear power plants with 37 additional under construction, generating about 17% of the worlds electricity, with France generating 75% of it's electricity by nuclear power.

    (a) Identify two justifications why the US may have decommissioned some of its nuclear power facilities.

    (b) Give 2 supplementary practical applications that nuclear energy is currently being used in.

    (c) Describe each of the following concepts regarding nuclear energy

        (i)   The fuel used in nuclear plants
        (ii)   Breeder reactors
        (iii)   Biological effects
        (iv)   Fusion reactors

    (d) Describe the potential hazards of nuclear power generation by providing an example of a nuclear accident that has already occurred.

2. After reading the following excerpt from an article used taken from Orlando Sentinel, Sunday July 14, 2002, Section K, about an issue relating to storm water, answer parts (a), (b), (c) which follow.

> ### Sewage Could Fill Street Again
> Sanford officials are trying to figure out how to prevent the kind of raw sewage leak that recently forced the city to close down a portion of Seminole Boulevard for more than a week. Heavy rainfall overloaded the city's sewer system at the start of the month, forcing storm water runoff and raw sewage to flow out of a manhole. An undetermined amount of storm water spilled onto the street through a drain hole pipe into Lake Monroe over a period of three days before the rain subsided. The problem arose because heavy rain caused a rise in groundwater levels.

    (a) Give another reason that sewage may leak into the ecosystem besides those given above.
    (b) In terms of point and nonpoint pollution, pathogens, organic wastes and chemical pollutions, describe what possible outcomes might occur to Lake Monroe.
    (c) State two water quality standards and the federal regulations that support water quality standards.

3. Students at Lake Highland High School found historical data collected on Lemming population cycles at Point Barrow, Alaska from 1946 to 1966. Lemming are small mouse like rodents that live in treeless tundra and subtundra habitats. On the next page are their findings:

A.P. Environmental Science Study Guide - Chapter Six   Awesome Guides, Inc.

Year	Lemming per Acre
1946	30
1947	4
1948	6
1949	30
1950	4
1951	4
1952	20
1953	40
1954	5
1955	15
1956	35
1957	6
1958	3
1959	8
1960	60
1961	5
1962	7
1963	20
1964	7
1965	30
1966	7

(a) Suggest reasons why the Lemming populations have fluctuated between 1946 and 1966?
(b) Describe the carrying capacity (K) of the Lemming population, as well environmental resistance, and density-dependent and independent mortality factors.
(c) Design an experiment that tests the relationship between Lemming populations and the introduction of a keystone species to the area.

4. World population is increasing exponentially.
   (a) Explain what exponential growth is, and under what circumstances it is occurring in human populations?
   (b) Compare the population growth rates among developing countries and developed countries, and justifications for any differences.
   (c) Diagram a population growth curve for a developed and developing country.
   (d) Discuss the concept of Agenda 21.

Awesome Guides, Inc. A.P. Environmental Science Study Guide - Appendix A

Appendix A Practice Test #1 Answer Sheet Key

1. E
2. E
3. C
4. D
5. A
6. E
7. E
8. E
9. A
10. B
11. A
12. E
13. A
14. C
15. D
16. E
17. A
18. E
19. C
20. E
21. E
22. E
23. C
24. A
25. E
26. C
27. C
28. E
29. B
30. E
31. A
32. E
33. D
34. E
35. B
36. C
37. D
38. D
39. D
40. C
41. A
42. E
43. C
44. A
45. E
46. D
47. B
48. E
49. D
50. C
51. E
52. E
53. E
54. D
55. B
56. E
57. D
58. E
59. C
60. B
61. D
62. A
63. C
64. B
65. E
66. D
67. A
68. C
69. B
70. C
71. E
72. B
73. D
74. D
75. E
76. B
77. C
78. E
79. A
80. D
81. E
82. E
83. D
84. D
85. E
86. C
87. D
88. A
89. E
90. D
91. D
92. A
93. E
94. E
95. D
96. D
97. A
98. E
99. E
100. D

A.P. Environmental Science Study Guide - Appendix B  Awesome Guides, Inc.

Appendix B Practice Test #1 Subject Index
Comparison

Compare the questions that you missed on Practice Test #1 to this subject index to see what areas or concepts that you are weak in.

- If you missed questions 1, 7, 23, 28, 31, 32, 45, 57, 61, 67, 72, 89, then you should review the concepts related to environmental rules and regulations, human communities and society, and environmental ethics and sustainability.
- If you missed questions 30, 34, 100, then you should review the concepts related to biodiversity, ecosystem destruction, and global changes.
- If you missed questions 2, 14, 36, 39, 42, 59, 64, 85, then you should review the concepts related to ecosystem structure and general ecology.
- If you missed questions 3, 4, 15, 26, 65, 91, then you should review the concepts related to ecosystems and how they function.
- If you missed questions 22, 23, 93, then you should review the concepts related to population ecology and ecological succession.
- If you missed questions 6, 8, 13, 41, 50, 73, 74, then you should review the concepts related to changes in ecosystems, natural selection, plate tectonics, environmental genetics, and evolution.
- If you missed questions 3, 9, 10, 16, 29, 71, 82, 88, 94, 98, then you should review the concepts related to human demographics and populations, comparisons of developing and developed countries.
- If you missed questions 18, 25, 33, 66, 70, then you should review the concepts related to geotechnical science (soils).
- If you missed questions 6, 35, 38, 52, 54, then you should review the concepts related to water environmental quality.
- If you missed questions 55, 84, then you should review the concepts related to food production.
- If you missed questions 24, 27, then you should review the concepts related to biodiversity of the world's wild species of animals and plants.
- If you missed questions 2, 5, 17, 68, 69, then you should review the concepts related to the worlds' resources.
- If you missed questions 20, 49, then you should review the concepts related to fossil fuels.
- If you missed questions 12, 19, 44, 53, 86, 92, then you should review the concepts related to nuclear power.
- If you missed questions 77, 78, 81, 83, 97, then you should review the concepts related to renewable energy.
- If you missed question 11, then you should review the concepts related to human environmental hazards, and toxicology.
- If you missed questions 21, 58, 76, 95, then you should review the concepts related to pests and their control.
- If you missed questions 37, 40, 43, 46, 51, 63, 75, 79, then you should review the concepts related to water pollution.
- If you missed questions 48, 99, then you should review the concepts related to solid waste.
- If you missed questions 62, 96, then you should review the concepts related to hazardous chemicals.
- If you missed questions 47, 56, 60, 80, 87, 90, then you should review the concepts related to the atmosphere.

Awesome Guides, Inc.   A.P. Environmental Science Study Guide - Appendix C

Appendix C Practice Test #1 Answer Key & Rubrics

1. e
Urban blight occurs when conditions within a city decline. This causes businesses to close resulting in unemployment. As the tax base declines cities can no longer afford to clean up and repair it's infrastructure, thus creating lower property values and reduction in local services.

2. e
Forest sustainability refers to the use of an intact forest and it's products. This is opposite to deforestation or clear cutting. An intact forest provides many services such as carbon storage, oxygen production, carbon dioxide reduction, biodiversity, and climate moderation. It also prevents erosion.

3. c
Population profiles may represent developed and undeveloped countries. Developed countries tend to have low fertility rates, and if the fertility rate continues to be low over a period of time, then the profile will show an increased older population with a declining population of children and young people.

4. d
Primary production within ecosystems is a very inefficient process, capturing only about 2% of the solar radiation from the sun. Even though this is a small fraction of the energy available it still accounts for a very large amount of energy produced.

5. a
The "tragedy of the commons" refers to a resource that may or may not be owned, but is used by many people. Examples of this include: private ranchers using federally owned grasslands or commercial fisheries using the open ocean. This concept of tens leads to the exploitation of these common resources and typically causes a decline or destruction of these resources.

6. e
The earth's crust is composed of large slabs of floating rock. These are called tectonic plates. Tectonic plates move slowly causing the plates to converge (coming together forming a subduction zone). They can diverge (move apart, spreading) or they can transform (move laterally past each other). All of these can cause volcanism, earthquakes, formation of mountains, oceanic ridges and continental drift.

7. e
A sustainable society means that resources are used and reused without permanently destroying or harming the environment. Sustainable societies can theoretically continue to survive indefinitely without depleting resources. Things like reducing your personal consumption of resources, reusing products, making sound environmental decisions and supporting environmental organizations all lead to a sustainable society.

8. e
Both plants and animals adapt to their environment. Among the most common adaptations organisms have are coping with abiotic factors (heavy fur, flying south, hibernation, cold hardiness, deciduous, bulbs), obtaining food (quick moving tongue, long neck, extensive roots and root hairs), escaping predation (running ability, quills, bad smell, cryptic coloration, thorns, poisonous chemicals), finding and attracting mates (exotic plumage, pheromones, bright colors) migration and seed dispersal (clinging burs, parachutes or wings on seeds).

A.P. Environmental Science Study Guide - Appendix C  Awesome Guides, Inc.

9. a
To calculate doubling time of a population increasing at a constant rate you would divide the percent of growth rate (4.5%) into 70 (derived from the population growth equation and has nothing to do with the population) .70/4.5% = 155 years

10. b
Developing countries typically show a fertility rate that is well above the replacement level. This means that the age structure has larger numbers of young people. Because of the large number of young people at reproductive age, a declining fertility rate will take many years to show a reduction in the overall population size.

11. a
Heavy metals such as arsenic, aluminum and mercury from industrial chemicals pollute air & water. Hydrocarbons, particulate matter (PAN's) and volatile organic compounds are found in the air of urban areas. Asbestos is found in insulation of some homes and commercial buildings.

12. e
Half life is the time for half of the amount of a radioactive isotope to decay and for plutonium that time is 24,000 years.

13. a
Gene Pool is the total sum of all of the individuals of a particular species.

14. c
Consumers in an ecosystem are those organisms that cannot produce their own food through raw materials. Consumers may be herbivores, carnivores, omnivores or parasites.

15. c
A calorie is the amount of heat it takes to raise one gram of water one degree celsius.

16. e
Environmental resistance is the sum of all factors that lead to population decline and keep them from growing or spreading. Some of these factors include, shortages of food and water, predation, and disease. Since developing countries continue to **increase** in their population and are continuing to spreading out, then by the strict definition of environmental resistance the choices above have not caused the population to decline. For factors to be considered environmental resistance they must cause the population to decline.

17. a
Coral bleaching is the loss of photosynthetic algae that shares a symbiotic relationship with the corals. The zooxanthellae algae are found in corals that occur in water 75 meters or shallower. This has resulted in the death of 15% of the world's coral reefs during the summer of 1998. It is associated with high temperatures and high light intensities, but the exact cause is unknown.

18. e
Salinization is the accumulation of salts in the soil due to excessive irrigation. Salinization occurs because fresh water used in irrigation contains between 150- 600 ppm of dissolved salts. As the water evaporates salt is left behind and accumulates in the soil.

Awesome Guides, Inc. A.P. Environmental Science Study Guide - Appendix C

19. c
Breeder reactors use nonfissionable uranium 238. U238 absorbs extra neutrons converting it into plutonium 239, which is fissionable. The plutonium is then used as a nuclear fuel.

20. e
More efficient cars, lowering speed limits, better building insulation and more efficient appliances, all decrease the demand for and consumption of fossil fuels.

21. e
A pest could be any organism that is noxious, destructive or troublesome. This includes both animals and plants.

22. e
All populations of organisms need a critical number of species to maintain a population. If the population drops below the critical number then factors such as inbreeding, disease and predation can stop population from increasing and may cause extinction.

23. c
Biotic potential is the rate at which organisms can increase in number under ideal conditions. Biotic potential factors include: reproductive rate, ability to migrate or disperse, defense mechanisms or the ability to cope with adverse conditions. Environmental resistance includes factors that limit population size. Environmental resistance factors include: disease, parasitism, adverse weather conditions, lack of water, food or nutrients and habitat destruction.

24. a
Biodiversity refers to the variety of life. Any disruption of a habitat can cause loss of biodiversity. These include: pollution, exotic species, physical alteration of habitats such as conversion and fragmentation. Controlled hunting limits the number and kind of organisms harvested. Some taxes from the purchase of hunting equipment are used to buy conservation and breeding areas. Many duck populations have actually increased since controlled hunting began.

25. e
Humus is the top layer of soil composed of surface litter and decomposing plant matter.

26. c
Anthropogenic refers to a human process. Forest fires, decomposition of leaf litter, aerobic respiration and volcanic eruptions are all natural processes. Internal combustion, burning of fossil fuels, is a human process.

27. c
The Endangered Species Act of 1973 expired and was reauthorized in 1988. Both environmentalists and developers criticize it because developers believe that the ESA is too strict and threatens jobs. Environmentalists criticize the act because species are not protected until they are listed as endangered or threatened.

28. e
Reducing pollution control techniques provides new jobs, cleans the environment, reduces worker illness and takes advantage of recycled materials.

A.P. Environmental Science Study Guide - Appendix C  Awesome Guides, Inc.

29. a
Replacement fertility rate refers to the rate that just replaces the parents, it's slightly greater than 2.0 and is slightly higher in developing countries.

30. e
A sustainable society is one that is able to maintain the resources it currently has. The use of sound science and stewardship in decision making provides the best opportunities towards a sustainable society.

31. a
Urban sprawl refers to the spreading out of a city and its services. If not for the automobile, more people and businesses would have remained in the cities.

32. e
Atmosphere pollutants from most human activities are confined to the troposphere, the 1st. layer of the atmosphere. The stratosphere, the second layer of the atmosphere, contains the majority of ozone and is polluted by CFC's. Ozone is a productive layer that filters out ultraviolet radiation.

33. d
A typical soil profile consists of an O horizon (humus), A horizon (topsoil), and E horizon (zone of leaching where less humus and minerals are present). The E horizon gets its name from elevation or leaching downward of minerals. The B-horizon is next, and is subsoil and an accumulation of leached material. Finally, the C-horizon is the parent material.

34. e
The environmental movement started when people began to see natural resources disappearing as early as the late 1800's. Air and water quality was declining and human wastes were seen almost everywhere. During the dust bowl in the 1930's, where large amounts of cropland were destroyed, people began to look more towards conservation and not the misuse of land. Environmentalists, actually a biologist, such as Rachel Carson shocked the world by her book "Silent Spring" in 1962. There she wrote how, the use of DDT, a pesticide now banned, would kill songbirds.

35. a
Condensation is the formation of water molecules to form a liquid or even ice. A high relative humidity of 100% means that the air is saturated with water vapor. Cooling causes the water molecules to form condensation.

36. b
Temperatures of around 78 degrees Fahrenheit characterize tropical rainforests, and frequent heavy rains. Although the temperate deciduous forest has rain throughout the year, the temperatures are variable from hot in the summer to below freezing during the winter months.

37. c
The general path of primary and secondary sewage follows these steps: raw sewage goes past a bar screen to remove large debris. From there it moves to a grit chamber where the velocity slows down allowing coarse grit to settle. Here fat and oil are skimmed off. Next it enters the primary clarifier where particulate organic matter settles, forming raw sludge, which is removed. The now clarified water moves to the aeration tank where microscopic organisms feed on the organic material in the oxygen rich environment. Following the aeration tank the material moves to a secondary clarifier where organisms settle. These settled organisms are called activated sludge. Activated sludge returns to the aeration tank where it is reused, while the remainder of the liquid is removed from the clarifier, disinfected and released.

Awesome Guides, Inc. A.P. Environmental Science Study Guide - Appendix C

38. e
Overdrawing of groundwater has serious consequences. Among these are, lower water tables, land subsidence, wells going dry and water shortages.

39. d
Grasslands are located in Central North America, Central Asia, subequatorial Africa, South America, southern India, and northern Australia.

40. c
The most common method of sewage treatment in the U.S. is preliminary, primary and secondary. Tertiary (advanced) treatment is often not cost effective to most communities. Over 90% of the organic matter is typically removed after secondary treatment.

41. a
Selective pressures are environmental resistance factors that effect individual organisms.

42. e
Terrestrial biomes are very large areas that exhibit similar types of vegetation, animal life, climate and soils. The climate, temperature and precipitation are the most important factors in determining what types of plants and animals can inhabit the area. Although soil type is important, temperature and precipitation are the main determining factors.

43. c
Environmental law has a major impact on ecosystems. Putting rules and regulations into strict laws, and executing severe penalties can avoid situations like "Tragedy of the Commons".

44. a
Chernobyl, Ukraine is the worst nuclear disaster to date. There was a complete melt down of the nuclear reactor caused by human error, which affected thousands of people. A lack of redundancy (backups) in the system was particularly to blame. Three-mile island is another nuclear accident caused by human error, but it did not cause a complete meltdown of the reactor. The Love Canal is a toxic waste dump.

45. e
After WWII people moved out of the cities (urban sprawl) and caused the inner cities to deteriorate due to the lower tax base and cut services. Moving to urban areas required more gasoline, automobiles and automobile parts. These increases in resources caused more air pollution, and required the use of valuable farm and parklands.

46. d
Cultural eutrophication is a human caused source of adding wastes to rivers, lakes and streams resulting in algae blooms and in rapid ageing of these resources.

47. b
Ozone depletion is considered by most experts to be primarily caused by CFC's. Stopping their production is the principle method of curbing ozone depletion.

48. e
Waste to energy (WTE) facilities burn solid wastes to produce electricity. By burning paper and removing many of the recyclables and toxic substances a significant savings of fossil fuels can be obtained.

A.P. Environmental Science Study Guide - Appendix C

49. d
Technology is currently available to harness the petroleum from oil shale and tar sands, however it is currently too expensive to mine in comparison to crude oil. Shale and tar sands do not provide enough energy to meet the demands of today.

50. c
There are many adaptive features that organisms develop, but it is closely tied to the particular environmental changes that occur. Therefore, a combination of traits enhances the organism's survival.

51. e
There are numerous water pollutants, among them are: sediments, toxic chemicals, solid wastes and additional nutrients.

52. e
Removing groundwater faster than it can be replenished can produce serious consequences. These include: decreased stream flow rates, saltwater intrusion, unproductive agricultural lands and lower property values.

53. e
We are constantly bombarded by radiation from the sun, modern technology and terrestrial sources. These include: x-rays, microwaves, cosmic rays, radon and uranium.

54. d
Storm water runoff is all of the material that comes from water running off of the streets, parks, etc. Included in storm water are fertilizers, pesticides, bacterial waste, oils, leaves and sticks. Activated sludge is found in the wastewater treatment process.

55. b
World food production has a great potential but is hindered by degradation of soil (desertification), depletion of water resources, and increased demand for meat and dairy products. Production of high-yield varieties of corn, rice, etc. has actually increased food production.

56. e
Global warming caused by greenhouse gases, will result in thermal expansion of oceans, melting of polar ice caps and glaciers, rise in sea level and change the position of major currents.

57. d
The gross national product (GNP) is a measure of a nation's wealth, the sum total of all goods and services produced in a country per unit of time, but it does not factor in the loss or decline of the nation's valuable national resources.

58. e
The earliest pesticides such as DDT, are called first generation pesticides and contained hazardous pollutants such as lead, arsenic and mercury. They were persistent in the environment, which means they were resistant to breaking down in an ecosystem. However, they were extremely useful in controlling pests on crops (increased food production) and in fighting disease carried by insects such as malaria (saving numerous lives). Although the U.S. has banned the use of these pesticides, developing countries still use these because they are effective and inexpensive.

Awesome Guides, Inc. A.P. Environmental Science Study Guide - Appendix C

59. c
A species is one kind of organism that has the potential to interbreed and produce fertile offspring. The key is, in order to be a "species", fertile offspring must be produced. This is not possible with any group of plant, animal, fungi or microbe not in the same species.

60. b
Acid precipitation refers to any precipitation that is more acidic than normal, even small differences in pH.

61. c
When suburbs were developed in the 1950's and 1960's many people moved out of the cities leaving the inner city areas in great need of repair. The handicapped and elderly people were not a mobile and remained. The tax base declined and "slums" began in many large cities.

62. a
The Cuyahoga River that flows through Cleveland Ohio once caught on fire. Indiscriminate release of pollution made the river devoid of life in the 1960's. Given time, and with environmental laws, many of the hazardous wastes disappeared making the river a model showing that pollution can be reversed.

63. c
Secondary treatment, also known as aeration, involves biological treatment of sewage waste. By this time, 90% plus of the organic material is removed and little to no pathogens. Pathogens are treated after secondary treatment in most cases with chlorine and then released into temporary ponds or wetlands.

64. b
Weather is the daily reading of a region's temperature and precipitation. Climate is the temperature and precipitation recorded over a long period of time.

65. e
Carbon dioxide is returned to the atmosphere through many processes, fires, volcanoes, internal combustion (burning of fossil fuels), and aerobic respiration. Only two know processes can remove CO_2 from the atmosphere, photosynthesis and the oceans (which act as CO_2 sinks).

66. c
Nitrifying and denitrifying bacteria in the soil convert nitrogen in the nitrogen cycle.

67. a
Local governments raise money through property taxes. The tax base is used for local services. Income tax, gasoline tax { unless a additional tax is added by local government) state lotteries all go to federal or state governments. All property owners must pay property taxes and are never directly billed.

68. c
The Magnuson Act of 1976 extended jurisdiction from 12 miles to 200 miles due to over fishing (which occurred mainly because of modern fish finding technologies).

69. b
"New Forestry" management mainly emphasizes sustainability. This stops clear cutting and provides a forest that can continue to be harvested theoretically indefinitely.

A.P. Environmental Science Study Guide - Appendix C

70. c
Desertification occurs when the land is misused through over irrigation (which causes salination of the soil), overgrazing, tilling of crop land and deforestation.

71. e
Cutting down of forests (deforestation) occurs because: developing countries use wood as fuel for heating and cooking and they use forestland for their agriculture. As well, in developing countries the sale of charcoal from the burning of wood is a business for many people and there are no laws or penalties in existence to prevent deforestation.

72. b
The Highway Trust was specifically designed to provide funds to build new roads through a gasoline tax and increases proportionately with increased commuting. It does not take into account the preservation of open space and agricultural land.

73. c
Selective breeding combines traits that are desirable from two or more different organisms. After an organism is breed selectively, more genes of that organism will be present, while others may be less abundant due to the new genes present.

74. d
Selective pressures that directly affects an organism and may cause physical and behavioral changes in an organism include: climate, resource availability, predation, parasitism and immigration of an organism of the same species to the area, among others. There is no such thing as the principle of the limits.

75. e
Organic wastes include: pathogens, cause pollution, fecal material and kitchen wastes.

76. b
DDT is a persistent pesticide that is banned in the U.S. It was discovered by Paul Muller who was awarded the Nobel Prize for his discovery. DDT is cheap and often used in developing countries where it has greatly increased crop production and saved lives due to the killing of insects that feed on crops and cause disease. Ecologists did not recognize the environmental problems that would occur when it was first introduced.

77. b
Renewable resources are these that typically can be renewed within one's lifetime or sooner. Wood, sunlight, wind, tides, hydroelectric energy, thermal energy are all considered renewable. Fossil fuels take millions of years to make therefore they are not renewable.

78. d
Conventional cars can run on fuels other than gasoline, with some minor conversions. These fuels include: methane gas, hydrogen gas, gasohol (gas mixed with alcohol). Petroleum is another name for gasoline. Sugar compounds cannot run a conventional car and in fact could do great harm to the engine.

79. a
Primary sewage treatment begins as raw sewage first comes to the wastewater treatment plant. It's primary purpose is to screen out large debris and them slow the water flow down in a grit chamber to collect the heaviest suspended solids. Pathogen removal takes place after secondary treatment, and biological treatment occurs after primary treatment.

Awesome Guides, Inc. A.P. Environmental Science Study Guide – Appendix C

80. d
The Clean Air Act (CAA) of 1990 required a 50% reduction of sulfur emissions, the addition of alcohol to some gasolines, development of maximum achievable control for 188 toxic pollutants. Radon, from natural decay of rock, is not human made and therefore is not part of the CAA.

81. d
Passive solar refers to the use of solar energy without the use of external energy (a pump to move water heated by the sun); active solar does use external energy. Passive solar costs less to install and maintain.

82. e
All people have the same biotic potential to reproduce, however developed countries have lower fertility rates, a higher standard of living and greater access to education.

83. c
Solar energy is a clean, renewable resource, but it does have disadvantages. They are: to provide enough useful energy it must be concentrated, it's only available intermittently, it varies greatly depending on the location, it can not be stored, and it can not solve the energy needs of our energy hungry world. It does not disrupt or affect the electromagnetic radiation from the sun.

84. d
World food production has increased over the last 50 years due to increased irrigation, fertilizers, genetically engineered higher yield crops and by using more land (hectares) worldwide.

85. c
An ecotone is the transitional zone between two adjacent ecosystems.

86. b
In nuclear fission the mass of a large atom (reactant) produces atoms (products) that have less mass.

87. c
A lake's buffering capacity represents its ability to lessen or neutralize the affects of acids in the water column.

88. a
The human population is growing exponentially and is currently increasing at the rate of 100 million per year.

89. e
Urban sprawl occurs when large numbers of people move out of the city and into suburban areas. Urban sprawl depletes fossil fuels because more cars are traveling more distances, which in turn causes more air and water pollution. This generates more solid wastes and requires more land clearing resulting in lost ecosystems and less biodiversity.

90. c
Sulfur dioxide comes from the burning of coal and higher smokestacks allow for the smoke to dissipate more readily, therefore making this method the best for reducing sulfur dioxide. Oil and gasoline, or refuse do not contain significant amounts of sulfur dioxide thus reducing their use would not lower the amount of sulfur dioxide in the troposphere.

A.P. Environmental Science Study Guide - Appendix C

91. c
The process of nitrogen fixation refers to the conversion of atmospheric nitrogen (N2) into forms that plants can use, nitrates. Many cyanobacteria and legumes (peas, beans, clover) have the ability to fix atmospheric nitrogen.

92. a
Nuclear power is a very clean and inexpensive source of energy. Unlike coal, the process does not involve any sulfur and doesn't cause acid rain, nor does it contribute to the green house gases.

93. e
Species with high biotic potential produce large numbers of offspring but do little to nothing toward the protection of their young. They have the ability to migrate long distances and invade new territories, and can adapt to different and changing environmental conditions.

94. e
The world's population is currently over 6 billion with one fifth living in poverty. This percentage also has no clean water, suffers from malnutrition and is illiterate.

95. d
DDT is a first generation (early) pesticide that is relatively harmless to humans. It is banned in the U.S. but because it is inexpensive, it is still used in many developing countries. It is persistent (long lasting) and broad spectrum (kills target and nontarget insects) .It was banned in the U.S. because it interferes with the calcium metabolism of birds causing their eggshells to become too thin.

96. d
Halogenerated hydrocarbons, also called organic chlorides, are organic hydrocarbons that have been altered synthetically by adding an atom from the halogen group of chemicals (chlorine, flourine, bromine and iodine). These compounds are very hazardous to human health because they are nonbiodegradable and bioaccumulate. Examples include Tetrachloroethylene and 1,2-dibromoethane. They are used as pesticides (DDT, Mirex), solvents and plastics.

97. a
Geothermal energy harnesses energy from hot groundwater aquifers found in geologically active parts of the world, by using the escaping steam to drive a turbogenerator, which produces electricity.

98. e
Many poor nations have rapidly increasing populations and the result is: low job base (high unemployment), loss of any economic gains and increased competition for available resources.

99. e
Landfills must deal with environmental problems such as, leachate moving towards groundwater, the venting of methane gas, cell liners and surface subsidence.

100. d
Ecosystems are divided into trophic (feeding) levels. All organisms are dependent upon the first level or beginning of the food chain. Autotrophs (green plants) represent the 1st. trophic level and usually have the most biomass, numbers and total amount of high-grade usable energy.

Appendix D - Practice Test #1 Free Response Question Answers

1. a) An algae bloom is a sudden excessive growth of planktonic algae. It causes the transparency of the water to go down.
   - It is usually characterized by the input of excessive nitrogen into the body of water.
   - Point sources are those areas that are putting nutrients directly into the body of water, and they are usually easier to identify and control. Examples include: discharge from sewer plants, power plants or factories.
   - Nonpoint sources are more difficult to identify because they are usually scattered over a large area and may be some distance from the body of water. Examples are: storm water or agricultural runoff, atmospheric or from farm animals.
   - A fecal coliform test can be performed to determine if the body of water is safe for human recreation.
   - The long-term consequences of this phenomenon include the removal of DO from the water when the algae die off and decompose. This in turn could cause a fish kill. The reduction of sunlight could affect beneficial aquatic plants and if cyanobacteria (blue-green algae) are present in high levels then their toxins can harm fish and other life that depend on the lake. All of these long-term consequences would then cause a loss of human recreational use.

   b) To remediate means to return the body of water or other ecosystem to an uncontaminated state. This is possible by applying several methods:
   - The first and most important step is to stop the source of pollution from going into the water.
   - The application of alum and the reduction of nitrogen into the water should be considered.
   - Aeration of the water body and the removal of excessive detritus are two other possibilities.
   - The water quality parameters that would meet the plan goals are: DO, nitrates, phosphates and BOD.

   c) Governmental regulations that might be used to control additional widespread pollution problems are:
   - National Pollution Discharge Elimination System
   - Total Maximum Daily Load
   - The Clean Water Act

2.) Sewage is the wastewater released by residences, businesses and industries in a community. It is 99.94 percent water, with only 0.06 percent of the wastewater dissolved and suspended solid material. The cloudiness of sewage is caused by suspended particles, which in untreated sewage ranges from 100 to 350 mg/l. A measure of the strength of the wastewater is biochemical oxygen demand, or BOD_5. The BOD_5 measures the amount of oxygen microorganisms require in five days to break down sewage. Untreated sewage has a BOD_5 ranging from 100 mg/l to 300 mg/l. Pathogens or disease-causing organisms are present in sewage. Coliform bacteria are used as an indicator of disease-causing organisms. Sewage also contains nutrients (such as ammonia and phosphorus), minerals, and metals. Ammonia can range from 12 to 50 mg/l and phosphorus can range from 6 to 20 mg/l in untreated sewage.

   a) See the wastewater plant diagram below for important process identifiers and read on for descriptions:

A.P. Environmental Science Study Guide - Appendix D

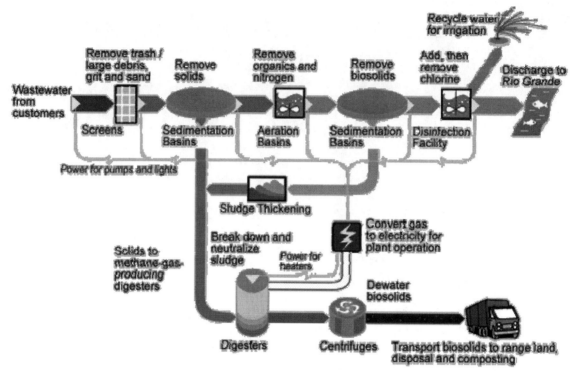

- Sewage treatment is a multi-stage process to renovate wastewater before it reenters a body of water is applied to the land or is reused. The goal is to reduce or remove organic matter, solids, nutrients, disease-causing organisms and other pollutants from wastewater. Each receiving body of water has limits to the amount of pollutants it can receive without degradation. Therefore, each sewage treatment plant must hold a permit listing the allowable levels of BOD_5, suspended solids, coliform bacteria and other pollutants. The discharge permits are called NPDES permits, which stands for the National Pollutant Discharge Elimination System.

Preliminary Treatment

- Preliminary treatment to screen out, grind up, or separate debris is the first step in wastewater treatment. Sticks, rags, large food particles, sand, gravel, toys, etc., are removed at this stage to protect the pumping and other equipment in the treatment plant. Treatment equipment such as bar screens, comminutors (a large version of a garbage disposal), and grit chambers are used as the wastewater first enters a treatment plant. The collected debris is usually disposed of in a landfill.

Primary Treatment

- Primary treatment is the second step in treatment and separates suspended solids and greases from wastewater. Wastewater is held in a quiet tank for several hours allowing the particles to settle to the bottom and the greases to float to the top. The solids drawn off the bottom and skimmed off the top receive further treatment as sludge. The clarified wastewater flows on to the next stage of wastewater treatment. Clarifiers and septic tanks are usually used to provide primary treatment.

Awesome Guides, Inc. A.P. Environmental Science Study Guide - Appendix D

Secondary Treatment

- Secondary treatment is a biological treatment process to remove dissolved organic matter from wastewater. Sewage microorganisms are cultivated and added to the wastewater. The microorganisms absorb organic matter from sewage as their food supply. Three approaches are used to accomplish secondary treatment; fixed film, suspended film and lagoon systems.
- **Fixed Film Systems** - Fixed film systems grow microorganisms on substrates such as rocks, sand or plastic. The wastewater is spread over the substrate, allowing the wastewater to flow past the film of microorganisms fixed to the substrate. As organic matter and nutrients are absorbed from the wastewater, the film of microorganisms grows and thickens. Trickling filters, rotating biological contactors, and sand filters are examples of fixed film systems.

- **Suspended Film Systems** - Suspended film systems stir and suspend microorganisms in wastewater. As the microorganisms absorb organic matter and nutrients from the wastewater they grow in size and number. After the microorganisms have been suspended in the wastewater for several hours, they are settled out as sludge. Some of the sludge is pumped back into the incoming wastewater to provide "seed" microorganisms. The remainder is wasted and sent on to a sludge treatment process. Activated sludge, extended aeration, oxidation ditch, and sequential batch reactor systems are all examples of suspended film systems.

- **Lagoon Systems** - Lagoon systems are shallow basins, which hold the waste-water for several months to allow for the natural degradation of sewage. These systems take advantage of natural aeration and microorganisms in the wastewater to renovate sewage.

Final Treatment

- Final treatment focuses on removal of disease-causing organisms from wastewater. Treated wastewater can be disinfected by adding chlorine or by using ultraviolet light. High levels of chlorine may be harmful to aquatic life in receiving streams. Treatment systems often add a chlorine-neutralizing chemical to the treated wastewater before stream discharge.

- Waste sludge as a result of the final treatment could be used as fertilizer because it is rich in organic compounds, and is no longer pathogenic. This would save additional space in landfills.

- Treated wastewater could be sold to power companies to use in the production of electricity.

- Treated wastewater could be used as irrigation.

- Treated wastewater could be used to supply wetlands with water during dryer months.

Three environmental policies that affect wastewater treatment facilities are:

- The discharge permits, called NPDES permits, stand for the National Pollutant Discharge Elimination System, state that each sewage treatment plant must hold a permit listing the allowable levels of BOD_5, suspended solids, coliform bacteria and other pollutants found in their discharge.

- In 1972, the U.S. Congress adopted the Clean Water Act to protect the nation's waters. Through this act, the U.S. Environmental Protection Agency and corresponding state agencies were given the responsibility to regulate activities that threaten the quality of the nation's water resources.

A.P. Environmental Science Study Guide - Appendix D  Awesome Guides, Inc.

- In the Federal Clean Water Act, Congress adopted a comprehensive water policy for the nation and set as a national goal the elimination of pollutant discharges to the navigable waters of the U.S. by 1985.

3. a) The answer of 325,000 KW hours/day is obtained by:

$$\frac{1,000,000 \text{ BTU/ton}}{10,000 \text{ BTU/KW hour}} \times (5000 \times .65) = (100)(3250) = 325,000 \text{ KW hours/day}$$

1 megawatt = 1000 kilowatts (1,000,000 / 1,000) so therefore 1 megawatt hour = 1,000 kilowatt hours

Thus: 325,000 kilowatt hours = 325,000/1,000 = 325 megawatt hours/day

b) (325)(.75) = 243.75 and (243.75)(1,000) = $24,375/day daily profit for the power plant

c) The disadvantages of using the waste to energy process are:
- Some of the recyclable material is used in the process.
- The possibility of toxic chemicals adding to air pollution is present.
- Disposal of fly ash can become a problem.

The advantages are:
- Combustion reduces weight and volume.
- Toxic wastes are easier to handle.
- The charges to dump garbage could be eliminated using profits from the power generation.
- Equipped with scrubbers, standards set by the Clean Air Act could be met.

d) The profit made from selling and recycling aluminum is:
(5,000 tons)(0.05) = 250 tons and (250 tons) / ($10.00) = $2,500/ day

e) The problems associated with the land filled material are:
- Methane gas is released
- Leachate contaminating ground water
- Site location
- Odor
- Settling of the land
- Cell liners breaking

4. a) No plant species will grow in solid ice, therefore when the glaciers retreat, leaving bare rock, then primary (bare rock) succession can take place.

- When studying this area for ecological succession it can be assumed that the moraines exposed first represent the oldest stages of succession while the moraines exposed last represent the pioneer (first) stages of succession.

- It is possible to study the stages of ecological succession by knowing the rate the glaciers are retreating, and examining what species are growing in those particular areas from south to north.

b) In both species, alders and dryas, the pH went down. The alders caused a steady decrease in the pH creating acidic conditions, while the dryas decreased the soil pH to 7.1 (near neutral) and then seemed to leveled off.

pH Levels Over Time

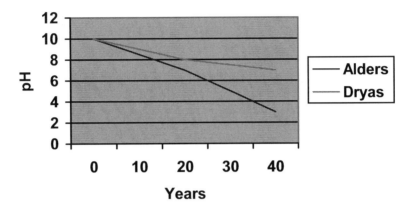

Since different plant species require different abiotic conditions, such as pH, moisture, shade, then as succession proceeds, and conditions change, the species (both plant and animal) that inhabit that area will also.

c) Sitka spruce lower the pH and do not fix nitrogen.

- Fixing nitrogen means using atmospheric nitrogen (N_2) and converting it into NO_3, after several processes in the nitrogen cycle. If sitka spruce were able to fix nitrogen, you would expect the nitrogen levels in the soil to go up (or at least remain constant) and not down.

The process is a facilitative one, because the changes that are taking place in the soil (previous to the sitka spruce), facilitate or help the abiotic conditions that will accommodate sitka spruce growth.

A.P. Environmental Science Study Guide - Appendix E

Awesome Guides, Inc.

Appendix E Practice Test#2 Answer Sheet Key

1. A( ) B( ) C(●) D( ) E( )
2. A( ) B(●) C( ) D( ) E( )
3. A( ) B( ) C( ) D(●) E( )
4. A(●) B( ) C( ) D( ) E( )
5. A( ) B( ) C(●) D( ) E( )
6. A(●) B( ) C( ) D( ) E( )
7. A( ) B(●) C( ) D( ) E( )
8. A( ) B( ) C( ) D(●) E( )
9. A( ) B( ) C( ) D(●) E( )
10. A( ) B( ) C(●) D( ) E( )
11. A( ) B( ) C(●) D( ) E( )
12. A( ) B(●) C( ) D( ) E( )
13. A( ) B( ) C( ) D( ) E(●)
14. A( ) B(●) C( ) D( ) E( )
15. A( ) B( ) C( ) D(●) E( )
16. A( ) B(●) C( ) D( ) E( )
17. A( ) B(●) C( ) D( ) E( )
18. A( ) B( ) C(●) D( ) E( )
19. A( ) B( ) C(●) D( ) E( )
20. A( ) B(●) C( ) D( ) E( )
21. A( ) B(●) C( ) D( ) E( )
22. A(●) B( ) C( ) D( ) E( )
23. A(●) B( ) C( ) D( ) E( )
24. A( ) B(●) C( ) D( ) E( )
25. A( ) B(●) C( ) D( ) E( )
26. A(●) B( ) C( ) D( ) E( )
27. A( ) B( ) C(●) D( ) E( )
28. A( ) B(●) C( ) D( ) E( )
29. A( ) B(●) C( ) D( ) E( )
30. A(●) B( ) C( ) D( ) E( )
31. A( ) B( ) C(●) D( ) E( )
32. A( ) B( ) C(●) D( ) E( )
33. A( ) B(●) C( ) D( ) E( )
34. A( ) B( ) C(●) D( ) E( )
35. A(●) B( ) C( ) D( ) E( )
36. A(●) B( ) C( ) D( ) E( )

37. A( ) B( ) C( ) D(●) E( )
38. A(●) B( ) C( ) D( ) E( )
39. A( ) B(●) C( ) D( ) E( )
40. A( ) B( ) C( ) D( ) E(●)
41. A( ) B(●) C( ) D( ) E( )
42. A( ) B( ) C( ) D(●) E( )
43. A( ) B( ) C(●) D( ) E( )
44. A( ) B( ) C(●) D( ) E( )
45. A( ) B( ) C( ) D( ) E(●)
46. A(●) B( ) C(●) D( ) E( )
47. A( ) B( ) C(●) D( ) E( )
48. A( ) B( ) C( ) D(●) E( )
49. A( ) B(●) C( ) D( ) E( )
50. A(●) B( ) C( ) D(●) E( )
51. A(●) B( ) C( ) D( ) E( )
52. A( ) B( ) C( ) D(●) E( )
53. A( ) B( ) C(●) D( ) E( )
54. A( ) B( ) C( ) D( ) E(●)
55. A( ) B( ) C(●) D( ) E( )
56. A(●) B( ) C( ) D( ) E( )
57. A( ) B( ) C(●) D( ) E( )
58. A(●) B( ) C( ) D( ) E( )
59. A( ) B(●) C( ) D( ) E( )
60. A( ) B( ) C(●) D( ) E( )
61. A(●) B( ) C( ) D( ) E( )
62. A( ) B( ) C( ) D( ) E(●)
63. A( ) B( ) C(●) D( ) E( )
64. A(●) B( ) C( ) D( ) E( )
65. A( ) B(●) C( ) D( ) E( )
66. A( ) B( ) C(●) D( ) E( )
67. A( ) B( ) C( ) D( ) E(●)
68. A( ) B( ) C( ) D(●) E( )
69. A( ) B( ) C(●) D( ) E( )
70. A(●) B( ) C( ) D( ) E( )
71. A( ) B( ) C( ) D(●) E( )
72. A( ) B( ) C( ) D( ) E(●)

73. A( ) B( ) C( ) D(●) E( )
74. A(●) B( ) C( ) D( ) E( )
75. A( ) B( ) C(●) D( ) E( )
76. A( ) B( ) C( ) D( ) E(●)
77. A( ) B(●) C( ) D( ) E( )
78. A( ) B( ) C( ) D(●) E( )
79. A( ) B( ) C(●) D( ) E( )
80. A( ) B(●) C( ) D( ) E( )
81. A( ) B( ) C( ) D( ) E(●)
82. A(●) B( ) C( ) D( ) E( )
83. A( ) B(●) C( ) D( ) E( )
84. A( ) B( ) C(●) D( ) E( )
85. A( ) B( ) C( ) D( ) E(●)
86. A(●) B( ) C( ) D( ) E( )
87. A( ) B( ) C( ) D(●) E( )
88. A( ) B( ) C( ) D( ) E(●)
89. A(●) B( ) C( ) D( ) E( )
90. A( ) B( ) C( ) D(●) E( )
91. A(●) B( ) C( ) D( ) E( )
92. A( ) B( ) C(●) D( ) E( )
93. A( ) B(●) C( ) D( ) E( )
94. A( ) B( ) C( ) D(●) E( )
95. A(●) B( ) C( ) D( ) E( )
96. A( ) B( ) C( ) D(●) E( )
97. A(●) B( ) C( ) D( ) E( )
98. A( ) B( ) C( ) D( ) E(●)
99. A( ) B(●) C( ) D( ) E( )
100. A( ) B( ) C(●) D( ) E( )

Awesome Guides, Inc.  A.P. Environmental Science Study Guide - Appendix F

Appendix F Practice Test#2 Subject Index Comparison

Compare the questions on Practice Test #2 that you missed to this subject index to see what areas or concepts that you are weak in.

- If you missed questions 33-42, 51, 54, 56, 58, 67, 82, 83, 86, 89-91, 95, 98 then you should review the concepts related to environmental rules and regulations, human communities and society, and environmental ethics and sustainability.
- If you missed questions 55, 68, 96, 97 then you should review the concepts related to biodiversity, ecosystem destruction, and global changes.
- If you missed questions 1-14 then you should review the concepts related to ecosystem structure and general ecology.
- If you missed questions 15-19, 59-62, 66 then you should review the concepts related to ecosystems and how they function.
- If you missed questions 53, 63, 65, 74 then you should review the concepts related to population ecology and ecological succession.
- If you missed questions 20-24, 100 then you should review the concepts related to changes in ecosystems, natural selection, plate tectonics, environmental genetics, and evolution.
- If you missed questions 25-28, 64, 69 then you should review the concepts related to human demographics and populations, comparisons of developing and developed countries.
- If you missed questions 52, 70-73 then you should review the concepts related to geotechnical science (soils).
- If you missed questions 92 then you should review the concepts related to water environmental quality.
- If you missed questions 99 then you should review the concepts related to food production.
- If you missed questions 93, 94 then you should review the concepts related to biodiversity of the world's wild species of animals and plants.
- If you missed questions 29-32 then you should review the concepts related to the worlds' resources.
- If you missed questions 29-32, 75 then you should review the concepts related to fossil fuels.
- If you missed questions 43-50, 76, 77 then you should review the concepts related to nuclear power.
- If you missed questions 85 then you should review the concepts related to renewable energy.
- If you missed question 87 then you should review the concepts related to human environmental hazards, and toxicology.
- If you missed questions 78, 79 then you should review the concepts related to pests and their control.
- If you missed questions 57, 80 then you should review the concepts related to water pollution.
- If you missed questions 81 then you should review the concepts related to solid waste.
- If you missed questions 84 then you should review the concepts related to hazardous chemicals.
- If you missed questions 85, 87, 88 then you should review the concepts related to the atmosphere.

Appendix G Practice Test #2 Answer Key & Rubrics

1. c.
2. b.
3. d.
4. a.

These all refer to the levels or hierarchy of the organization of life, which begins with atoms and ends with the biosphere. The hierarchy goes from the smallest particle (atom) to the largest entity (biosphere). Environmental ecology is concerned with, in hierarchy order: species, population, community, ecosystem, biome and biosphere.

5. c.
6. a.
7. b.
8. d.

A trophic level refers to a feeding level. All of the trophic levels make up a food chain. Energy is transferred along a food chain beginning with autotrophs (green plants/algae) on level 1, Primary consumers (herbivores) on level 2, secondary consumers (carnivores) on level 3 and secondary carnivores (carnivores feeding on other carnivores) on level 4.

9. d.
10. c.
11. c.
12. a.
13. e.
14. b.

For these questions you should review the concepts about the various biomes in your study guide or A.P. Environmental Science textbook. The review in your study guide is found on pages 27 - 28.

15. d.
16. b.
17. a.
18. c.
19. c.

The graph represents a typical population or growth curve also known as an "S" (sigmoid) curve. Usually populations in a new environment will, after a lag or adjustment phase, grow exponentially because resources are high and competition is low. After exponential growth the population is at equilibrium or the carrying capacity. Carrying capacity population numbers will fluctuate above and below the carrying capacity. If the carrying capacity is greatly increased, then extinction my occur.

20. b.
21. b.
22. a.
23. a.
24. b.

A vulnerable species has a more difficult time adapting than an adaptive species. Among the characteristics of vulnerable species are: narrow distribution, small population, limited genetic variation, large physical size, low biotic potential, limited ability to migrate, small number of offspring, and a long generation time. Panda bears are an example of a vulnerable species.

Among the characteristics of highly adaptive species are: wide distribution, large population, high degree of genetic variation, small physical size, high biotic potential, large numbers of offspring, short generation time, and the ability to migrate. Insects have the characteristics of a highly adaptive species.

Awesome Guides, Inc. A.P. Environmental Science Study Guide - Appendix G

25. b.
26. a.
27. c.
28. b.

The diagrams represent an age profile, showing the number of individuals in each age group also called a cohort. An age profile like diagram A has a small base, meaning that the number of people who will be of reproduction age is relatively small, thus a slowing population growth. This is typical of developed countries. However the opposite is true of diagram B and is typical of developing countries.

29. a. See chart on test

30. a. (43)(5.7) = 245.10 quadrillion BTUs

31. c. See chart on test

32. c. See chart on test

33. b.
34. c.
35. a.
36. a.
37. d.

These four environmental disasters are among the most commonly known. Review your textbook for more information on these events.

38. a.
39. b.
40. e.
41. a.
42. d.

Review your study guide pages 81-85 for more information on important environmental laws and regulations. You should be able to quote some of these usually on the free response questions.

43. c.
44. ac.
45. e.
46. abc.
47. c.
48. d.
49. ab.
50. ad.

Be familiar with the general operation of nuclear, coal, oil, and natural gas power plants. There are informative numerous websites that can provide diagrams and additional information.

A.P. Environmental Science Study Guide - Appendix G  Awesome Guides, Inc.

51. a.
The Cairo Conference in September 1994 was the third U.N. conference on population and development, attended by 15,000 leaders and representatives, from 179 nations and almost 1,000 non-governmental organizations.

52. d.
Mollisols are very fertile soils with a deep A horizon and rich in humus and minerals.

53. c.
A praying mantis is a carnivore, eating insects, and occupies the same tropic level as other carnivores, such a weasels, wolves, etc. and is on the third level.

54. e.
The more value you can give to saving a forest the better changes you would have to meeting your objective. All of the choices would strengthen your case.

55. c.
Biodiversity, the variety of life, is found in all ecosystems, but is much greater in tropical regions, such as a coral reef.

56. a.
The Chernobyl incidence was a complete meltdown of a nuclear reactor and was caused by human error that was also combined with the lack of redundancies, or backups.

57. b.
The secondary sewage treatment process follows the processes, removal of debris and girt …Removal of particulate organic materials… …Removal of colloidal and dissolved material…Disinfection

58. a.
Experience has shown that when people own their property, they will take an active role in maintaining their investment. Policies, volunteers, and more housing have not been successful in curtailing urban blight.

59. b.
Plants require nitrogen, and nitrogen is also a plant macronutrient. Plants however can't use nitrogen in it's elemental form. Plants require nitrogen in the form of either ammonium, or nitrite.

60. c.
For any experiment to be considered valid there must be a control. Without a control group there is no way to know if the parameter you are testing, nitrogen, makes a difference in plant growth. The plants may have shown poor growth anyway, with or without nitrogen-fixing bacteria, there is not way to tell without the control group.

61. a.
Carbon to put in the environment/ecosystem in many ways through; internal combustion, decomposition, fires, volcanoes, respiration etc. but is only removed by to major processes, photosynthesis, and absorption in the ocean by marine algae (sometimes the oceans are called carbon "sink")

62. e.
Competition among organisms has no winners. Even though one larger stronger animal, for example, may get the resource, that animal will still have to expend energy to get that resource. By separating themselves for each other, warblers use resource partitioning to avoid or lessen competition.

63. c.
Estuaries are places where marshes, lakes, or rivers meet the ocean. These areas are very important because many young organisms find protection from the harsh open ocean; in other words, they get their start there. It's also ideal because lots of nutrients are present in estuaries.

64. a.
In curve A, population is growing exponentially; this represents population growth under ideal conditions, no or few limiting factors. After reaching way above the carrying capacity, the population crashes. In curve B the population fluctuates around its carrying capacity.

65. b.
Adverse weather conditions can slow a population's growth. Some animals for example will NOT breed under drought conditions. All of the other factors may actually increase a population's growth.

66. c.
Mutualism is a relationship between two organisms where both organisms benefit from the relationship. In the case of trees and epiphytic, or air plants the epiphyte benefits by attaching to the tree where it can more efficiently acquire nutrients, while the tree benefits by the small amounts of nutrients that are gathered by the epiphyte through the collection of rainfall. Many people believe that these air plants are parasitic to the trees since they are attached to them, however, the air plant DOES NOT take any nutrients from the tree or weaken its growth.

67. e.
Ecosystems get rid if their wastes, and recycle some but not all the elements.

68. d.
For enhanced reproductive success an organism must be able to migrate or spread seeds. Migration allows organism to find mates, and have a better mate selection, while dispersal of seeds allows plants to germinate and grow without competing with the parent plant.

69. c.
After World War II returning soldiers started families that had relativity large numbers of children, around 4 per family was typical. This is known as the post World War II "Baby Boom". This group of babies, known in population ecology as a cohort (a group born at about the same time) is now nearing retirement age.

70. a.
Loam, considered at the BEST soil for agriculture, is made up of 40% sand, 40% silt, and 20% clay. This mixture allows some water to be held without the soil becoming waterlogged, and provides a good mix of nutrients.

71. d.
The "O" horizon consists of surface litter and decomposing plant matter. The "O" stands for organic, since it contains dead organic matter.

A.P. Environmental Science Study Guide - Appendix G  Awesome Guides, Inc.

72. e.
For roots to thrive they must have good aeration, oxygen, and some water holding capacity, however, water MUST be able to move through the soil. Soils that allow water to stand too long, reduce oxygen, and cause "root rot" to many species of terrestrial plants.

73. c.
Humus is extremely important towards improving soils. Mineralization refers to the gradual oxidation of organic matter, and leaves a gritty mineral component to soil. This is caused by declining humus content and leads to decline in nutrient holding capacity, infiltration and aeration, and eventual collapse of the topsoil.

74. a.
Production of pollutions is not considered a service.

75. c.

76. a.
235U is the fissionable form used in nuclear power plants.

77. b.
Neutrons are the subatomic particle that starts and sustains a nuclear reaction. It takes a neutron hitting the 235U nucleus at just the right speed to cause fission. When the neutron hits 235U at just the right speed, 236U, a highly unstable product, undergoes fission immediately into lighter atoms called fission products. The fission reaction then gives off several more neutrons and releases tremendous amount of energy. Usually these neutrons are traveling too fast to cause fission, but can be controlled and slowed down to cause more fission in a domino like effect called a chain reaction.

78. d.
First generation pesticides were among the first pesticides produced and contain toxic heavy metals, such as lead, and mercury. These early substances are very accumulating in soils, and inhibit plant growth and poison other organisms, including humans.

79. c.
Biological controls are a means of using living organisms to control unwanted pests. These may include certain bacteria's like BT, bacillus thuringiensis, or insects such as ladybugs. Another effective method of insect or pest control is by using sterile males, since many female insect only breed once in a lifetime.

80. b.
Coliform bacteria are found in the intestines of many animals. The presence of this type of bacteria is an indication that animal waste material is in that body of water. Since animal wastes may contain many pathogenic bacteria, the water is considered unsafe to drink or swim in.

81. e.

82. a.

83. b.

84. c.

85. e.
Ozone, O_3, is a naturally occurring mainly in the stratosphere. It acts as a shield that protects organisms from UV, ultra violet radiation.

86. a.

87. d.
VOC's or volatile organic compounds will evaporate into the air in a vaporous state, and are considered a major air pollutant. They are a result of incomplete combustion of fuels and wastes.

88. e.
Due to strict government regulation of gasoline, which formally contained lead, gasoline of today are lead free, resulting in a sharp decline of lead in the atmosphere.

89. a.
In engineering practices and design cost benefit is extremely important, by comparing the estimated costs to the benefits. Sometimes extra costs at the beginning of a project might save $$ in the long run for maintenance costs, repair of rundown parts etc.

90. d.
Automobiles simply encourage people to move out of the cities, cause air pollution, and clog public transportation.

91. a.
Urban sprawl, moving from the cities to urban areas, results in a great loss of agricultural land.

92. c.
Saltwater intrusion occurs when saltwater flows into the underground freshwater aquifer. Lowering of the water table, which normally provides pressure significant enough to keep saltwater out, causes this problem. The ground water becomes contaminated with salt making it unusable or very expensive to purify.

93. b.
The Lacy Act of 1900 prohibits interstate commerce from dealing with illegally killed wildlife making it more difficult for hunters to sell their kill.

94. d.
A keystone species is vital for the survival of other species, for example, reintroduction of wolves into Yellowstone Park in Wyoming, increased the number of songbirds in the park. This occurred because the wolves preyed on animals at rivers and streams, keeping their numbers in check. This lowered population of these animals, and allowed vegetation at the riverbanks to grow, (before the wolves there were too many grazers, which trampled the plants). The result was that many songbirds were attracted to the new vegetation.

95. a.
CITES, or the Convention on Trade in Endangered Species, is an international treaty conveying some protection to endangered and threatened species by restricting trade of those species or their products.

96. d.
Destruction is habitat is foremost in most environmental problems. All organisms on this planet MUST have a habitat for their survival.

97. a.
Forest fragmentation, the destruction of some areas, while leaving others, has the greatest affect on specialized species. These species have a very limited ability to adapt to new or changing environments.

98. e.
Humans are the major component of the treaty.

99. b.
The maximum sustainable yield is the amount of a renewable resource that can be taken year after year without depleting that resource. It refers to the maximum harvest that is balanced by the regenerative capacities of that ecosystem.

100. c.
Tragedy of the Commons refers to the idea that many people use a common resource, often depleting it, where no one owns or takes care of the resource.

Appendix H Practice Test #2 Free Response Question Answers

1.
    (a) Autotrophs (first trophic level/producers)---pigeons (second trophic level/herbivores)--- red-tailed hawks (third trophic level/carnivores) Energy flow in food chains is one way, that is to say that energy must always be put into an ecosystem. Energy cannot be created or destroyed, First Law of Thermodynamics, and in every energy transfer, energy is converted into low-grade heat and escapes the ecosystem, Second Law of Thermodynamics. Since some energy escapes, that according to the First Law of Thermodynamics, energy must be put back into the ecosystem. It can be said that energy cannot be recycled.

    Biotic potential is the maximum rate that organisms can reproduce under ideal conditions. This is possible when environmental resistance is at a minimum. Environmental resistant factors include, predation, disease, competition, pollution etc. The pigeons at Disney World were kept under near ideal conditions and released in larger numbers than they naturally occur in the area. This practice attracted the red-tailed hawks. With the new and increased resources, it is possible through migration, and reproduction that the red-tailed hawk population probably increased. Where resources are available organisms tend to increase their numbers.

    (b) Disney could make wise use of its property and keep enough "green areas" so that a natural population of red-tailed hawks can exist.

    Disney could try releasing homing pigeons at different times during different events to see if that discourages the red-tailed hawks

    (c) An exotic species is a non-native organism. In many cases exotic species thrive and increase their populations because of lack of natural predators. Many times exotics are very robust species and out compete naturally occurring species. When natural species are eliminated, weakened or declining then the organisms that depend on them also decline, starting a "snow-ball" effect. Examples of exotic species are kudzu vine, water hydrilla, and fire ants.

2.
    (a) Costal ecosystems are very vulnerable to high winds and storms. These cause beach erosion and property damage. Many habitats are lost. In southern beaches these storms many disturb sea turtle nesting sites, many of which are endangered species.

    (b) Many scientists believe that the rise in sea level is due to global warming, thus melting the polar ice caps. Global warming is most likely caused by the addition of greenhouse gases, such a carbon dioxide, and methane. Looking for alternative energy sources that do not release greenhouse gases and, curtailing the release of methane gas from landfills and other sources could stop this phenomena.

- (c) Montreal Protocol —1987 to cut back CFC'S by 50% by the year 2000.
- Clean Air Act —of 1970 to control and greatly cut back air pollution.
- National Ambient Air Standards —to set laws requiring any business that releases air pollutants to stay within certain values.

3.
    (a) <u>Curve A</u> has an arithmetic (straight line showing steady growth) and a geometric (curved line) growth. <u>Curve B</u> represents a typical "S" or sigmoid curve, where a population shows a lag phase or adjustment at in beginning, then starts to grow exponentially, and then levels off when the carrying capacity is realized. <u>Curve C</u> is an oscillating curve that shows seasonally or yearly fluctuations in a population of slightly above and slightly below the carrying capacity. Many stable or equilibrium populations have this type of growth curve. <u>Curve D</u> represents an extinction curve, where the population losses all of its members. This could be caused by the introduction of an exotic species, overuse of resources, weather or climatic changes, poaching, or even the lack of proper hunting regulations.

    (b) 70/20 = 3.5 Years

    (c) Curve C, See above answer

(d) Curve D. See above answer, and add...An exotic species, due to lack of competition and predators could increase very rapidly outnumbering natural species, and using their resources. This use of these resources would produce an increase limiting factors (such as food, disease, predation), and could eliminate the natural population.

4.

(a) Species diversity, or biodiversity, is representative of the variety of life. This entire ecosystem has a very small biodiversity, with only 20 plant and 10 animal species. This is quite small when you consider that a rainforest often has hundreds of species, especially insects, for every hectare. There are more bird species in the Small Country of Costa Rica, for example, than are in the entire Untied States.

(b) Actual numbers are not possible in this case, but a range can be calculated for the data. At 90% accuracy, there is a 10% error, from that:

- Redwood Trees (200)(0.1) = plus or minus 20, thus numbers would be between 180 and 220, times 100 hectares = between **18,000 and 22,000 actual trees.**
- Small Mammals (15)(0.1) = plus or minus 1.5, thus numbers would be between 13.5 and 16.5 times 100 hectares = between **1,350 and 1,650 actual small mammals.**
- Invertebrates (100)(0.1) = plus or minus 10, thus numbers would be between 90 and 110, times 100 hectares = between **9,000 and 11,000 actual invertebrates.**
- Birds (300)(0.1) = plus or minus, 30 thus numbers would be between 270 and 330, times 100 hectares = between **27,000 and 33,000 actual birds.**

(c) Many bird species migrate seasonally over great distances. During a migration, it is possible to see 1000's of birds of a particular species at one time. Tree swallow during a migration, for example, can literally blacken the skies for several miles during this migration. This would not violate the 10% rule, which states that 90% of the energy is lost on each trophic level of the food chain or food web, and only 10% is transferred to the next level. It would be expected in an ecosystem to have more trees, first trophic level, than birds, second or third trophic levels, however these birds are not a permanent part of this ecosystem and travel over many ecosystems to reach their destination, thus balancing out the 10% rule

(d) In many cases it is either physically or economically impossible to study an entire ecosystem in its entirety. Thus environmental scientists look at representative samples of an ecosystem to determine an estimate of what resources or other characteristics exist. This could be compared to conducting a survey using a representative sampling of a population. Done properly, this technique can be very accurate.

Appendix I Practice Test#3 Answer Sheet Key

1. C
2. C
3. D
4. C
5. B
6. D
7. C
8. C
9. C
10. D
11. C
12. C
13. D
14. C
15. A
16. C
17. D
18. C
19. D
20. E
21. B
22. D
23. B
24. A
25. A
26. C
27. B
28. E
29. A
30. D
31. A
32. D
33. C
34. A
35. A
36. A
37. A
38. B
39. C
40. D
41. A
42. D
43. B
44. C
45. E
46. A
47. C
48. C
49. C
50. A
51. B
52. C
53. B
54. E
55. D
56. A
57. D
58. A
59. B
60. C
61. D
62. A
63. E
64. C
65. C
66. A
67. B
68. B
69. A
70. A
71. D
72. D
73. A
74. A
75. D
76. B
77. D
78. A
79. C
80. B
81. C
82. B
83. C
84. D
85. B
86. A
87. E
88. E
89. A
90. C
91. B
92. C
93. D
94. C
95. E
96. A
97. E
98. B
99. C
100. B

A.P. Environmental Science Study Guide - Appendix J  Awesome Guides, Inc.

Appendix J Practice Test #3 Subject Index Comparison

Compare the questions on Practice Test #2 that you missed to this subject index to see what areas or concepts that you are weak in.

- If you missed questions 1, 10, 11, 15, 17, 39, 47, 48, 72, 74, 98 then you should review the concepts related to environmental rules and regulations, human communities and society, and environmental ethics and sustainability.
- If you missed questions 77, 81, 84, 87, 88 then you should review the concepts related to biodiversity, ecosystem destruction, and global changes.
- If you missed questions 8, 9, 16, 18, 19, 44 then you should review the concepts related to ecosystem structure and general ecology.
- If you missed questions 2, 21, 23, 33, 42, 57, 73, 75 then you should review the concepts related to ecosystems and how they function.
- If you missed questions 3, 34, 50, 65, 76, 78 then you should review the concepts related to population ecology and ecological succession.
- If you missed questions 24, 50, 56, 70, 77, 79-81 then you should review the concepts related to changes in ecosystems, natural selection, plate tectonics, environmental genetics, and evolution.
- If you missed questions 20, 50, 83, 84, 86, 90 then you should review the concepts related to human demographics and populations, comparisons of developing and developed countries.
- If you missed questions 8, 24-26, 85 then you should review the concepts related to geotechnical science (soils).
- If you missed questions 34, 36, 82, 93, 94 then you should review the concepts related to water environmental quality.
- If you missed questions 8, 25, 26, 31, 32, 36, 69, 86 then you should review the concepts related to food production.
- If you missed questions 51-55 then you should review the concepts related to biodiversity of the world's wild species of animals and plants.
- If you missed questions 1, 25, 66 then you should review the concepts related to the worlds' resources.
- If you missed questions 22, 89 then you should review the concepts related to fossil fuels.
- If you missed questions 4, 28, 29, 58-62, 68 then you should review the concepts related to nuclear power.
- If you missed questions 5, 6, 8, 12, 14, 30 then you should review the concepts related to renewable energy.
- If you missed question 31, 32, 40, 41, 47, 63, 64, 96 then you should review the concepts related to human environmental hazards, and toxicology.
- If you missed questions 31, 32, 69, 91 then you should review the concepts related to pests and their control.
- If you missed questions 13, 33-35, 49, 71, 92-94 then you should review the concepts related to water pollution.
- If you missed questions 37, 38, 95, 96 then you should review the concepts related to solid waste.
- If you missed questions 31, 32, 35, 40, 41, 47, 69, 90, 91, 97, 99 then you should review the concepts related to hazardous chemicals.
- If you missed questions 3, 13, 27, 43, 45, 46, 67, 73, 100 then you should review the concepts related to the atmosphere.

Appendix K Practice Test#3 Answer Key & Rubrics

1. c.

2. c.
Abiotic and biotic factors include ALL living and nonliving components of an ecosystem.

3. d.
This occurs in the nitrogen cycle

4. c.
Due to stringent regulations nuclear is currently not cost efficient for new construction projects.

5. b.

6. d.

7. c.
For hydroelectric power a large amount of moving water is required. This is simply not available in most locations.

8. c.
Modern farming practices actually partially created the erosion of soil, this coupled with an extended drought led to large amounts of topsoil being lost due to wind erosion. Use of new farm machinery without knowledge of conservation proved to be a dangerous combination.

9. c.
Ecosystems include both biotic (living) and abiotic (nonliving) components.

10. d.

11. c.
By owing cars, people had easy access to the cleaner and quieter suburbs.

12. c.
Since everyone produces wastes, this source of energy is readily available.

13. d.
Although environmental scientists are concerned with all kinds of detrimental affects to the earth's ecosystems, CO_2 and CFC's are of most concern, because of the high potential to damage large populations at one time. CO_2 is a major greenhouse gas, while CFC's, from refrigerants, damages the valuable protective O_3, ozone layer.

14. c.
In the northeastern part of the United States, as with most of the US, the sun shines on southern exposures most of the day, thus receiving the largest amount of radiant energy and heat during the day. Deciduous trees, those that loose their leaves in the winter, would provide shade during the warmer months, and heat during the colder months.

15. a.

A.P. Environmental Science Study Guide - Appendix K

16. c.
Denitrification is the result of soil bacteria, opposite from nitrifying bacteria, which converts certain forms of nitrogen to atmospheric nitrogen, N_2.

17. d.
Scientific experimentation answers, but as questions are answered, more are generated. Science is a slow, changing, and continuing process.

18. c.
Phosphorus is a major plant nutrient and macronutrient for plants.

19. d.
A pyramid has a large base, and gets smaller with height. Trophic, feeding, levels of food chains and food web have a similar character tics. There are large numbers and high biomass at the beginning trophic level, green plants/algae, and due to a large energy loss, about 90% per trophic level, the numbers and biomass gets smaller along the higher trophic levels, in the general order; green plants/algae…herbivores…carnivores…top carnivores.

20. e.
Optimum range refers to the abiotic and biotic conditions at their most ideal levels for organisms to grow.

21. b.

22. d.
Potential energy is ability to do work and is often referred to as stored energy.

23. b.
Balanced herbivory is the balance of plant species that keeps a diversified population, and avoids monocultures (genetically equal), kept in check by various herbivores.

24. a.

25. a.
Tilling up the soil exposes valuable topsoil to erosion. No-till farming avoid this.

26. c.
Even the freshest irrigation water contains some salt. After the water evaporates or is absorbed by plants, salts are left behind and build up over time. This has been a major problem worldwide, and is seen, for example, in the Western US, from diverting water from the Colorado River for irrigation.

27. b.
Descending air absorbs moisture.

28. e.
Nuclear wastes isotopes will be active for 10,000-100,000 years. Currently the consensus is to store the wastes in geological burial sites. Scientists have found either earthquake, volcanic, or ground water leaching problems with most of the sites investigated.

Awesome Guides, Inc. A.P. Environmental Science Study Guide - Appendix K

29. a.
Breeder reactors are designed so that nonfisssionable 238U absorbs extra neutrons. When this occurs, ^{238}U is converted to plutonium ^{239}Pu, which is fissionable. There are generally 2 neutrons in addition to the one that is added originally to start the reaction, and the 2 neutrons can help sustain the chain reaction, thus producing more fuel than it consumes. This process also makes good use out of uranium ore, since most of the ore, 99.7% is nonfissionalble ^{238}U. Breeder reactors present special problems because ^{239}Pu has a very high half-life, 24,000 years, and can be purified and made into nuclear weapons more easily, providing opportunities for terrorists.

30. d.
Hydrogen fuel cells are currently used in some buses in Vancouver and Chicago. They are very efficient, not dependent on foreign oil reserves, and cause much less pollution than internal combustion engines. Among the drawbacks are the lack of an in place infrastructure for refueling.

31. a.

32. d.

33. c.

34. a.
Eutrophic or hypereutrophic lakes are usually older lakes, and/or ones that have had a high nutrient loading from anthropogenic (human) sources.

35. a.
Chlorine is very effective in killing bacteria, but is a dangerous chemical to handle in it pure concentrated form.

36. a.

37. a.

38. b.

39. c.
CERCLA stands for Comprehensive Environmental Response Compensation and Liability Act, of 1980, more commonly known as the Superfund, primarily adopted to clean up toxic waste dumps.

40. d.

41. a.

42. d.
Light as part of the electromagnetic spectrum contains the colors in order of longest to shortest wavelength; red, orange, yellow, green, blue, indigo, and violet.

43. b.
The layers of the atmosphere for the ground level up are; troposphere, stratosphere, mesosphere, and the thermosphere.

44. c.

A.P. Environmental Science Study Guide - Appendix K   Awesome Guides, Inc.

45. e.
Loss of ozone would harm external tissues of organisms, but not internal organs, directly, such as the lungs.

46. a.
Nitrogous oxide for internal combustion absorbs light and is largely responsible for the brownish color of photochemical smog.

47. c.
Nitrogen and sulfur oxides, resulting from internal combustion can form acids in the atmosphere, namely, nitric acid and sulfuric acid.

48. c.

49. c.
People have gotten used to relativity inexpensive water, an large increase would be very unpopular.

50. a.
Transgenic organisms are those that are genetically engineered. If the transgenic genes are spread to other non-target organisms, than undesirable weeds, for example, may be able to develop resistance to herbicides, or grow out of control.

51. b.

52. c.

53. b.

54. e.

55. d.
Think locally/act globally! This statement means that **you** can have a great impact in your community; however laws must be international, and accepted by all nations. Even though many nations ban whaling, several do not, causing a decline in whale populations. This is also true of DDT, a pesticide, and its use. Even though the US bans DDT Mexico still applies it. Consequently, since DDT has no borders, it still shows up in US food chains especially those on bordering states and near its use.

56. a.
Zooxanthellae algae live in a symbiotic relationship with tropical corals, called mutualism. The algae gives corals its color. High temperatures are suspected as the reason of coral bleaching, the whiting of coral, due to demise of the zooxanthellae algae.

57. d.

58. a.

59. b.

60. c.

Awesome Guides, Inc. A.P. Environmental Science Study Guide - Appendix K

61. d.

62. a.

63. e.
Wind turbines located in migratory birds paths could greatly lower these bird populations. Among other disadvantages of wind power are, aesthetic, and the fact that it's only an intermittent source of energy, and would require backup or storage if the wind is light or stops.

64. c.
There is virtually NO free hydrogen on earth. All of the hydrogen is bonded into water or other compounds. Although plants produce free hydrogen by breaking apart the chemical bonds of the water molecule in photosynthesis, scientists have not yet developed a method to duplicate this process.

65. c.
Current world population is just over 6 billion. With the current exponential growth the world is experiencing human population is expected to be 9 billion by the year 2054.

66. a.
Habitat destruction is a major reason that causes a decline in the variety of life (biodiversity). Fragmentation, the destruction of some wild areas while leaving others intact, also causes loss of biodiversity, especially to specialized species that require a complete intact forest for survival. Erosion controls, an asset to the environment, and keystone species, ones that help the survival of many other species, are both important towards biodiversity.

67. b.
The addition of the many greenhouse gases is expected to cause climatic changes, such as global warming. Even minute changes in CO_2, such as a few 10th of a % would be devastating. A 2% increase would kill most aerobic life.

68. b.
Less than 1% of the fuel mined is separated into fissionable $235U$, by the very small differences in weight. This process requires extremely sensitive and highly technical equipment, which is why many developing countries cannot use nuclear fuel, due to this lack of technology.

69. a.
Even though DDT is blamed for major environmental damage to organisms, such as the thinning of bird shell eggs, and biomagnification of its toxins, it has saved countless human lives through the control of diseases like malaria. Although banned in the US, it is still used in other countries.

70. a.
Nonpoint pollution sources are ones that are difficult to "pinpoint" the source. Runoff form cropland is one such nonpoint pollution source. Direct dumping of wastes such as direct factory or wastewater discharges are called point pollution.

71. d.
BOD or biological oxygen demand represents the rate at which oxygen is depleted from a body of water. The higher the number, the greater the rate of oxygen depletion.

A.P. Environmental Science Study Guide - Appendix K

72. d.
Urban sprawl, or the movement of people from the cities to urban areas outside of the city, causes a loss of agricultural land because many farms are abandoned for housing, shopping centers etc.

73. d.
Lighting, with about 24 million volts, is able to break down the incredibly strong triple covalent bond in atmospheric nitrogen. The elemental nitrogen chemically combines with oxygen and is acted upon by soil bacteria to produce nitrates. Nitrates, not water, are responsible for the grass greening. In fertilizers, the % nitrogen, a major plant nutrient, is the first number of 3, given on the outside of the bag, such 24-8-8, means that there is 24% nitrogen.

74. a.
Theories result from the retesting of an hypothesis, and would be tested in the same manor as a hypothesis. A theory is formulated after a hypothesis is tested many times with the same results.

75. d.
Energy is ONEWAY through an ecosystem. It must ALWAYS be imputed into an ecosystem. Energy is NEVER recycled, only changes into lower levels, entropy that are not useable by organisms. Minerals, water, gases are recycled.

76. b.
The process of ecological succession in southern forests follows the steps of grasses first, small perennials (woody shrubs) pine trees, and finally a climax forest of hardwood trees such as, oaks and hickory.

77. d.
Synergistic effects are ones, that when combined, have a much greater effect than they would have individually. For example: pollutants in the environment may cause organisms to be more vulnerable to disease, drought, predators etc.

78. a.
Tropical Rain Forests have poor soils, due to the high erosion from the frequent rains, an average temperature of $78°F$ or $28°C$ have epiphytes, are plants, dense canopy(overhead), and a little under story due the lack of adequate light. Many colorful insects are found, in a great variety, along with broadleaved trees, and year round consistent climate.

79. c.
When an exotic animal, not native, is introduced into an ecosystem it can either adapt to the new surrounding, migrate out of the area, die. In many cases organisms introduced to a new ecosystem with similar climate than the one they came from, usually flourish and increase their numbers exponentially due to lack of natural predators. Examples is exotic species introductions are numerous, such a melaluca trees into Florida, kudzu vine in the south eastern United States, and rabbits in Australia.

80. b.
Forest fires are a natural part of ecosystems. They recycle materials, burn leaf litter(that may prevent annual plants from growing, and cause catastrophic fires if too thick), and usually don't burn too hot or fast to kill native animals.

Awesome Guides, Inc.  A.P. Environmental Science Study Guide - Appendix K

81. c.
Speciation is the gradual change or an organism's physical characteristics. This occurs when organisms are isolated from each other reproductively, and are in different habitats that they must adapt to.

82. b.
The earth's crust is made up of many tectonic plates. These plates are dynamic, moving, which cause continental drift, earthquakes, volcanoes etc.

83. c.
Developing countries have distinct difference from developing countries. Among those, developing countries have a lower GNP, gross national product, higher birth rate, and less education per capita.

84. d.
Increases of human populations cause over cultivation, poaching, loss of biodiversity, and increased disease resistance due to overuse of antibodies. Mitigation is a process that restores an ecosystem.

85. b.
Sands are very easily workability for cultivation. Clays are very difficult to work because they become sticky, have a high shrink, swell ratio, are muddy and harden to brick like consistency, with even small additions of water.

86. a.
Land suitable for agriculture is the most rare on earth.

87. e.
The blue whale, the largest animal to live on planet earth is critically endangered.

88. e.
Sustainable logging allows timber reserves to continue generation to generation. Ecotourism gives people a new appreciation and respect for natural areas, while providing quality recreation opportunities. Cacao and rubber plantations are natural flora and also provide homes for native animals. Extractive reserves use resources but leave enough to continue sustainable environments and wildlife habitats.

89. a.
A nations power grid is a network of all major power lines that is sold to power suppliers on the open market. Electricity produced from power plants is uploaded to the power grid and shipped via power lines to transfer stations and them consumers.

90. c.
In developed countries, the control of indoor pests causes indoor pollution. Asbestos has been removed for most indoor environments, and is no longer used in new construction. Animal wastes and parasites are typically associated with developing countries.

91. b.
DDT is a persistent pesticide, meaning that it does not break down in the environment quickly and accumulates and concentrates in organisms, biomagnification, or bioaccumulation.

A.P. Environmental Science Study Guide - Appendix K  Awesome Guides, Inc.

92. c.
Biological oxygen demand or BOD is a measure of the oxygen using potential of water, wastewater, or other organic substances.

93. d.
Sewage and storm water have very different qualities. Collecting them together causes unnecessary loading at the sewage treatment facility, since both are treated differently. The cost would also be prohibitive. While it is true that using wastewater for irrigation is a good idea, storm water is polluted water, and usually not appropriate for irrigation because it contains oils, grease, etc. Tertiary treatment, chemical, is cost prohibitive in most applications.

94. c.
Primary sewage treatment is the second step; preliminary (removal of sticks rags, etc.) is the first, which removes suspended organic materials, and particulates by slowing down the water movement and allowing materials to settle.

95. e.
Some plastics, glass, paper and metal can all be recycled.

96. a.
WTE facilities provide a way to make large amounts of energy from MSW, but still require land filling of combustion materials.

97. e.
Among the problems with toxic waste dumps are: liver disease, birth defects, nervous system disorders, and cancer.

98. b.
The Love Canal is an example of how toxic wastes were dumped before certain regulations were put into effect. This is an old toxic waste dump that was covered up and sold to build houses, schools etc. The dump began to collapse exposing barrels of chemical wastes. Fumes leaked in to the area causing health problems for many residents.

99. c.
The EPA, and other agencies have a ZERO tolerance for carcinogens, cancer-producing substances.

100. b.
Anthropogenic or human produced, substances include halogenated hydrocarbons, a class of synthetic organic compounds that one or more hydrogen atoms of fluorine, bromine, chlorine, or iodine. These compounds are real environmental problems. Although humans product methane, nitrogen oxides, water vapor and carbon dioxide, so do many other natural processes.

Appendix L Practice Test #3 Free Response Question Answers

1.
 (a) Public "outcry" against new plants, cost is prohibitive, problems with nuclear wastes (no set long-term solutions), safety issues, the NIMBY principle (Not In My Backyard, where would new plants be built?).

 (b) Medical applications (x-rays and nuclear medicine), military (weapons, power for submarines and ships)

 (c)
  (i) The fuel used in most nuclear energy applications is ^{235}U or Uranium 235. This is the fissionable uranium that accounts for only 0.7% of all uranium fuel ore mined. It must be enriched by separating ^{235}U from ^{238}U.

  (ii) A breeder nuclear reactor uses nonfissionable ^{238}U by converting it into fissionable ^{239}P (plutonium) by allowing the extra neutrons from the typical nuclear reaction with ^{235}U to hit ^{238}U. It can produce its own fuel.

  (iii) Causes mutations of genetic material, such as genes, tissue damage, either permanent or death to the organisms.

  (iv) Nuclear fusion is the combining of, in contrast to splitting of, nuclear materials. The sun is an example of nuclear fusion, combining two hydrogen atoms and producing helium as a by-product. The problem of nuclear fusion is that requires extremely high temperatures, 3,000,000 degrees C, plus pressure. At the present time, there is no material or other technique to contain the high temperatures

 (d) Nuclear reactors have a potential for a complete meltdown, such as was the case of the Chernobyl accident. Engineers shut down the plants' safety system, took out the control rods, and decreased the flow of coolant water. The fuel core unknowing increased its heat without the coolant. The extra steam produced by the heating reactor causes a power surge 100 times the maximum level allowed, blowing the top off of the reactor, causing a meltdown to occur, that burned for days. Over 50 tons of dust and debris with 90 million curies of radioactivity spread over thousands of square miles.

2.
 (a) It is possible that the underground pipes developed leaks, as they often due over time.

 (b) Spilling raw sewage into a body of water directly (point pollution) or over a large undetermined area (nonpoint pollution) can have detrimental effects on the lake. For example organic wastes have a high BOD, biological oxygen demand. This in effect would lower DO, dissolved oxygen to the lake, killing the aerobic organisms that depend on an adequate supply of oxygen. Chemical wastes such as heavy metals (lead, mercury, and cadmium), oils from automobiles, and pesticides, could cause death to the biota of the lake, since at even low concentrations, they are very toxic. Raw sewage can also contain pathogens, disease causing, bacteria such as fecal coliform, cholera, and dysentery.

 (c) <u>The Clean Water Act of 1972</u> —federal program with goals of protecting and restoring the physical, chemical and biological integrity of bodies of water.

 <u>Water Quality Act of 1987</u> —Provides amendments to the Clean Water Act, creating a fund to support construction of treatment plants and address water shed issues of nonpoint pollution.

3. The fist task would be for you to construct a graph using the given data! There are several possibilities, such as a bar graph!

 (a) As is typical in many animal populations, there are seasonal and yearly population variations. This may be due to predator-prey relationships, or migration/immigration or availability of resources.

 (b) Carrying capacity refers to the numbers of an organism that an ecosystem can comprise and sustain that population. Availability of resources, fluctuations in weather patterns (density independent),

A.P. Environmental Science Study Guide - Appendix L    Awesome Guides, Inc.

and may also play a role. Density dependent factors such as disease, or increased competition for resources and mates could cause populations to fluctuate.
Environmental resistance is any factor that would limit population growth, and includes, competition, predation, and disease.

(c) Hypothesis: The introduction of a keystone species will have no effect on the Lemming populations.(This is a Null hypothesis, a typical way to state a hypothesis where a scientist doesn't have to prove every possible situation, an impossible task, making his/her research more credible)

Experimental procedure: Locate two areas that are the same in size, Lemming population, available resources, weather, cover, population structure etc. Maintain all factors equally among each area, but introduce a keystone species to one area, or the experimental site. Observe the Lemmings over a range of 5 years and keep track of the population size, behavior, migration/immigration patterns, etc. in each site, both experimental and control (no keystone species).

4.
(a) Exponential growth is very rapid growth of a population. The worlds' population is currently experiencing this type of growth. When limiting factors, or environmental resistance is low, or nonexistent, then populations can grow very rapidly. Limiting factors include, availability of mates, and resources, disease, famine, competition, predation.

(b) Populations of developing countries account, for a large part, to exponential growth of the worlds' population. There are large numbers of people at pre-reproduction age. In developed countries the numbers at pre-reproduction are comparatively lower. Even though population increases have slowed in developed countries, populations will continue to increase rapidly for many years until a balance is reached for zero population growth be truly achieved. Rationalization to explain these differences include: education, increased crop yields, better technology, cures for disease, pest management, clean drinking water, increases lifespan, control of predation, biotechnology, and modern medicine. Developed countries have a much lower fertility rate (number of children born), than developing countries due to the high numbers of individuals at pre-reproduction age.

(c) See diagrams of developing and developed countries on page 34 of your study guide.
(d) See definitions of Agenda 21 on pages 5 of your study guide.

Appendix M Measurement Units

Distance:
1 centimeter (cm) = 0.39 in
1 decimeter (dm) = 3.94 in.
1 meter = 1.09 yards
1 kilometer (km) = 0.62 mile

1 inch = 2.54 cm
1 foot = 3.05 dm
1 yard = .091 meter
1 mile = 1.61 kilometer

Area:
1 centimeter squared (cm^2) = 1.55 square inches (sq in)
1 sq in = 6.45 cm^2
1 meter squared (m2) = 1.20 square yards (sq yd)
1 sq yd = .836 m2
1 hectare (ha) = 2.47 acres
1 acre = 0.405 ha

Volume:
1 liter (L) = 1.06 quarts (qt)

1 quart = 0.95 liters

Mass:
1 gram (g) = 0.035 ounces (oz)
1 kilogram (kg) = 2.2 pounds (lbs)

1 ounce = 28.4 grams
1 pound = 0.45 kilograms

Appendix N Energy Measurement Units

- 1 calorie = the amount of heat it takes to raise 1 gram of water 1 degree Celsius (1.8 degree F)

- 1 BTU = the amount of heat it takes to raise one pound of water 1 degree Fahrenheit

- 1 joule = the force of one Newton over 1 meter

- 1 calorie = 3.968 BTU's = 4,186 joules

- 1 BTU = 0.254 calories = 1,055 joules

- 1 therm = 100,000 BTU's

- 1 quad = 1 quadrillion BTU's

- 1 watt = 1 watt of energy for one hour = 3.413 BTU's

- 1 kilowatt (kw) = 1000 watts

- 1 kilowatt hour (kwh) = 1 kilowatt for 1 hour = 3413 BTU's

- 1 megawatt (Mw) = 1,000,000 watts

- 1 gigawatt (Gw) = 1,000,000,000 watts = 1,000 Mw

- 1 horsepower = 0.7457 kilowatts = 2,545 BTU's

- 1 gallon of gasoline = 125,000 BTU's

- 1 barrel of oil = 25,000,000 BTU's

- 1 cubic foot of natural methane gas = 1,031 BTU's

- 1 short of coal = 25,000,000 BTU's

Appendix O Important and Helpful Web Sites

- Course Overview: http://apcentral.collegeboard.com/article/0,1281,151-162-0-4357,00.html

- FAQ'S: http://www.collegeboard.com/ap/students/faq/faq003.html

- AP Products: http://cbweb4p.collegeboard.org/cgi-bin/ncommerce3/ExecMacro/tcb/tcbsearch.d2w/report?options=1&global_search=environmental+science

- The College Board: http://www.collegeboard.com/

Awesome Guides, Inc.  A.P. Environmental Science Study Guide - Appendix P

Appendix P Practice Test Answer Sheet Key

1. A( ) B( ) C( ) D( ) E( )
2. A( ) B( ) C( ) D( ) E( )
3. A( ) B( ) C( ) D( ) E( )
4. A( ) B( ) C( ) D( ) E( )
5. A( ) B( ) C( ) D( ) E( )
6. A( ) B( ) C( ) D( ) E( )
7. A( ) B( ) C( ) D( ) E( )
8. A( ) B( ) C( ) D( ) E( )
9. A( ) B( ) C( ) D( ) E( )
10. A( ) B( ) C( ) D( ) E( )
11. A( ) B( ) C( ) D( ) E( )
12. A( ) B( ) C( ) D( ) E( )
13. A( ) B( ) C( ) D( ) E( )
14. A( ) B( ) C( ) D( ) E( )
15. A( ) B( ) C( ) D( ) E( )
16. A( ) B( ) C( ) D( ) E( )
17. A( ) B( ) C( ) D( ) E( )
18. A( ) B( ) C( ) D( ) E( )
19. A( ) B( ) C( ) D( ) E( )
20. A( ) B( ) C( ) D( ) E( )
21. A( ) B( ) C( ) D( ) E( )
22. A( ) B( ) C( ) D( ) E( )
23. A( ) B( ) C( ) D( ) E( )
24. A( ) B( ) C( ) D( ) E( )
25. A( ) B( ) C( ) D( ) E( )
26. A( ) B( ) C( ) D( ) E( )
27. A( ) B( ) C( ) D( ) E( )
28. A( ) B( ) C( ) D( ) E( )
29. A( ) B( ) C( ) D( ) E( )
30. A( ) B( ) C( ) D( ) E( )
31. A( ) B( ) C( ) D( ) E( )
32. A( ) B( ) C( ) D( ) E( )
33. A( ) B( ) C( ) D( ) E( )
34. A( ) B( ) C( ) D( ) E( )
35. A( ) B( ) C( ) D( ) E( )
36. A( ) B( ) C( ) D( ) E( )
37. A( ) B( ) C( ) D( ) E( )
38. A( ) B( ) C( ) D( ) E( )
39. A( ) B( ) C( ) D( ) E( )
40. A( ) B( ) C( ) D( ) E( )
41. A( ) B( ) C( ) D( ) E( )
42. A( ) B( ) C( ) D( ) E( )
43. A( ) B( ) C( ) D( ) E( )
44. A( ) B( ) C( ) D( ) E( )
45. A( ) B( ) C( ) D( ) E( )
46. A( ) B( ) C( ) D( ) E( )
47. A( ) B( ) C( ) D( ) E( )
48. A( ) B( ) C( ) D( ) E( )
49. A( ) B( ) C( ) D( ) E( )
50. A( ) B( ) C( ) D( ) E( )
51. A( ) B( ) C( ) D( ) E( )
52. A( ) B( ) C( ) D( ) E( )
53. A( ) B( ) C( ) D( ) E( )
54. A( ) B( ) C( ) D( ) E( )
55. A( ) B( ) C( ) D( ) E( )
56. A( ) B( ) C( ) D( ) E( )
57. A( ) B( ) C( ) D( ) E( )
58. A( ) B( ) C( ) D( ) E( )
59. A( ) B( ) C( ) D( ) E( )
60. A( ) B( ) C( ) D( ) E( )
61. A( ) B( ) C( ) D( ) E( )
62. A( ) B( ) C( ) D( ) E( )
63. A( ) B( ) C( ) D( ) E( )
64. A( ) B( ) C( ) D( ) E( )
65. A( ) B( ) C( ) D( ) E( )
66. A( ) B( ) C( ) D( ) E( )
67. A( ) B( ) C( ) D( ) E( )
68. A( ) B( ) C( ) D( ) E( )
69. A( ) B( ) C( ) D( ) E( )
70. A( ) B( ) C( ) D( ) E( )
71. A( ) B( ) C( ) D( ) E( )
72. A( ) B( ) C( ) D( ) E( )
73. A( ) B( ) C( ) D( ) E( )
74. A( ) B( ) C( ) D( ) E( )
75. A( ) B( ) C( ) D( ) E( )
76. A( ) B( ) C( ) D( ) E( )
77. A( ) B( ) C( ) D( ) E( )
78. A( ) B( ) C( ) D( ) E( )
79. A( ) B( ) C( ) D( ) E( )
80. A( ) B( ) C( ) D( ) E( )
81. A( ) B( ) C( ) D( ) E( )
82. A( ) B( ) C( ) D( ) E( )
83. A( ) B( ) C( ) D( ) E( )
84. A( ) B( ) C( ) D( ) E( )
85. A( ) B( ) C( ) D( ) E( )
86. A( ) B( ) C( ) D( ) E( )
87. A( ) B( ) C( ) D( ) E( )
88. A( ) B( ) C( ) D( ) E( )
89. A( ) B( ) C( ) D( ) E( )
90. A( ) B( ) C( ) D( ) E( )
91. A( ) B( ) C( ) D( ) E( )
92. A( ) B( ) C( ) D( ) E( )
93. A( ) B( ) C( ) D( ) E( )
94. A( ) B( ) C( ) D( ) E( )
95. A( ) B( ) C( ) D( ) E( )
96. A( ) B( ) C( ) D( ) E( )
97. A( ) B( ) C( ) D( ) E( )
98. A( ) B( ) C( ) D( ) E( )
99. A( ) B( ) C( ) D( ) E( )
100. A( ) B( ) C( ) D( ) E( )

Awesome Guides, Inc. A.P. Environmental Science Study Guide - Appendix P

Appendix P Practice Test Answer Sheet Key

1. A ( ) B ( ) C ( ) D ( ) E ( )
2. A ( ) B ( ) C ( ) D ( ) E ( )
3. A ( ) B ( ) C ( ) D ( ) E ( )
4. A ( ) B ( ) C ( ) D ( ) E ( )
5. A ( ) B ( ) C ( ) D ( ) E ( )
6. A ( ) B ( ) C ( ) D ( ) E ( )
7. A ( ) B ( ) C ( ) D ( ) E ( )
8. A ( ) B ( ) C ( ) D ( ) E ( )
9. A ( ) B ( ) C ( ) D ( ) E ( )
10. A ( ) B ( ) C ( ) D ( ) E ( )
11. A ( ) B ( ) C ( ) D ( ) E ( )
12. A ( ) B ( ) C ( ) D ( ) E ( )
13. A ( ) B ( ) C ( ) D ( ) E ( )
14. A ( ) B ( ) C ( ) D ( ) E ( )
15. A ( ) B ( ) C ( ) D ( ) E ( )
16. A ( ) B ( ) C ( ) D ( ) E ( )
17. A ( ) B ( ) C ( ) D ( ) E ( )
18. A ( ) B ( ) C ( ) D ( ) E ( )
19. A ( ) B ( ) C ( ) D ( ) E ( )
20. A ( ) B ( ) C ( ) D ( ) E ( )
21. A ( ) B ( ) C ( ) D ( ) E ( )
22. A ( ) B ( ) C ( ) D ( ) E ( )
23. A ( ) B ( ) C ( ) D ( ) E ( )
24. A ( ) B ( ) C ( ) D ( ) E ( )
25. A ( ) B ( ) C ( ) D ( ) E ( )
26. A ( ) B ( ) C ( ) D ( ) E ( )
27. A ( ) B ( ) C ( ) D ( ) E ( )
28. A ( ) B ( ) C ( ) D ( ) E ( )
29. A ( ) B ( ) C ( ) D ( ) E ( )
30. A ( ) B ( ) C ( ) D ( ) E ( )
31. A ( ) B ( ) C ( ) D ( ) E ( )
32. A ( ) B ( ) C ( ) D ( ) E ( )
33. A ( ) B ( ) C ( ) D ( ) E ( )
34. A ( ) B ( ) C ( ) D ( ) E ( )
35. A ( ) B ( ) C ( ) D ( ) E ( )
36. A ( ) B ( ) C ( ) D ( ) E ( )
37. A ( ) B ( ) C ( ) D ( ) E ( )
38. A ( ) B ( ) C ( ) D ( ) E ( )
39. A ( ) B ( ) C ( ) D ( ) E ( )
40. A ( ) B ( ) C ( ) D ( ) E ( )
41. A ( ) B ( ) C ( ) D ( ) E ( )
42. A ( ) B ( ) C ( ) D ( ) E ( )
43. A ( ) B ( ) C ( ) D ( ) E ( )
44. A ( ) B ( ) C ( ) D ( ) E ( )
45. A ( ) B ( ) C ( ) D ( ) E ( )
46. A ( ) B ( ) C ( ) D ( ) E ( )
47. A ( ) B ( ) C ( ) D ( ) E ( )
48. A ( ) B ( ) C ( ) D ( ) E ( )
49. A ( ) B ( ) C ( ) D ( ) E ( )
50. A ( ) B ( ) C ( ) D ( ) E ( )
51. A ( ) B ( ) C ( ) D ( ) E ( )
52. A ( ) B ( ) C ( ) D ( ) E ( )
53. A ( ) B ( ) C ( ) D ( ) E ( )
54. A ( ) B ( ) C ( ) D ( ) E ( )
55. A ( ) B ( ) C ( ) D ( ) E ( )
56. A ( ) B ( ) C ( ) D ( ) E ( )
57. A ( ) B ( ) C ( ) D ( ) E ( )
58. A ( ) B ( ) C ( ) D ( ) E ( )
59. A ( ) B ( ) C ( ) D ( ) E ( )
60. A ( ) B ( ) C ( ) D ( ) E ( )
61. A ( ) B ( ) C ( ) D ( ) E ( )
62. A ( ) B ( ) C ( ) D ( ) E ( )
63. A ( ) B ( ) C ( ) D ( ) E ( )
64. A ( ) B ( ) C ( ) D ( ) E ( )
65. A ( ) B ( ) C ( ) D ( ) E ( )
66. A ( ) B ( ) C ( ) D ( ) E ( )
67. A ( ) B ( ) C ( ) D ( ) E ( )
68. A ( ) B ( ) C ( ) D ( ) E ( )
69. A ( ) B ( ) C ( ) D ( ) E ( )
70. A ( ) B ( ) C ( ) D ( ) E ( )
71. A ( ) B ( ) C ( ) D ( ) E ( )
72. A ( ) B ( ) C ( ) D ( ) E ( )
73. A ( ) B ( ) C ( ) D ( ) E ( )
74. A ( ) B ( ) C ( ) D ( ) E ( )
75. A ( ) B ( ) C ( ) D ( ) E ( )
76. A ( ) B ( ) C ( ) D ( ) E ( )
77. A ( ) B ( ) C ( ) D ( ) E ( )
78. A ( ) B ( ) C ( ) D ( ) E ( )
79. A ( ) B ( ) C ( ) D ( ) E ( )
80. A ( ) B ( ) C ( ) D ( ) E ( )
81. A ( ) B ( ) C ( ) D ( ) E ( )
82. A ( ) B ( ) C ( ) D ( ) E ( )
83. A ( ) B ( ) C ( ) D ( ) E ( )
84. A ( ) B ( ) C ( ) D ( ) E ( )
85. A ( ) B ( ) C ( ) D ( ) E ( )
86. A ( ) B ( ) C ( ) D ( ) E ( )
87. A ( ) B ( ) C ( ) D ( ) E ( )
88. A ( ) B ( ) C ( ) D ( ) E ( )
89. A ( ) B ( ) C ( ) D ( ) E ( )
90. A ( ) B ( ) C ( ) D ( ) E ( )
91. A ( ) B ( ) C ( ) D ( ) E ( )
92. A ( ) B ( ) C ( ) D ( ) E ( )
93. A ( ) B ( ) C ( ) D ( ) E ( )
94. A ( ) B ( ) C ( ) D ( ) E ( )
95. A ( ) B ( ) C ( ) D ( ) E ( )
96. A ( ) B ( ) C ( ) D ( ) E ( )
97. A ( ) B ( ) C ( ) D ( ) E ( )
98. A ( ) B ( ) C ( ) D ( ) E ( )
99. A ( ) B ( ) C ( ) D ( ) E ( )
100. A ( ) B ( ) C ( ) D ( ) E ( )

Copyrighted material – do not duplicate!

Appendix P Practice Test Answer Sheet Key

1. A( ) B( ) C( ) D( ) E( )
2. A( ) B( ) C( ) D( ) E( )
3. A( ) B( ) C( ) D( ) E( )
4. A( ) B( ) C( ) D( ) E( )
5. A( ) B( ) C( ) D( ) E( )
6. A( ) B( ) C( ) D( ) E( )
7. A( ) B( ) C( ) D( ) E( )
8. A( ) B( ) C( ) D( ) E( )
9. A( ) B( ) C( ) D( ) E( )
10. A( ) B( ) C( ) D( ) E( )
11. A( ) B( ) C( ) D( ) E( )
12. A( ) B( ) C( ) D( ) E( )
13. A( ) B( ) C( ) D( ) E( )
14. A( ) B( ) C( ) D( ) E( )
15. A( ) B( ) C( ) D( ) E( )
16. A( ) B( ) C( ) D( ) E( )
17. A( ) B( ) C( ) D( ) E( )
18. A( ) B( ) C( ) D( ) E( )
19. A( ) B( ) C( ) D( ) E( )
20. A( ) B( ) C( ) D( ) E( )
21. A( ) B( ) C( ) D( ) E( )
22. A( ) B( ) C( ) D( ) E( )
23. A( ) B( ) C( ) D( ) E( )
24. A( ) B( ) C( ) D( ) E( )
25. A( ) B( ) C( ) D( ) E( )
26. A( ) B( ) C( ) D( ) E( )
27. A( ) B( ) C( ) D( ) E( )
28. A( ) B( ) C( ) D( ) E( )
29. A( ) B( ) C( ) D( ) E( )
30. A( ) B( ) C( ) D( ) E( )
31. A( ) B( ) C( ) D( ) E( )
32. A( ) B( ) C( ) D( ) E( )
33. A( ) B( ) C( ) D( ) E( )
34. A( ) B( ) C( ) D( ) E( )
35. A( ) B( ) C( ) D( ) E( )
36. A( ) B( ) C( ) D( ) E( )
37. A( ) B( ) C( ) D( ) E( )
38. A( ) B( ) C( ) D( ) E( )
39. A( ) B( ) C( ) D( ) E( )
40. A( ) B( ) C( ) D( ) E( )
41. A( ) B( ) C( ) D( ) E( )
42. A( ) B( ) C( ) D( ) E( )
43. A( ) B( ) C( ) D( ) E( )
44. A( ) B( ) C( ) D( ) E( )
45. A( ) B( ) C( ) D( ) E( )
46. A( ) B( ) C( ) D( ) E( )
47. A( ) B( ) C( ) D( ) E( )
48. A( ) B( ) C( ) D( ) E( )
49. A( ) B( ) C( ) D( ) E( )
50. A( ) B( ) C( ) D( ) E( )
51. A( ) B( ) C( ) D( ) E( )
52. A( ) B( ) C( ) D( ) E( )
53. A( ) B( ) C( ) D( ) E( )
54. A( ) B( ) C( ) D( ) E( )
55. A( ) B( ) C( ) D( ) E( )
56. A( ) B( ) C( ) D( ) E( )
57. A( ) B( ) C( ) D( ) E( )
58. A( ) B( ) C( ) D( ) E( )
59. A( ) B( ) C( ) D( ) E( )
60. A( ) B( ) C( ) D( ) E( )
61. A( ) B( ) C( ) D( ) E( )
62. A( ) B( ) C( ) D( ) E( )
63. A( ) B( ) C( ) D( ) E( )
64. A( ) B( ) C( ) D( ) E( )
65. A( ) B( ) C( ) D( ) E( )
66. A( ) B( ) C( ) D( ) E( )
67. A( ) B( ) C( ) D( ) E( )
68. A( ) B( ) C( ) D( ) E( )
69. A( ) B( ) C( ) D( ) E( )
70. A( ) B( ) C( ) D( ) E( )
71. A( ) B( ) C( ) D( ) E( )
72. A( ) B( ) C( ) D( ) E( )
73. A( ) B( ) C( ) D( ) E( )
74. A( ) B( ) C( ) D( ) E( )
75. A( ) B( ) C( ) D( ) E( )
76. A( ) B( ) C( ) D( ) E( )
77. A( ) B( ) C( ) D( ) E( )
78. A( ) B( ) C( ) D( ) E( )
79. A( ) B( ) C( ) D( ) E( )
80. A( ) B( ) C( ) D( ) E( )
81. A( ) B( ) C( ) D( ) E( )
82. A( ) B( ) C( ) D( ) E( )
83. A( ) B( ) C( ) D( ) E( )
84. A( ) B( ) C( ) D( ) E( )
85. A( ) B( ) C( ) D( ) E( )
86. A( ) B( ) C( ) D( ) E( )
87. A( ) B( ) C( ) D( ) E( )
88. A( ) B( ) C( ) D( ) E( )
89. A( ) B( ) C( ) D( ) E( )
90. A( ) B( ) C( ) D( ) E( )
91. A( ) B( ) C( ) D( ) E( )
92. A( ) B( ) C( ) D( ) E( )
93. A( ) B( ) C( ) D( ) E( )
94. A( ) B( ) C( ) D( ) E( )
95. A( ) B( ) C( ) D( ) E( )
96. A( ) B( ) C( ) D( ) E( )
97. A( ) B( ) C( ) D( ) E( )
98. A( ) B( ) C( ) D( ) E( )
99. A( ) B( ) C( ) D( ) E( )
100. A( ) B( ) C( ) D( ) E( )